Anatomy of Foolishness

Anatomy of Foolishness

*The Overlooked Problem of
Risk-Unawareness*

Stephen Greenspan
Foreword by Robert B. Shilkret

Hamilton Books

Lanham • Boulder • New York • Toronto • London

Published by Hamilton Books
An imprint of The Rowman & Littlefield Publishing Group, Inc.
4501 Forbes Boulevard, Suite 200, Lanham, Maryland 20706
Hamilton Books Acquisitions Department (301) 459-3366

6 Tinworth Street, London SE11 5AL

British Library Cataloguing in Publication Information Available

Library of Congress Cataloging-in-Publication Data Available

ISBN 978-0-7618-7162-0 (pbk. : alk. paper)
ISBN 978-0-7618-7163-7 (electronic)

∞™ The paper used in this publication meets the minimum requirements of American National Standard for Information Sciences Permanence of Paper for Printed Library Materials, ANSI/NISO Z39.48-1992.

This book is dedicated to the memory of three much-loved colleagues: Michael J. Chandler, an early mentor who made it possible for me to become a psychologist, who nurtured my interest in social incompetence, and who rescued me from jams caused by my own social incompetence; A. J. "Pappy" Pappanikou, a later mentor who tried to get me to behave less foolishly; and Pappy's daughter Lisa Pappanikou Glidden, a peer who found my foolishness hilarious.

Contents

List of Figures

Foreword

This is a very wise book on foolishness. Stephen Greenspan did his undergraduate work at The Johns Hopkins University, where he graduated in 1962, having studied American history and political science. After serving in the Army (a requirement in those days), he then worked at the Department of Commerce in Washington and at a public policy institute in Rochester, New York, before deciding to go to graduate school in psychology. After completing his PhD in developmental psychology at the University of Rochester, Steve was a postdoctoral fellow in developmental disabilities at UCLA's Neuropsychiatric Institute; then he was a research scientist at the Boys Town Center for the Study of Youth for six years, where he also had an appointment at the University of Nebraska. He was then on the faculty of George Peabody College for Teachers at Vanderbilt University, before moving to the University of Connecticut, Department of Educational Psychology. He was at the University of Connecticut for the longest period, moved through the academic ranks there, and is now an emeritus professor, retiring early in 1998, a few years before he was sixty years old. It was then that he moved to follow his wife, Helen Apthorp, to the Denver area, where Helen had a career opportunity. Steve was an independent scholar in Colorado for twenty years, until after Helen's recent retirement, when they moved to Northern California to be near their two adult sons.

In truth, Steve has been an independent scholar his whole professional life. His thinking has always been highly original, and his productivity is prodigious. He can write faster than I can read. But he is certainly not an academic loner, as testified by his dozens of articles and book chapters with a wide range of colleagues and student coauthors. While he was extraordinarily productive and creative throughout his career, his work really zoomed since this so-called retirement from academia. I love the word "zoomed"—it is the word used by Mary Ainsworth (who taught a course both of us took at Johns Hopkins) to describe the work in attachment theory, influenced primarily by her, shortly before she died.

Beneath these basic facts, Steve has really had three careers. Maybe there is a fourth, and a fifth, of which I am still unaware. The first was as a developmental psychologist. His first published paper, with his mentor Michael Chandler, was as a graduate student and it appeared in the journal *Developmental Psychology*. (He started at the top and it has been just upward ever since!) That first paper was titled "Ersatz Egocentrism."

It noted, among other things, that true perspectivism or empathy (the converse of egocentrism) must involve understanding something that one has *not* experienced oneself, and includes an awareness of the limits of one's ability truly to know another's experience. Thus, his earliest work in psychology dealt with Piagetian psychology, but the social aspect of that school of thought, which was highly underdeveloped, despite Piaget's dozens of books, indeed, his cognitive developmental factory in Geneva. Piaget always kind of sneered at the social side of development. Greenspan's ground-breaking work on foolishness really grew out of his early attempts to apply Piagetian concepts to the study of social development years (actually decades) earlier.

Greenspan's subsequent work in developmental psychology centered on parenting, also a highly social aspect of the child's world. Steve's three careers have been continuing and overlapping, in that he later returned to this early interest in parenting and published a book on it a few years ago. But parenting and social development has always been an important part of Steve's thinking. I think I first saw a version of the manuscript for the parenting book as early as the 1970s. (If Steve is nothing else, he is perseverant).

Secondly, and the career Steve is most noted for, has been his work in intellectual disability (ID, formerly called mental retardation). Steve's big theory has argued and demonstrated convincingly that so-called ID is really as much social as intellectual (or cognitive), and involves particularly these people's being overly-trusting of others. This realization led to a decades-long interest in gullibility in general, an under-studied topic in psychology. Steve's book of a few years ago, *Annals of Gullibility* went a long way toward remedying that. The publication of *Annals* is one of the most fortuitous events I know of in publishing, generally. Its publication came just at the moment of the uncovering of Bernard Madoff's massive financial fraud, a topic dealt with at some length as an example in Steve's current book. When Steve realized he had been swindled himself in the Madoff scandal, he quickly published an intriguing piece in *Skeptic* magazine, which, in turn, interested the *Wall Street Journal*, which had him do a long piece in its weekend edition shortly after the Madoff story broke. The hook was "gullibility expert gets gulled by Bernie Madoff." Steve is remarkably unbothered by embarrassment, especially when it provides a teaching opportunity, and this one certainly did. Maybe Steve is fundamentally a teacher, after all.

His work in intellectual disability (ID) has been recognized nationally and internationally by several awards, including the Dybwad Humanitarian Award of the American Association on Intellectual and Developmental Disabilities (AAIDD) and the Jacobson Award for Critical Thinking of the American Psychological Association. He also was recently added to the "Wall of Fame" of the National Organization on Fetal Alcohol Syndrome (NOFAS) for his important writing on the social incompetence of individuals with this disorder (the number one known cause of ID in the United States).

Thirdly, Steve has become nationally known in legal circles for his work as a mitigation expert witness in so-called "Atkins hearings. These are cases in which a person with ID is facing a death sentence. As a result, he is consulted about such things as measuring IQ, neuropsychiatric disabilities, forensic quandaries, the assessment of "adaptive behavior" (thanks to Steve an increasingly important diagnostic criterion), and he has served as an expert witness, almost always for the defense, in numerous death penalty cases in which a diagnosis of ID (which is often disputed) will bring the death penalty off the table. Steve has had considerable success in saving peoples' lives, literally. There are probably two more books to be written drawing from this phase of Steve's life: "Surmounting IQ" and "Ending the Death Penalty."

More personally, I have known Steve for a long time. We met in college. I was a first-year student at Johns Hopkins and Steve was a graduating senior that year. We overlapped only that one year, and we were amazed later that we ended up in closely-related fields. Steve had a great influence on my own development in college. He was the first person I knew who was truly interested in ideas (as opposed to being interested in doing well in school). We have been close friends and colleagues ever since that time, over fifty years ago now. If you are lucky, as I was, you do make your longest and closest friendships in college. Read Stephen Greenspan's new book on foolishness. It will change your life, no fooling!

—Robert B. Shilkret
South Hadley, MA

Preface

To a large extent, we are defined by the decisions we make, good or bad. A behavioral economist (which I am not) will generally focus on the elements of good decisions, especially those that involve optimal use of resources. Conversely, I am more interested in bad decisions, especially those that could have disastrous consequences (something which, for the most part, does not ensue from the non-optimal choices studied by economists). A sobering thing about bad decisions is that it only takes one bad decision to ruin or destroy a life. Thus, even for someone whose life is generally marked by good decisions, he or she is only one bad decision away from disaster. I describe such a decision as *foolish* because it involves a failure to take into account a risk that usually can be anticipated as a possibility, sometimes even as a probability. This book, therefore, can be seen as an attempt to make readers aware that becoming a competent person involves developing an ability to recognize and to accurately weigh risk when making everyday decisions. When I say "weigh" risk I am not suggesting it is necessary to become an overly anxious and fearful person. But developing a basic level of risk-awareness must become part of the equation for anyone hoping to survive outside of, say, a cloistered monastery.

This is the second of what I hope will be several books addressing aspects of human foolishness. I say "hope" because I am in my late seventies. I stumbled across the topic when well over the age of sixty and (despite Robert Shilkret's kind words) I do not consider myself a fast writer. The first book in the series was *Annals of Gullibility* (Greenspan 2009a). It explored, though illustrative stories, "social-induced foolishness" (my jargon term for gullibility), one of three major types of foolishness. Although a four-factor causative theory of foolishness was mentioned in the book's first chapter, the theory was not used systematically to analyze the book's many gullibility stories.

The current book is broader in scope, but narrower in execution. Its breadth stems from a focus on all three types of foolishness: induced-social (gullibility), noninduced-social, and practical /physical. Its narrowness stems from a decision to use a few examples to illustrate each type of foolishness, rather than attempt to be encyclopedic (an impossible task, given that every day brings several new foolishness stories to my attention). Another difference is that the four-factor causative theory is used here systematically to explain many if not most of the examples of foolishness that are discussed. Additional books will, if I live long enough, address specific applications of the foolishness concept, in areas such as disability and criminal justice.

Interest in *Annals of Gullibility*—and by extension my theory of foolishness—was enhanced by the amazing coincidence that on December 12, 2008, two days after I held the first copy in my hand, I discovered that I had been hoodwinked by Bernard Madoff's Ponzi scheme, or more accurately the Madoff "feeder" fund I had invested in. I managed to publish lengthy articles on the topic a few weeks later as featured essays in both *Skeptic* and the *Wall Street Journal* (Greenspan 2008, 2009d). Those essays, which can be accessed on my website (stephen-greenspan.com), attracted widespread interest.

This interest reflected, in part, to some, the amusing irony of a gullibility expert being gulled (a Canadian financial columnist, Robert Fulford (2008), wrote (to paraphrase) "the first Greenspan, Alan, will be remembered as the former Fed chairman who didn't see it coming while the other Greenspan, Stephen, will be remembered as the gullibility expert who forgot to read his own book"). However, interest in the piece also reflected the view—expressed by many readers (some quite knowledgeable about finance)—that I provided a thoughtful and largely valid answer to the question "how could so many reasonably smart people—including an authority on gullibility—have behaved so foolishly when investing their life savings?" A condensed version of my Madoff essay is contained in chapter 7.

A WORD ABOUT THE TITLE

Almost 400 years ago, Robert Burton (1621) wrote what Samuel Johnson described as the only book that could get him out of bed two hours early. That work, which spanned four volumes, had the lengthy title *The Anatomy of Melancholy, What It Is: With all the Kinds, Causes, Symptomes, Prognostickes, and Several Cures of It. In Three Maine Partitions with their several Sections, Members, and Subsections. Philosophically, Historically, Opened and Cut up*. It is rightly considered one of the great scientific and satiric books in the English language.

In calling the current book *The Anatomy of Foolishness*, I share with Burton only the wish to explore and "cut up" the various kinds, causes, prognostic outcomes and, when possible, cures for foolishness. Burton used melancholy as an umbrella to cover much of what was understood about human knowledge and behavior in the seventeenth century. In contrast, I am content to stick more narrowly to foolishness, not that it is a small topic. I make no claim to be in Burton's class as a writer or intellectual, although I share with him, and most writers, some obsessive tendencies. Burton was all-inclusive in his coverage of the topic of melancholy, while I am content to just scratch the surface of a topic that, like Burton's, has been explored much less than one might think.

UPDATING OF ERASMUS

The current book covers some of the same territory as was addressed by the great humanist author Desiderius Erasmus (1509) of Rotterdam, in his book *The Praise of Folly*. A lengthy essay written in Latin during a stay when Erasmus spent time in the English countryside in 1509, it was later expanded (with illustrations by Hans Holbein the Younger), translated and published in several countries where it attracted much notoriety. Mostly a comic work, inspired by Greek and Roman satires, it portrays Folly as a goddess who was nursed by nymphs named "inebriation" and "ignorance" and with companions named "self-love," "flattery," "oblivion," "laziness," "pleasure," "madness," "wantonness," "intemperance," and "deep sleep." Folly elaborately praises various forms of foolishness, such as superstition and madness and, of course, has many good things to say about herself (along the lines of "stick with me and you'll get rich and have a good time"). Although Erasmus was a Catholic cleric, much admired by church authorities in Rome, his devastating critique of the phony piety and corrupt practices then prevalent in the church, is considered to have been a catalyst for the Reformation.

HOW I CAME TO THIS TOPIC

I have, for many years, explored the topic of social and practical competence and incompetence, first in normally developing children, then in youth and adults with cognitive and behavioral impairments, and more recently in people generally. Initially, I approached competence as a broad personality trait that one brings to all situations, but at some point I went through a personal paradigm shift and started to see competence in terms of how wisely or foolishly one deals with specific situations. Looked at in this way, it is possible for someone to be generally very competent but to fail miserably (sometimes with life-altering consequences) when facing a particular challenge. Looking at foolishness in terms of failure to manage a specific challenge, one can thus explain how anyone—no matter how socially or practically effective they generally are—can be done in (sometimes literally) by a single act of foolishness. Examples of potentially catastrophic foolish acts are: lighting a cigarette in a car with gasoline cans on the back seat (a practically foolish act), agreeing to waive one's right to have an attorney present when interrogated by the police (an induced socially foolish act), and resisting a demand by an armed robber to hand over one's wallet (a noninduced socially foolish act) (see figure 2.1).

The aspect of foolishness that first drew my attention was "gullibility" (Greenspan, Loughlin, and Black 2001), a term that describes being duped or tricked by one or more other persons into believing or doing something that is not in one's interest. My interest in gullibility grew out of my involvement as an expert or advocate in several cases of false confession to murder, starting with Richard Lapointe, a Connecticut man born with a brain malformation that made him especially vulnerable to social pressure and manipulation. Lapointe's gullibility made him a sitting duck in a police interrogation (which when skillfully carried out can entrap an innocent or socially vulnerable person) and he was given a life sentence which was not overturned until he had spent over twenty-five years in prison.

I admit to having a personal interest in the topic as well. I had few friends as a child, a function of growing up in the years before the invention of the polio vaccine and having an overprotective mother who would not let me play with other children for fear that I would catch the dreaded disease from fecal contamination, a popular theory at that time. (Howard Hughes also experienced such polio-driven maternal over-protectiveness, which explained his morbid and crippling fear of germs). As a result of this social isolation, when I started school I had a great desire to be accepted by other children, combined with little understanding of how to attain that end. As a result, I often behaved foolishly, sometimes as the victim of the cruel tricks which kids will play on peers who are unusually naïve or clueless.

Although, like most people, I became less prone to foolishness as I got older, I continue to have foolish moments as an adult, such as recently when I paid a guy who approached me on the street to patch my rear bumper with what later turned out to be cardboard backed by aluminum foil and covered up with wax which I was advised to leave undisturbed for a few hours. (Putting wax on supposedly wet paint should have been a dead giveaway). The writing of this book is motivated, in part, by my desire to understand how to avoid behaving foolishly in the future. Hopefully, some preventive benefit will also accrue to readers who have a similar propensity or who have loved ones whose foolish tendencies have placed them in harm's way on occasion.

THE CENTRALITY OF RISK-UNAWARENESS

The main contribution of this book to the literature on foolishness is the identification of risk-unawareness as its central defining feature. While articles and books about foolishness often depict behaviors where obvious bad consequences were not anticipated, risk-unawareness (or at least risk-ignoring) is almost never mentioned as the core problem. Hopefully, one outcome of this book will be a greater understanding that being *smart* in the everyday world (as opposed to doing well in school) is to a large extent a matter of knowing when a proposed course of action is safe or, more importantly, knowing when it is not safe.

MULTIDIMENSIONAL APPROACH TO FOOLISHNESS

In addition to emphasizing risk-unawareness as an overlooked core aspect of foolishness (and, conversely, risk-awareness as an overlooked core aspect of wisdom), I also argue that any foolish, or wise, act must be understood as resulting from the confluence of several internal and external factors coming together to determine how well or how poorly an individual handles a particular risk-based challenge. This is one of the reasons why specific foolish acts are difficult to predict, as each situation poses different challenges, each person differs somewhat in which cognitive or affective buttons are pushed by that situation, and the person themself may be in a usual (alert, sober) or altered (exhausted, anxious) state when the challenge materializes. Such a multidimensional approach to behavior is hardly the norm in the social sciences, and certainly not in my discipline of psychology, where scholars typically focus on a single factor (in the case of foolishness, cognition) as the basis for an attempt to explain a complicated phenomenon. While a study using a single independent variable is easier to carry out, the amount of variance accounted for is usually small, and the contribution to understanding someone's behavior is, thus, minimal.

FOCUS ON FOOLISHNESS RATHER THAN FOOLS

One distinction I try to make (not always successfully) is between foolish behavior and foolish people. Obviously, some people behave foolishly on a very frequent basis, and when that happens the temptation is to assign them a label, whether it is a common pejorative such as "fool" or a clinical designation such as "personality disorder." I am definitely interested in people who, because of some disability or disorder (such as autism or Intellectual Disability) have a pervasive and potentially dangerous inability to recognize social or physical risk. In fact, I devote chapter nine to this topic; a fuller treatment of this topic is saved for a planned future book tentatively titled "Disorders of Common Sense." For the most part, the current book avoids labeling people and focuses instead on the nature and causes of foolish behavior in everyday situations which most of us exhibit or encounter at one time or another. This exploration of foolish behavior in the general population builds on a monthly blog, "Incompetence: Of foolishness and gullibility," that I have been writing for the online edition of *Psychology Today* (www.psychologytoday.com/us/blog/

incompetence). Many of the stories in this book first appeared in that column.

AUTOBIOGRAPHICAL NATURE OF SOME MATERIAL

This book is a throwback in some ways to the early days of psychology, when authors used autobiographical introspection (for example, Sigmund Freud on his dreams, William James on his mystical experiences) as a source of data. In line with one semi-serious definition of a psychologist as someone who studies things he is bad at, I have had more than my share of foolish (particularly gullible) moments. A few of these made their way into this book, mostly identified as mine, with one or two of the more embarrassing ones attributed to a pseudonym. An advantage of using such material is that, having attained some degree of self-understanding, I can better discuss how all four explanatory factors affected my own foolish behavior than I can when analyzing the foolish behavior of a person (say in the news) I do not personally know, and where my analysis is, by necessity, speculative.

—Stephen Greenspan
Nicasio, CA

Acknowledgments

Several people inspired or sustained me while I was writing this book. I owe these "support persons" my deepest appreciation for their encouragement and advice. Here is a list of the most notable of my benefactors:

- Harvey Switzky, who urged me to add motivation to my model
- The late Jim Granfield, who urged me to do the same for situations
- Laraine Glidden, who offered me early publishing outlets for my ideas
- John Driscoll, Gail Loughlin, and Peter Love, students who taught me much
- Robert Shilkret, for his wonderful Forward and for educating me about Freud
- Martin Ford, whose motivation model inspired my four-factor framework
- Lybi Ma, who invited me to blog about foolishness for *Psychology Today*
- Alan Taddiken, for letting me use his art and for incessantly providing ideas
- James Patton, a long-time collaborator in the study of adaptive behavior
- George Woods, who has taught me what little I know about the brain
- Gail Kara and Phillip Guddemi, who educated me about systems theory
- Flash Gordon, my physician, who prodded me to celebrate St. Stupid's Day
- My sons Alex and Eli, who luckily failed to inherit my foolishness gene
- My loving wife Helen Apthorp, who encourages, helps, and tolerates me

I

Overview of Foolishness

Foolishness is one of those constructs that are used a great deal in common parlance, but which are poorly defined and little studied by psychologists or other social scientists. One starting point, used in chapter 1, for understanding a poorly defined construct is to look at how it is approached in literature and in popular culture. A salient outcome of this exercise is that foolish behavior is marked by unrecognized or unheeded risk or danger. But a perusal of the limited scholarly literature on foolishness (in chapter 2) finds almost no mention of risk-unawareness as a component, let alone as a key, for understanding the construct. In chapter 3, a provisional theory of foolish behavior is described, while in chapter 4 the elements in the model are spelled out and illustrated. This theory provides the framework for analysis of the many examples of foolish action that are scattered throughout the balance of the book.

ONE

Popular and Religious Conceptions of Foolishness

Foolishness is a common theme in popular culture and in literature. The term "foolishness," and related terms such as "fool," "foolish," and "folly," have long been used in literature, folk expressions, and popular culture, not to mention in everyday parlance. As an example, the terms occur repeatedly throughout major religious texts, such as the Quran and both the Jewish and Christian Bibles. In the current chapter, I shall review some, but by no means all, of this use. A common theme that emerges in most of this use is the view that foolish conduct is *risky* conduct. In other words, a person behaves foolishly when they ignore or fail to recognize undesired consequences that are both obvious and potentially very dangerous for the actor.

MONOTHEISTIC CONCEPTIONS OF FOOLISHNESS

Foolishness and the risks faced by fools are described frequently in the three related monotheistic religions of Islam, Judaism, and Christianity. In the Quran, the term "foolish" comes in very early, in Surah 2 ("The Cow," the longest of the Surahs), which is the very first Surah after the opening. The focus of this Surah (Library of Islam 1994) is on the "hypocrites," lukewarm supporters of Islam, implied in the translator's notes to include Jewish rabbis who were contemporaries of Mohammed. The hypocrites are described thusly: "and when it is said unto them: Believe as the people believe, they say: Shall we believe as the foolish believe? Behold they are indeed the foolish but they know not." (2:13). Why are the non-believers foolish? Because they will wind up facing the fires of Hell, a fate for non-believers that is stated repeatedly and more explicitly in later Surahs. Thus, in the Quran, people who do not embrace the teachings of Islam are described as foolish in that they are playing a very dangerous game, in which they run the risk of eternal damnation.

In the Jewish Bible, the terms "foolish" and "fools" are used in a very similar fashion as in Islam, namely to describe someone who is running a risk of severe punishment, including ruin, death, disfigurement or damnation at the hands of a very quick-to-anger deity. For example, in Ecclesiastes—which along with Proverbs, can be viewed as an extended essay on foolishness—it is written (all Biblical quotes are from the Oxford New Revised Standard Version [NRSV], 1989), "when you make a vow to God, do not delay fulfilling it; for he has no pleasure in fools" (Eccles. 5:4). Later in that section (5:6) the likely consequence of offending God is made more explicit: "[why should you run the risk that] God be angry at your words, and destroy the work of your hands?" In other words, it is sheer foolishness to behave in a way that would cause a vengeful God to take negative notice of you.

More direct evidence that conduct in defiance of God brings serious consequences in the Jewish Bible can be found in Numbers 12. Out of hearing of Moses, Miriam and Aaron criticized him for marrying a Cushite woman. They also puffed themselves up, boasting that the Lord spoke through them as much as through Moses. At that point, God appeared in a cloud and asserted that Moses is the only person through whom he speaks directly face-to-face and not through a cloud and in riddles. Who, therefore, do Miriam and Aaron think they are "to speak against my servant Moses. And the anger of the Lord was kindled against them and he departed. When the cloud went away from over the tent, Miriam had become leprous. . . . Then Aaron said to Moses, 'Oh my Lord, do not punish us for a sin that we have so foolishly committed'" (Num. 12:8-11). Again, what makes an act foolish in this story is that the consequences are so dire and so easily predictable, given God's omniscience and his tendency to severely punish those who defy him.

That it is extremely foolish to mess with a vengeful God is a theme developed even further in Deuteronomy, where Moses warns a rebellious people by saying "Do you thus repay the Lord, O foolish and senseless people?" (Deut. 32:6), later quoting the Lord as saying "For a fire is kindled by my anger, . . . I will heap disasters upon them, spend my arrows against them: wasting hunger, burning consumption, bitter pestilence. The teeth of beasts I will send against them, with venom of things crawling in the dust" (32:22-24). Later, the Lord describes the people of Israel as "a nation devoid of sense; there is no understanding in them. If they were wise, they would understand this; they would discern what the end would be" (32:28-29).

The book of Proverbs contains some passages that focus on foolish thought processes rather than outcomes; examples are "doing wrong is like sport to a fool; but wise conduct is pleasure to a person of understanding" (Prov. 10:23); "one who is clever conceals knowledge, but the mind of a fool broadcasts folly" (12:23). But Proverbs also contains many consequence-related warnings: "a babbling fool will come to ruin" (10:8); "fools die for lack of sense" (10:21); "the fool will be servant to the wise" (11:29); "the talk of fools is a rod for their back" (14;3); "fools mock at the guilt offering, but the upright enjoy God's favor" (13:9); "folly is the punishment of fools" (16: 22); "one's own folly leads to ruin" (19:3); and "precious treasure remains in the house of the wise, but the fool devours it" (21:20).

In line with its less punitive orientation, the Christian Bible discusses foolishness less in terms of the risk of punishment and more in terms of the risk of not being rewarded. In Matthew 7:26-27, Jesus states "everyone who hears these words of mine and does not act on them will be like a foolish man who built his house on sand. The rain fell, and the floods came, and the winds blew against that house, and it fell—and great was its fall!" Again, a foolish person is foolish because his action, or in this case inaction, will have a long-term consequence, implied as failure to achieve salvation, a risk which a wise person (described in Matthew 7:25 as building his house on rock) will not encounter.

FOOLISHNESS IN EASTERN RELIGIONS

Eastern religions, such as Buddhism and Taoism, also tend to view foolishness and wisdom as polar opposites. But while there is more emphasis on foolishness (God-alienating behavior) in the three Abrahamic religions, there is more emphasis on wisdom (attainment of enlightenment) in Eastern religions. Furthermore, in the writings of generally deity-free Eastern religions, the risk discussed as likely to accrue to foolish actors is not so much a matter of God-inflicted plague or leprosy (Jewish Bible) or next-world damnation (Islam and Christianity) as it is a matter of failure to attain peace, happiness, and success in one's life. One exception to that is in Tibetan Buddhism, a relatively mystical branch which places much emphasis on reincarnation. In a classic of Tibetan Buddhism, *The Sutra of the Wise and Foolish*, the argument is advanced that troubles in one's current life were likely caused by foolish behavior in a former life, and that foolish action in the present is likely to bring bad consequences in one's next life (see Takakusu 1901).The essence of foolishness in Buddhism is to be found in the reliance on inadequate thinking, whose inadequacy stems from the fact that one does not recognize danger, even when such danger is fairly obvious or pointed out by wiser heads.

An example can be found in the story of the "Wise Birds and Foolish Birds" told in *Buddhist Tales for Young and Old* (Anderson 2007). The story involved many birds that lived in a giant tree in a forest. The wisest bird, who was their leader, saw two branches rubbing together, and noticed a wisp of smoke starting to form, and realized a fire could start that could burn down the forest. He called a meeting of the other bird residents and told them that they needed to vacate for another land, as staying there was too dangerous. The birds who were wise followed the leader's advice, while the birds that lacked wisdom felt he was an alarmist and they decided to stay in their comfortable homes and trust the tree would remain a safe place to live. Needless to say, the leader's words proved true and the forest caught fire. The birds that took the leader's advice survived while the others were blinded by smoke and many of them perished. The moral is: Those who ignore the advice of the wise do so at their own risk. (Anderson 2007, vol. 1, 169-70).

This definition of foolishness as a failure to heed wise warnings of danger can be found in many of the parables in the *Lotus Sutra*, a book whose attribution to the historic Buddha is disputed but which is, nevertheless, considered to be one of the most evolved statements of Buddhist doctrine. In one important parable, the Buddha tells a story (also involving fire) to a disciple about a rich man who had many children living in a large house that was in bad repair. A fire broke out and the man had the sense to run outside but his children did not recognize the danger. Even when the man called to them and told them of the need to come outside, the children refused to leave because they were too attached to their carts and other playthings inside the house. Knowing that his children cared mainly about their possessions, the man bribed them by telling them that they would each receive three carts if they came outside. This ruse worked and the man's children finally heeded his warning. Most of the commentary on this parable (the Buddhist equivalent of hairsplitting musings in the Jewish Talmud) focuses on the importance—for formal Buddhist doctrine—of the old man giving his sons one big cart rather than three smaller ones, and fails to make note (perhaps because it is so obvious) of the dangers flowing from an over-emphasis on material possessions.

In Buddhism, foolishness is considered, along with anger and greed, to be one of the "three evils," also known as the "three poisons," but is more fundamental because greed and anger are thought to be facilitated by foolishness. These are considered destructive impulses that "are the essence of all the delusions and negative workings of life that impede the realization of our full potential for happiness and creativity" (SGI Quarterly 2005). Foolishness, also known as "fundamental darkness," is defined in Buddhist writings as ignorance of the true nature of life. This true nature involves connectedness to others and to the broader good. Foolishness can be willful (driven by competitive impulses, for example) or passive (a failure to examine how one's behavior is undermining one's values). Thus, foolishness in Buddhism has a cognitive component (lack of knowledge of what is important) and a motivational component (holding incorrect values). As the parables show, the consequence of being foolish, in line with the other two evils (greed and anger), is that one will behave in a manner that has ultimate negative consequences for oneself and for society.

Taoism, like Buddhism, is an Eastern philosophical and religious system that has much to say about how to live a wise, contented, and valued life. One of the key concepts in Taoism is *wu-wei*, a Chinese term meaning "non-acting." This basically means that one acts naturally and without egoistic investment, in order to achieve what Liu Xiaogan termed a "balance between minimal effort and best result" (Fowler 2005) . Foolishness enters into this formulation, as action that is forced (that is motivated by excessive concern about outcome) has a high potential to backfire and, thus, to be foolish. Wisdom, therefore, has a "brake" mechanism against hasty action, a theme that is developed further later in this book. Because foolishness usually occurs in response to challenging or motivating situations, wu-wei enables one to become less foolish as a function of becoming more detached from external temptations or provocations.

FOOLS IN LOVE

One of the most common uses of the term "fool" is in conjunction with the word "love." It is reflected in dramatic works (such as *Fool for Love*, a 1983 play by Sam Shepard made into a movie, directed by Robert Altman), multiple songs with that title (written by songwriters as diverse as Ike Turner, Sandy Rogers, Das Pop, Tara Blaise, and Paul Burch). Numerous poems with that title emphasize four related forms of love-foolishness: (a) reactivating a mutually destructive relationship based on a reoccurring sick pattern; (b) staying in a relationship that is abusive or exploitative; (c) risking a good relationship through an affair; and (d) a state of blind dependency and compliance with any demand.

A somewhat different form of love-foolishness, which involves an error of omission rather than commission, involves being prevented by narcissism, rigidity, excessive perfectionism, or a meddling parent, from ever entering into or consummating a love relationship. This is reflected in these words from the song "What Kind of Fool Am I?" recorded by Sammy Davis Jr.: "What kind of fool am I? Who never fell in love. It seems that I'm the only one that I have been thinking of." (Bricusse and Newley 1962).

Although love-based foolishness can be found at all ages from adolescence up, a particularly risky form of love-foolishness can be found in the elderly. The expression "there is no fool like an old fool" was first recorded in 1546 ("But there is no foole to the olde foole, folke saie") in John Heywood's (1963) collected *Dialogue of Proverbs* and has been repeated in numerous works of literature ever since. It refers mainly to people (usually men) of an advanced age acting as if they were young again, particularly in undertaking sexual relationships with much younger partners, whose true motives (typically pecuniary) are disguised. In this, as in other forms of love-foolishness, we see people behaving in a manner detrimental to their own self-protective interests. Davis' song may be considered an alternative statement on elder love-foolishness, as it reflects recognition—near the end of one's life—of the damage to one's ultimate happiness caused by a failure to open oneself up to love.

FOOLS IN ROYAL COURTS

Examples of court fools can be found in many ancient societies, such as Greece, Rome, and India. However, the practice was especially widespread in medieval Europe, where virtually every royal court employed a "fool," known also as a jester. A jester's job was to entertain the monarch and his courtiers, by telling jokes and riddles and singing songs, many of them containing satirical and biting political commentary. What made such comments foolish (in the sense of courting danger) is that if told by anyone else, the jokester would likely be thrown into a dungeon or executed. Fools had a degree of immunity, in that they could get away with ridiculing the king in the name of fun or (sometimes the case) being viewed as a simpleton. However, even a fool could go too far, as was learned by Archibald Armstrong, a famous jester to King James I of England, who found himself dangerously out of a job when he made one insulting comment too many.

William Shakespeare, who wrote during the reigns of James, and his predecessor Elizabeth I, peopled his plays with many court fools. In *Twelfth Night*, Shakespeare described Feste the jester as "wise enough to play the fool" (act 3, scene 1). While this could have various interpretations, it likely was a recognition that a successful jester needed to know how far he could go and when he needed to play it safe. Implicit in the royal fool role, therefore, was the notion that one was playing a risky game that required a fair amount of skill to pull it off successfully.

Shakespeare's company of players, the Lord Chamberlain's men (later the King's men) always employed a fool specialist, initially Will Kempe (a clownish fool), later replaced by Robert Armin (a more serious fool). Shakespeare wrote several jester roles for Armin, who wrote a mock-scholarly treatise on the subject, the full title of which is "*Fool upon fool, or six sorts of sots: A fat fool and a flat fool, a lean fool and a clean fool, a merry fool and a very fool, showing their lives, humors and behaviors, with their want of wit in their show of wisdom. Not so strange as true*" (Armin, 1605).

A particular focus of Armin's analysis was the distinction between "natural" and "artificial" fools. A natural fool in Armin's typology is what today we would term someone with an intellectual disability, while an artificial fool is someone pretending to be a natural fool, whether an actor such as Armin (the first fool in the title) or a "wise fool" such as Feste in *Twelfth Night*.

Armin broke down this distinction somewhat, by considering himself a hybrid, whose natural foolishness came from having a physical deformity and whose artificial foolishness came from careful study and emulation of natural fools (for example, by wearing a towel to clean up drool). The history of royal fools went through such a distinction, with early medieval jesters tending to be individuals with actual cognitive or emotional impairments whose humor tended to be crude, while later Elizabethan jesters were more likely to be professionals whose humor tended to be witty.

The main risk for natural fools in courts is that they were ridiculed and socially isolated, although their roles as jesters gave them an otherwise unattainable degree of social status (Wolfensberger 2003). Witty fools ran the risk of alienating their royal protectors when their jokes went too far, as in the above-mentioned case of Archibald Armstrong. This is the main theme in a novel by Nicole Galland (2009) set in twelfth-century Wales. Titled, appropriately, *The Fool's Tale*, the novel tells the story of an elfish court jester named Gwirion. A foundling who was a childhood friend of the crown prince Maelgwyn (nicknamed "Noble"), Gwirion became even more loved by his royal friend when he saved his life by refusing to divulge the wounded prince's hiding place after they were both surprised in an ambush that killed Noble's father. Now elevated to king, Noble showed remarkable tolerance of Gwirion's frequent outrageous, and usually sexually tinged, pranks.

Tension developed between the two friends, however, when the king entered into a politically-arranged marriage of which the jester disapproved. Gwirion, expressing jealousy at this rival for his friend's affection, behaved in a very rude and contemptuous manner towards the new queen. She responded in kind, and a game of mutual nastiness persisted for quite a while. Because of his love for his friend, Noble was willing to overlook the jester's disrespectful conduct towards the queen. However, Gwirion took his foolishness to a new, and very irresponsible, level with a disastrous prank that affected the ability of the court to feed itself. Infuriated, the king subjected Gwirion to a terrifying mock execution, warning him afterwards that he needed to begin choosing his pranks more carefully. Chastened, Gwirion made an effort to behave himself and stopped taunting the queen. She, on the other hand, developed a crush on her former tormenter. During a time when the king was off at war, she started pressuring Gwirion to enter into a sexual relationship. Gwirion, although now in love with the queen, was very conflicted over this betrayal of his friend, and also feared that the affair, if discovered, could result in a real execution. Nevertheless, he could not help himself and began behaving very recklessly, even sneaking under the covers on the queen's bed when her ladies-in-waiting were asleep on the other side of a flimsy partition. As might be expected, such dangerous behavior nearly resulted in catastrophe for both the queen and Gwirion. *The Fool's Tale* is, thus, a story about someone who is a fool in both senses of the word: a man who functions as a court jester, and a man (and woman) who lack the sense or self-control to avoid pursuing a very risky course of action.

HOLY FOOLS

The term "holy fool" is used to describe a very spiritually evolved person who puts his life and well-being in jeopardy not because of unawareness of risky consequences but as a calculated move born out of moral courage and conviction. Jesus, in overturning the money lending tables in the Temple, and Gandhi, in leading the Salt March, are often held up as examples of "holy fools" whose deliberate and dangerous defiance of established, but to them immoral, convention or law, were signs of their saintliness or divinity (E.-A. Stewart 1999).

Holy fools can be found throughout the Judeo-Christian tradition, as in the many stories of prophets and saints who did bizarre, even psychotic, things in order to prick the conscience of the larger society. An example of such a character is Saint Simeon, a sixth-century monk and ascetic who supposedly simulated madness and asked God to permit him to behave in a way that would cause others to despise him and not acknowledge his service to them. A justification for holy foolishness was supposedly provided by the Apostle Paul who said in 1 Corinthians 4:10 "we are fools for Christ's sake." By this, he meant that to be a true Christian one should reject worldly cares and attempt to emulate Jesus. Thus a Holy Fool is one who understands the social risks but chooses to ignore them in the service of a higher purpose.

In popular music, the notion of a holy fool is addressed in the Beatles' "The Fool on the Hill," included in their *Magical Mystery Tour* album. The song was written by Paul McCartney (1967) and was inspired by a mystical experience he had one day when a man in a raincoat with a silly grin suddenly appeared on top of a hill, said a few pleasant words, and then disappeared just as suddenly. The man, who may be considered a modern-day holy person, is belittled and ridiculed for his other-worldly demeanor but actually has attained a degree of contentment that most people can only wish for.

THE MARCH OF FOLLY

The term "folly" is basically a synonym for foolishness, as in the first two definitions of folly in wiktionary.com (2018): (1) "foolishness" and (2) "thoughtless action resulting in tragic consequence." While foolishness refers to a broad range of human activities, the term folly usually refers to political acts, as in "Seward's Folly" (the US purchase of Alaska, at that time considered a worthless wilderness) and in the following sentence: "If we stay in Iraq until 2010 or 2012, as Secretary of Defense Donald Rumsfeld has warned we might, Bush's folly could consume a trillion dollars" (Beatty 2005).

One of the best books on political folly was written by Barbara Tuchman (1984) and bears the title *The March of Folly*. She defined a folly as an act engaged in stubbornly by a government or quasi-political entity (such as the Catholic Church, which at one time functioned as a state and whose Vatican headquarters still technically is) which is clearly against its own interests. Another way of putting this, which jibes with most of the popular uses detailed in this chapter, is that a folly is a course of action that a state or organization continues to pursue in spite of obvious signs that the policy is failing and is likely to bring about consequences far worse than if the policy had been avoided or abandoned earlier.

Tuchman had three criteria for the follies that she profiled: (a) the course of action must have been seen as foolish (and described as such) by numerous contemporaries, (b) there must have been a reasonable alternative course of action available to the actors; and (c) it must have been perpetrated by a group rather than just a single individual (Tuchman 1984, 6-7). In *The March of Folly*, Tuchman provided an in-depth profile of four such follies: (1) the decision by the Trojans to bring the large wooden horse left by the Greeks into the walls of their city; (2) the egregious abuses by the Renaissance popes that led inevitably to the Protestant Reformation; (3) the unwillingness of the British Crown and government to placate the increasingly alienated American colonies before they declared their independence; and (d) the inability of the United States to avoid becoming ensnared in the Vietnam War.

Taking the second case—the abuses that led to the Protestant Reformation—as example, one can see that all three of the conditions specified by Tuchman were met:

a. there were many critics, over several generations, who pointed to the rising tide of discontent created by flagrant abuses by Popes, including: their appointment of relatives (including their own illegitimate children) to important positions, including bishoprics; their openly maintaining mistresses in violation of their vows of celibacy; their engaging in politics and warfare as if they were secular rulers; and their profligate spending and the resultant need to devise corrupt methods of revenue such as the selling of indulgences (reductions in the amount of time to be spent in Purgatory after death);

b. the reasonable alternative course of action was to stop these abuses, and to rule in a less corrupt and more collegial manner, such as by convening a church Council; and

c. this behavior was not an aberration by one or two Popes, but represented systemic corruption that pervaded the entire Papacy, over
various Renaissance Popes, from Sextus IV (1471-1484) to Clement
VII (1523-1534).

All efforts to alert the Papacy to the need to reform its conduct were
rejected, for an obvious reason: the existing system was too lucrative and
comfortable for the church rulers and their relatives and cronies. The
resulting Protestant Reformation brought about the defection of half of
Catholicism's membership and precipitated reforms which, if conducted
sooner and voluntarily, could possibly have headed off a catastrophe that
was quite predictable.

SHIP OF FOOLS

There have been several creative works titled "Ship of Fools." They all
comment on the phenomenon of capable people risking much or throwing their lives away, through poor lifestyle choices. An example is the
1974 Grateful Dead song of that title, which appears to be a warning
against the damage to oneself likely to accrue from drugs, alcohol and
blind ambition.

The first known use of that expression was in the title of a late fif-
teenth-century satirical book in German by a Swiss theologian named
Sebastian Brant (1494/1944), *The Ship of Fools*. The book was an instant
sensation, translated into Latin and other languages, and it spawned a
series of copycat works termed "fool's literature." Several famous works
of art were produced, including the book's woodcut illustrations attributed to Albrecht Durer and a famous triptych (c. 1490–1500) of that title
by Hieronymus Bosch.

The book tells the story, in 112 chapters, of a voyage by a ship filled
with individuals traveling to a desired utopia named Narragonia (from
German "Narr," or "fool"), a place that is in fact a fool's paradise. The
chapters tell of the various ways in which men and women undermine
their chance for happiness and salvation through foolish behavior. As a
devout Christian, Brandt equated foolishness with ungodliness, and
quite often the danger these fools were flirting with was rebuke from
God. This is illustrated in an etching caption: "Who wants good service
every day, / But never "thank you" wants to say, / His thunder God on
him will vent." However, there are many examples of likely negative
secular consequences, as in these other etching captions: "He merits future poverty / Who always lives in luxury, / And joins the spendthrifts'
revelry"; and "Who lights his lamp here warm and bright / And lets the
oil give cheering light, That man shall never have delight."

A modern take on the subject was found in a novel titled *Ship of Fools*,
by Katherine Anne Porter (1962), and a 1965 film adaptation by screen-

writer Abby Mann that was directed by Stanley Kramer. It tells the story of a group of disparate passengers on a freighter, making a voyage in 1933 from Veracruz, Mexico to Bremerhaven, Germany. The movie is a commentary on the failings—including a dissolute exhaustion of the will by civilized people, in and outside of Germany—that contributed to the rise of Hitler. It also looks metaphorically at the progress of the world on its voyage to disaster, as reflected in the dire fate awaiting many of the soul-sick characters in the movie as they sail unknowingly into the jaws of their own destruction.

A FOOL AND HIS MONEY

A folk idiom that comes to mind when thinking about foolishness is "a fool and his money are soon parted." The folk saying, which was coined in the sixteenth century by English poet Thomas Tusser (1580/1878), refers to two foolish tendencies that are common threats to any sizeable (or non-sizeable) bank balance: (a) a tendency to make unnecessary expensive purchases, and (b) a susceptibility to scam artists, promoting fraudulent or dubious schemes. Many humorous variations of this idiom have been devised, my favorite being one attributed to Will Rogers, "a fool and his money are soon elected" (goodreads.com, 132444). The truth of the original saying can be found in the common experience of many professional athletes and entertainers, who accrue large sums in their (typically) short peak earning years and manage to blow much or all of it on showy purchases, expensive gifts, and questionable investments. As with other uses of the word fool, this expression is based on the idea that behind a seemingly safe situation (having a high income) lies a hidden yet foreseeable threat (having a sharp drop-off in that income at some point), with the consequence being that one can become poor again if one does not save and invest wisely.

A FOOL'S ERRAND

A "fool's errand" is a task that cannot be accomplished, either because the problem to be solved is impossibly difficult or because the object to be attained does not exist, as when a practical joker hands a gullible person a sack after dark and tells her to go off and capture a snipe (a fictional bird, although one can find the "Common Snipe" in Iowa in March). This is a form of "wild goose chase" that is often used in summer camps, when naïve younger campers are given ridiculous instructions (such as banging rocks together) for carrying out this impossible task.

There are several classic works of literature that are accounts of a Fool's Errand, with the two most famous probably being Voltaire's 1759 *Candide* and Jonathan Swift's 1726 *Gulliver's Travels* (an earlier book from which Voltaire derived some inspiration). People who engage in a fool's errand are typically portrayed as overly trusting and gullible, and as seeking something (such as enlightenment or happiness) which both Candide and Gulliver eventually concluded was more likely to be found at home in one's own back yard.

FOOLISH SITCOM CHARACTERS

The *Seinfeld* sit-com, one of the most popular TV shows of all time, is described by its creators and principals as "a show about nothing" (reddit.com). In fact, like many predecessors such as *I Love Lucy*, *The Honeymooners*, *My Little Margie*, and *Life of Riley*, the show is about something, namely foolish behavior and the difficulty in getting out of messes created by characters who show consistently poor judgment. One is reminded, for example, of the recurring refrain of William Bendix's radio (and later TV) character in *Riley*: "what a revoltin' development this is," (Dunning, 1998) and the similar refrain of Gail Storm's TV character in *Margie*: "I've got a problem" (Terrace, 1979). All four of the central characters in *Seinfeld* behave foolishly, but Kramer clearly takes first prize in the foolishness sweepstakes. This is reflected in the very end of "The Wife" episode (so named because Jerry pretends to be married to his girlfriend so he can get her drycleaning discount). Kramer wants to look his best when he goes to meet his new girlfriend's family, so he spends time in a tanning studio, where he falls asleep in the tanning bed and comes out looking like he is in blackface. When he rings the doorbell, his girlfriend's father, who is Black, opens the door, takes one look at Kramer, and says angrily: "I thought you were bringing a white boy home. I don't see a white boy, I see a damn fool" (Mehlman 1994).

A brief look at some of the messes resulting from Kramer's profound lack of common sense serves to illustrate that he is a fool first and foremost because he rarely anticipates the likely risky consequences—physical or social—of his actions or verbalizations. A good example of this occurred in the 1994 episode "The Hamptons" (also known popularly as "ugly baby" and "shrinkage"), in which the four main characters spend a weekend at a vacation home at the seashore. During the episode, Kramer finds a tethered lobster trap and thinks it is acceptable to take the contents home. He cooks a lobster feast for his friends and is later arrested for theft and sentenced to pick up roadside trash.

The lobster incident illustrated Kramer's chronic failure to take social perspectives, recognize social convention or anticipate sometimes serious social consequences (in the Hamptons episode also mentioning to George that he had seen his date sun-bathing topless). As example, Kramer: failed to understand ("The Puerto Rican Day," 1998) that stomping in public on an accidentally incinerated Puerto Rican flag could get him attacked by a crowd watching New York's annual Puerto Rican Day parade; failed to understand ("The Nose Job," 1991) that commenting negatively on a woman's appearance could be deeply offensive (although here, as was often the case, he got away with it); failed to understand ("The Keys," 1992) that visiting excessively could endanger a friendship; and failed to anticipate that parking in a prohibited parking area ("The Handicap Spot," 1993) or urinating in a parking garage ("The Parking Garage," 1991) could get one arrested.

Dramatic as were Kramer's many socially foolish acts, it was in the arena of Practical foolishness that he came close to getting himself and others killed or seriously injured. Examples are: when Kramer failed ("The Doodle," 1995) to appreciate the seriousness of the fumigation warning on Jerry's door and spent ninety minutes in his friend's gas-filled apartment eating and reading; when he painted over the white lines ("The Pothole, " 1997) to make the lanes wider on the highway he had adopted, without understanding the potential for causing crashes; when he failed to understand the danger in telling someone about to have surgery ("The Jimmy," 1995) to ignore the advice not to eat before anesthesia, saying "Oh no, you got to eat before surgery, you need your strength" (Kavet and Robin, 1995); when he failed to anticipate the danger to himself and his pet chicken ("The Little Jerry," 1997) of getting involved in cock fighting; and when he attempted to get water out of his ear ("The Finale," 1998) by bouncing violently on one leg in the aisle of a small private plane, causing it to go out of control and make a crash landing. A later sitcom, *Curb Your Enthusiasm*, by *Seinfeld* cocreator Larry David, is even more a show about foolish behavior, as every episode (indeed every five minutes) shows the protagonist doing or saying something with no apparent awareness or concern about the likely consequences.

FOOL TALES

Many folk tales feature central characters who are described as foolish. These "fool tales" are often used as teaching devices, to make some point about elements of morality or efficacy. Fool tales are especially widely used in Jewish folk literature. There are many Yiddish words for fool, some of them (for example, shmuck, putz, shmendrick) variations on "penis." One non-penis Yiddish term for fool is "shlemiel" Here is a definition of a shlemiel from the children's book *Kibitzers and Fools: Tales My Zayda Told Me*: "A shlemiel (a fool) will dump a plate of hot soup into the lap of a shlimazel (unlucky person). . . . Farshtayst (do you understand?)" (Taback 2005).

One of the most widely known fool tales in Jewish literature is the short story "Gimpel the Fool," by Isaac Bashevis Singer (1957). The story—which clearly confirms my view (expressed in later chapters and in my book *Annals of Gullibility* [2009a]) that gullibility is maybe the most common form of foolishness—begins with Gimpel lamenting that others in his village of Frampol saw him as a fool because he was "easy to take in." He worked as a baker, a job where he had many opportunities to be tricked. One day, Rietze the candle dipper told Gimpel that his parents had returned from the grave and were outside asking for him. Although Gimpel suspected a trick, he went in search of his parents anyway, as he reasons "What did I stand to lose just by looking?" (Singer 1957).

Ridiculed for his gullibility, Gimpel goes to Frampol's rabbi for counsel. The rabbi consoles the baker by saying "It is written, better to be a fool all your days than for one hour to be evil. . . . They are the fools. For he who causes his neighbor to feel shame loses Paradise himself" (Singer 1957). (This also confirms my view of foolishness as risk-unawareness, as the severe consequence that the rabbi implies is in store for the tormentors is eternal damnation by a judgmental and unforgiving deity).

Gimpel considers leaving Frampol, but the villagers fix him up with a wife, Elka. He expresses reservations about Elka, because she is an unmarried mother and because she walks with a limp. But the townspeople convince him that her young son is actually her baby brother, that the limp is deliberate and, furthermore, they threaten to have the rabbi fine him for bad-mouthing Elka. She refuses to have sex with Gimpel and when she gives birth four months later, she tells Gimpel that the child was premature. Gimpel has doubts but the schoolmaster persuades him it is true because the same thing happened to Adam and Eve.

Gimpel sleeps at the bakery during the week, but one night he comes home unexpectedly and catches his wife having sex with another man. Gimpel moves out for awhile and eventually moves back in after deciding he was mistaken. This scenario repeats itself when Gimpel finds his apprentice in bed with Elka. She tells him to go out and check on the goat and when he returns the young man is gone and she denies everything. Elka has many more children by different men and each time Gimpel believes her assurances that she has been faithful. On her deathbed, Elka asks Gimpel for forgiveness and admits that none of the children are his. Gimpel has a crisis of faith and decides to deceive the world as it had deceived him by urinating in the bread dough. The crisis is resolved when Elka appears in a dream and tells him "You fool! Because I was false is everything false too? I never deceived anyone but myself. I'm paying for it all, Gimpel." He realizes that by becoming a deceiver he is jeopardizing his immortal soul. Gimpel buries the contaminated bread dough, divides his property among his several children, and leaves Frampol for good. He becomes an itinerant story teller, who weaves tall tales. He is now treated well by others, even though he still tends to believe lies. He looks forward to joining Elka in a place "without deception . . . [where] even Gimpel cannot be deceived" (Singer 1957).

FOOLS IN STREET SLANG

Mr. T is a former professional wrestler turned actor who starred as B.A. (Bad Attitude) Baracus in the 1980s television adventure series *The A-Team*. He was once voted in a BBC poll as the fourth most influential American, behind only Homer Simpson, Abraham Lincoln, and Martin Luther King Jr. A very muscular Black man who sported a Mohawk (the result of a failed attempt to carve a T in his head) and lots of jewelry, Mr. T's famous catchphrase "I pity the fool who . . ." [messes with me] actually came from his role in the 1982 film *Rocky III*. Implicit in this expression is that T is one dangerous dude and anyone who thinks that he can defeat him is making a very big mistake. A fool, in Mr. T's lingo, is thus someone who is putting himself at severe physical risk by miscalculating his ability to take on a person as tough as he.

Another example of the use of "fool" in urban US street slang is the expression "Boo Boo the fool." I first heard this when watching a sports news show when the topic of conversation was a Nike commercial in which basketball star Kobe Bryant was showing off his new pair of shoes by appearing to jump over a car that was speeding right at him. When the sports journalist Stephen A. Smith was asked if he thought the stunt was real, he replied by saying "Who do you take me for, Boo Boo the Fool?" Apparently inspired by Yogi Bear's ineffectual and often-tricked sidekick Boo Boo, this expression is widely used in urban slang to refer to someone who is easily taken in by others, as in "Man after I drove 100 miles to see that girl and I found out she gave me the wrong address I felt like Boo Boo the fool" (urbandictionary.com, 2018). Boo Boo's foolishness lies in his gullibility, that is, his overly trusting nature, which puts him constantly in danger of being victimized and taken advantage of.

TWO

Foolishness as Inattention to Risk

In contrast to the emphasis on risk-unawareness in the popular literature on foolishness, the few scholars who write about foolishness have tended to focus on process or capacity (for example, failure or inability to use reason) and rarely even mention risk or outcome. In part, this reflects the tendency of intelligence researchers (who are most likely to study foolishness) to emphasize academic and ignore non-academic (that is, social and practical) uses of intelligence, and in part it is a failure of psychologists in general to address specific context as a contributor to human behavior. Furthermore, I am unaware of any definition or treatise on foolishness that incorporates all four of the explanatory factors that I emphasize in this book.

In this chapter, I present an explanatory theory of foolish behavior which builds on the limited scholarly literature on the topic, but adds elements taken from the more general psychology literature on motivational contributors to human behavior. In line with the popular—including fictional and religious—literature on foolishness reviewed in chapter 1, and contrary to what other scholars have emphasized, I define foolish action as behavior which fails to recognize or give sufficient weight to the risk that is both serious and likely to be apparent to most people.

RELATIVE ABSENCE OF SCHOLARLY WORK ON FOOLISHNESS

Given the prevalence of the terms "foolish," "fool," and "folly" in popular culture and everyday parlance, one would expect a fair amount of scholarly writing by psychologists on the topic. However, a *Psych Info* search using keywords such as "foolishness" and "stupidity" (another, somewhat harsher, term for foolishness) turned up only around one hundred overlapping hits, with many of them coming from the fields of

19

literature, philosophy, or history rather than from individual differences in human behavior. A notable example of a work of literature dealing with the topic of foolishness is Dostoevsky's (1869) *The Idiot*, about a saintly man whose naïve gullibility made him too foolish to survive outside of a monastery. Within the field of philosophy, Avital Ronell's (2002) *Stupidity* provides an overview of how the topic has been addressed by various philosophers from Plato and Kant on. My favorite of the non-psychological works on foolishness is *The Encyclopedia of Stupidity*, by Dutch literary historian Matthijs van Boxsel (2003). Among the delights to be found in van Boxsel's book is this short poem by seventeenth-century Dutch poet Jeremias de Decker: "Stupidity is twice your lot: An ignoramus, you, my friend! And yet you know it not!" (Van Boxsel 2003, 00). The tiny nature of the psychological literature on foolishness can be put into perspective when considering that a *Psych Info* search using the keyword "intelligence" turned up approximately 60,000 hits, compared to maybe fifty works (half of the above-mentioned hits) on foolishness by psychologists. Undoubtedly, a major reason for the absence of research by psychologists into foolishness is the love affair that psychologists have with intelligence quotient (IQ), which some consider the psychology field's main contribution (or detriment) to culture and science. There is an assumption, therefore, that foolishness, or stupidity, is nothing more than low IQ. In fact, some dictionary definitions of foolishness start off with low IQ and then go on in later definitions to mention deficient common sense and poor judgment about everyday matters.

The recent surge of interest in multiple intelligences, which many attribute to Howard Gardner (1983), but was in fact proposed by Edward Thorndike (1921) many decades earlier, has encouraged an understanding that one can be stupid in ways not tapped by IQ tests. To understand this, it would help to know that French pioneering psychologists Alfred Binet and Theodore Simon—who around 1905 invented the test after which most subsequent IQ tests have been modeled—generated their test's content by sampling items from the school curricula at different grades. Thus, an IQ test can be considered an alternate form of an educational achievement test, which explains why IQ scores are very strongly correlated with (both test and report card) measures of academic functioning, but are considerably less strongly correlated with other aspects of competence. Interestingly, Binet and Simon started their study of intelligence much more broadly, including a more descriptive (and less test-based) approach to aspects that included social and everyday judgment. However, they narrowed their approach when asked by the French government to come up with a test to identify children unlikely to benefit from a new social invention: universal free public education.

The psychologist who has done the most to study non-IQ aspects of intelligence is Robert J. Sternberg, and it is no coincidence that he is also the scholar who has done the most to advance the study of foolishness.

For the most part, Sternberg has used the term "foolish" in his writings, although he gave the title *Why Smart People Are So Stupid* (Sternberg 2002a) to an edited book on the topic. In his own chapter in that book, Sternberg (2002b) indicated that he prefers the term "foolishness," leading me to speculate that the publisher felt that a book with "stupid" in the title was likely to sell better.

Sternberg indicates that he believes people who behave foolishly are deficient in "common sense," which he also describes as an absence of "tacit knowledge" about everyday and work roles and functions (2009a; 2009b). As a cognitive psychologist, it is not surprising that Sternberg, along with his longtime collaborator Richard Wagner (2002), has viewed foolishness mainly in cognitive terms, specifically as an absence of awareness of the unwritten rules that affect success in various settings. However, in spite of their preference for a cognitive view of foolishness, Sternberg and Wagner recognized that tacit knowledge alone cannot fully explain all cases of foolish behavior. For example, using the example of former president Bill Clinton's disastrous affair with Monica Lewinsky (which was much in the news around the time of the mini-conference that became the basis for his edited book), Sternberg asserted that Clinton surely possessed tacit knowledge that workplace sex with a young intern is neither ethical nor smart. Sternberg thus attributed Clinton's foolishness to certain personality traits, specifically arrogance and a sense of entitlement and immunity. Interestingly, Sternberg left sexual arousal, and Clinton's chronic sleep deprivation out of the causative equation, and also failed to mention situational components, such as Lewinsky flirtatiously snapping her thong at the priapic president (Sternberg 2009b).

Similarly, Wagner (2002) wrote about a bright college president who was fired because he had a fiercely combative style which caused him to frequently insult his board members. Presumably the college president possessed tacit knowledge that this was not a good idea, but his need to be combative was so ingrained that he was unable to control his behavior, even when dealing with people who possessed the power to fire him. For Wagner, this personality trait was so controlling that it probably amounted to a mental illness.

This idea that foolish behavior can be a reflection of mental illness was proposed even more strongly by psychoanalyst Edmund Bergler. In *A Talent for Stupidity*, Bergler (1998) labeled foolish patients of his with the acronym "B.I.I." ("the bungler, the incompetent and the ineffectual"). He suggested that virtually all foolishness, even when rising to the level of "pseudo-mental deficiency," could be attributed entirely to neurotic processes, such as repressed hostility. This view of habitually foolish behavior as reflecting self-destructive personality processes was also developed in a paper by Louis Birner (1984) titled "The Schlemiel and the Shlep: A

Psychoanalytic Note on Two Masochistic Styles," in the journal *Modern Psychoanalysis.*

A third explanatory factor, besides cognition and personality, has been emphasized by Toronto-based psychologist Keith Stanovich (1994) among others, and that is the role of affect and impulsivity. Under the rubric of "irrationality" (that is, non-intelligent decisions in people seemingly capable of making intelligent decisions), Stanovich (1999) has concentrated his attention on impulsivity-induced failure to use logic in addressing problems of the kind favored by economists and decision theorists such as Amos Tversky and Eldar Shafir (1992). Like most of the contributors to Sternberg's edited book, Stanovich (2002) avoided addressing problems that pose grave threats to an individual's existence or well-being; a major exception is a fatal truck accident discussed by David N. Perkins (2002, discussed later) in relation to situational time pressures. And, as I make clear throughout this book, true foolishness is reflected not in whether one makes a trivial mistake such as making an economically non-optimal purchase, but in whether one does something that puts one's (or others') well-being, safety, fortune, freedom, or life at risk.

A fourth factor that might contribute to explaining foolish action attracted little systematic attention by any of the contributors to Sternberg's (2002a) book, and that is the role of context or situation. Obviously, one is more likely to behave foolishly when dangers are less obvious, when there are aspects of a situation (such as an influencer using coercive or manipulative tactics) that induce fear or longing, or when there are no others in the immediate context who are able and willing to intervene on one's behalf. Although not emphasized by Sternberg or his contributors, situational influences on human functioning have been emphasized strongly in the work of social psychologists, such as Robert Cialdini (1984), whose book *Influence* explains how sales agents such as telemarketers use various ploys that are intended to get people to make purchases they neither want nor need. The role of situations is also a major part of the motivational theory of Martin Ford (1992), from whom I got much of the inspiration to develop my four-factor causative model of foolish action.

THREE FORMS OF FOOLISH ACTION

In the balance of this chapter, I lay out a four-factor explanatory model of foolish action that will provide the conceptual framework for the analysis of foolish acts in the balance of the book. This model is basically an elaborated and much more differentiated approach to the ideas touched on above (for example, "cognition" is much more than tacit knowledge and "personality" is more than arrogance). Before laying out this causative theory of foolish action, however, I need to say a little more about what I believe foolishness to be and about the three major forms or subtypes of foolish behavior.

In line with the popular and religious conceptions of foolishness discussed in chapter 1, I define foolish behavior as action which fails to recognize or attach sufficient attention to risk, particularly risk that is potentially serious and relatively obvious. (In this, I depart from the monotheistic religion literature, in that I am concerned with risk in this world rather than in the next). In figure 2.1, I identify three major types of foolish (that is, risk-ignoring) actions: "Practical," "Noninduced-Social," and "Induced-Social."

Practical foolish action involves behavior where the ignored risk is physical. An example, would be someone who decides to save money by cutting down a large high-hanging tree branch by himself rather than hiring a professional tree surgeon, thus exposing himself to the very real possibility of injury or death, as happened to an acquaintance when a large branch swung back at him, fatally knocking him off a high ladder.

Social foolish actions involve behavior where the ignored risk is societal (losing a job or one's savings) or interpersonal (rejection, humiliation). The distinction between social foolishness that is induced rather than non-induced has to do with whether or not the socially risky action is triggered by manipulative pressure from one or more other people (induced) or originates almost entirely from within the person him or herself (non-induced). Induced-Social foolish action is pretty much another word for "gullibility," which was the aspect of foolishness addressed in my earlier book *Annals of Gullibility* (Greenspan 2009a).

The foolish action typology is illustrated with numerous case examples in later chapters. Therefore, the typology will not be explained further here. One possible limitation of the typology is that Practical foolish action, while generally non-induced (for example, someone smoking in a closed car with a gasoline can in the back seat) can occasionally be induced (for example, adolescents daring each other to do a dangerous stunt). Furthermore, while the consequences of a Practically foolish act are always physical, they can also be social.

An example of a Practically foolish act that also had a Social (in this case induced) component occurred in California in 2007 (Goldstein 2017). A Sacramento radio station was featuring a "Hold Your Wee for a Wii" contest where a contestant, 28-year-old Jennifer Strange—hoping to win an electronic game device—died after she allowed herself to be pressured by DJ's to keep on ingesting water after she tried to stop and started showing signs of physical distress. This tragic example can be considered mainly Practical in that the risk which the victim and the contest organizers failed to recognize was physical: a bodily chemical imbalance which could (and did) result in serious illness and even death.

The induced component of this practically foolish action involved the social pressure that the radio announcers placed on Ms. Strange to keep

Types of Foolish Action

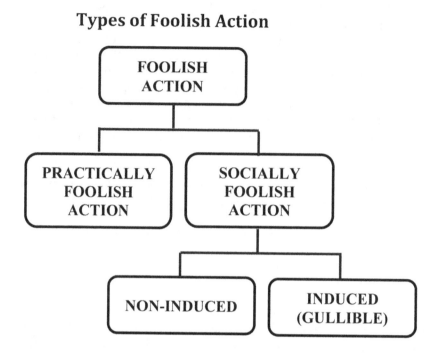

Figure 2.1.   Types of Foolish Action *Source: Chart by author.*

going. The organizers also were practically foolish in their failure to understand the need to have on hand medical personnel, both to monitor the contestants and to inform the station of the physical danger to which they were exposing the contestants. However, the act was also socially foolish in that the organizers of the stunt—who never intended anything other than humiliating the contestants in the service of entertaining their radio audience—failed to appreciate the social risks (condemnation, termination, lawsuits) to which they were exposing themselves and the company they worked for after the stunt backfired. While this example shows that the three-fold typology of foolish acts may be overly simplified, I shall still use it as a convenient framework for organizing and presenting the case materials which follow in subsequent chapters.

PLACING FOOLISHNESS ON A DEVELOPMENTAL CONTINUUM

As noted in chapter 1, foolishness and wisdom are often discussed in the vernacular literature as polar opposites. But as neither of them are very well defined, the precise nature of this polarity has for the most part not been well explained. The concept of risk awareness does, I believe, provide such an explanation, as long as one accepts my basic argument that foolishness is mainly a matter of lacking the ability or willingness to recognize and avoid obvious risk, while wisdom is mainly a matter of possessing an ability to recognize and avoid non-obvious risk. Or, given that I discuss foolishness in action terms, foolish action can be described as behavior which puts an actor in the path of foreseeable risk, while wise action involves behavior which allows the actor to avoid being in the path of relatively hidden and non-obvious risk. I believe that such a formulation is justified, even though I can accept that a somewhat broader formulation (for example, relative ability to understand consequences of action as well as inaction) which includes risk-awareness but is not limited to it, might also be valid.

To place foolishness and wisdom on a full developmental continuum, it is necessary to add a third construct: "common sense." Although Sternberg (2004) uses the terms wisdom and common sense interchangeably, and describes them as both characterized by "tacit knowledge" (understanding of unwritten social or practical rules that govern success in different settings), I believe wisdom and common sense to be related but different, and involving far more than tacit knowledge (Sternberg 2002a or 2002b or 2004). They are related in that both can be characterized by the possession of risk-awareness, but they are different in that the degree of risk-awareness associated with wisdom is greater than the degree of risk-awareness associated with common sense.

In this scheme, as portrayed in figure 2.2, common sense is defined by an awareness of obvious risk, while wisdom is defined by an awareness of both obvious and non-obvious (subtle and hidden) risk. People who have common sense, thus, may or may not (and typically do not) also have wisdom. Thus, there is a developmental continuum from foolishness (unawareness of obvious risk) to common sense (awareness only of

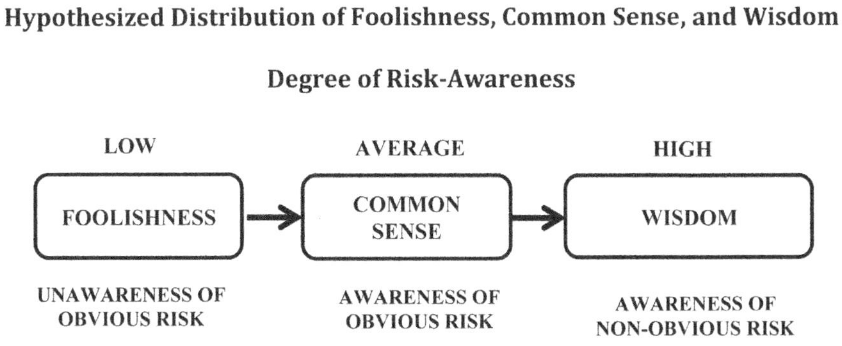

Hypothesized Distribution of Foolishness, Common Sense, and Wisdom

Degree of Risk-Awareness

Figure 2.2. Hypothesized Distribution of Foolishness, Common Sense, and Wisdom *Source: Chart by author.*

obvious risk) to wisdom (awareness of non-obvious as well as obvious risk).

Support for the notion of foolishness as unawareness of obvious risk can be found in the vernacular literature covered in chapter 1, and in most of the foolish action stories recounted throughout this book. Support for the notion of wisdom as awareness of non-obvious risk (and also for the idea that it is a scarce commodity) can also be found in vernacular uses of the word "wise" found in the media and elsewhere. An example of such usage can be found in accounts of victims of the Bernard Madoff Ponzi scheme, namely to describe the relatively few people in the investment community who possessed the wisdom to say "this looks fishy to me, and I will pass on it."

A poignant example was told by me when I was serving on a panel only a few months after the Madoff fiasco, where a mix of mental health and investment experts were attempting to make sense of the psychology of the victims (including yours truly). A consultant hired by hedge funds to check out investment targets, told the story of a man who asked him to evaluate Madoff, to whom the man's company had given over a billion dollars to invest. After spending a few weeks on this assignment, the consultant reported that he told the man he had identified several prominent red flags indicating that Madoff was running a fraudulent scheme. These included hand-written and non time-stamped trading slips, and the impossibility that such large reported trades would go unnoticed by other brokerage firms. The consultant urgently advised the man to immediately withdraw client funds, including those belonging to the man himself and many of his friends and family members. The (in hindsight, wisdom-challenged) man refused to follow this advice, telling the consultant that he considered Madoff a friend, and closed by saying "the SEC has given Bernie a clean bill of health, so why should I listen to you?" (this story is told in Greenspan and Woods 2016, 141-66).

The speaker did not publicly divulge the identity of his client but during a break he responded to my curiosity by telling me that the man was René—Thierry Magon de la Villehucet, the 65-year-old French aristocrat and hedge fund CEO, who committed suicide in his New York office by cutting his wrists with a box cutter. This (from a Japanese standpoint) extremely honorable man showed his decency in another way, by encasing his wrists in a plastic garbage bag, in order to not make too big a mess for the cleaning crew to have to deal with.

The largest vernacular literature on wisdom is probably to be found in the writings of Buddhist and other Eastern religious leaders, as well as in the related writings of Western moral philosophers such as Epictetus and Spinoza. A constant refrain to be found in these writings is the importance of not seeking or over-valuing fame, fortune, status, and material objects. Such superficially appealing goals are to be resisted for one simple reason, and that is that while those things may bring short-term happiness, they are highly likely, by making one a slave to external happenstance, to bring long-term unhappiness and frustration.

Common sense is a term first coined by Aristotle to refer to an intuitive path to everyday knowledge. As such, it is a lower-level skill than wisdom, in that the advanced risk-awareness shown by wise people—such as the hedge fund consultant who tried to warn Mr. Magon de la Villehucet about the danger Bernard Madoff posed to his business (and, unfortunately, to his life)—is the result of considerable knowledge and experience. Common sense, as an intuitive process, on the other hand, does not depend as much on in-depth knowledge or experience; in fact, it is most often learned incidentally and without instruction. This is found in such pieces of advice as to look both ways when crossing the street or to not look upward upon hearing someone shout "below" when rock climbing, in order to protect one's face from dislodged rocks. These lay conceptions of common sense appear to differ from lay conceptions of wisdom in the degree of obviousness of the risk-awareness that is involved.

The developmental nature of the proposed continuum can be described in several ways. One way involves the distribution of these kinds of behaviors in the general population. In terms of the "normal" (bell-shaped) curve that describes most human competencies (see fig. 2.3), wise and foolish actions (and even more so, people who habitually behave wisely and foolishly) are relatively infrequent occurrences, as indicated by their falling at the far right (roughly top 10 percent) and far left (roughly bottom 10 percent) tails of the curve. Finally, as common sense is a quality that is found most of the time in most people, it falls in the middle (80 percent) of the distribution, although undoubtedly the distribution varies as a function of the complexity of the specific challenge facing an actor. (A more extended discussion of common sense is contained in chapter 13).

Another, more explicitly "developmental" way of discussing this progression, is to talk about the typical life-course, and the kinds of protections against risk-unawareness that might be needed for individuals at different ages and stages of development. It is well-established in the cognitive-developmental literature that children and adolescents go through a sequence of qualitatively different stages of cognitive functioning, with the ideas of the Swiss developmental scholar Jean Piaget and his collaborator, Bärbel Inhelder, being especially influential (Piaget and Inhelder 2011). To my knowledge, they did not specifically address the subject of risk or risk-awareness, but it is possible I believe to extract ideas about risk-awareness from their general theory. Furthermore, the legal system already has some provisions—such as about what constitutes child neglect and what limitations there are on contractual or decision-making autonomy—that closely track Piagetian findings about the

Developmental Continuum of Foolishness to Wisdom

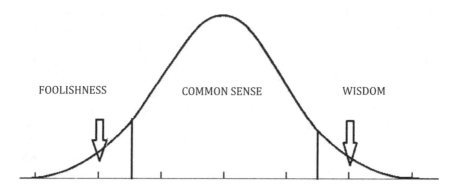

Figure 2.3.   Developmental Continuum of Foolishness to Wisdom *Source: Chart by author.*

growth of cognitive competence in childhood, adolescence, and young adulthood.

There are four basic stages in the Piaget-Inhelder scheme: the sensori-motor stage (roughly birth to 2), the stage of preoperations (roughly 2 to 7), the stage of concrete operations (roughly 7 to 12) and the stage of formal operations (roughly 12 through adulthood) (Piaget and Inhelder 2011). Infants (sensoriotor) period) basically have no risk awareness at all, which is why leaving an infant unattended, even for a little while, is a dangerous act which could result in grievous harm to the child and consequences ranging from loss of custody to jail time for the caregiver. The same is largely true as well for preoperational children, but risk-based protections can be relaxed a little bit (for example, by allowing a child to play outside without constant monitoring), especially as the child approaches the higher end of that stage.

It is when we get to the concrete and formal operations stages that things become a little more complex and interesting. Primary-age (roughly comparable to concrete operational) children can do many things in the practical sphere, such as operate a power mower, cook a meal, operate industrial equipment, and even drive a motor vehicle, and in some settings (such as a farm) or cultures (for example, the US and Great Britain in the nineteenth century, before the imposition of child labor laws), one can find examples of that happening. But for the most part, children prior to approximately twelve years old cannot be trusted to do practical (mechanical) tasks on their own in a fully satisfactory or safe manner. However, the real deficit in concrete operational children is more to be found in their inability to recognize social risks, which is reflected in the ease with which they can be tricked into being molested sexually (and then keeping quiet about it) by manipulative predators, such as trusted, but morally-depraved, family members or religious figures.

With adolescents who attain formal operations, there are few practical tasks of an everyday nature (that is, which do not require advanced training) that cannot be performed adequately, but they are still at risk socially, which is why in most places young people are not allowed to independently sign contracts, get married, take out loans, purchase property, etc. until they are eighteen years of age. Here the issue is not just the ability to recognize social risk, but also the ability to resist social pressure in which one's "will can be overborne" (a basic legal concept used to describe the social vulnerability of young people or others in need of legal protection). While fluid (brain structure-based) intelligence is largely fully formed by the onset of formal operations, crystallized (information-based) intelligence is still a work-in-progress, as are the "executive functions" (self-regulatory processes associated with the still-developing frontal lobes of the brain). It is for this reason, in addition to the over-dependence of teenagers on the approval and modeling of peers, that youths up to eighteen years old are considered so prone to behaving foolishly that they have their own judicial system and are generally exempted from the severe criminal penalties reserved for adults.

While increasing age in adulthood brings experiences and training that in some cases result in wisdom, the majority of adults are stuck in the realm of common sense, possessing neither substantial wisdom nor substantial foolishness (although glimpses of each may surface on occasion). However, when approaching the end of life, many elderly persons experience a diminution of cognitive ability as a result of biologically-based changes in brain structures and functioning. The behavior of individuals with Alzheimer's or other forms of dementia (loss of cognitive ability) is often described as "childlike," a consequence of which is a loss in the ability to recognize or avoid risk. For this reason, protective arrangements—such as conservatorships or guardianships—are often put in place to protect demented individuals from making poor decisions, usually initiated by others who would exploit the gullibility (that is, foolish trust) which comes with the loss of risk-awareness in the frail elderly. Thus, another "developmental" way of discussing foolishness is as a stage that many adults with brain-based disorders either regress to (dementia) or in the case of developmental disabilities, never fully grow out of. It is because of their younger mental ages, that adults with developmental disabilities are less able to recognize or avoid risk than are others at the same chronological age. My colleagues and I have argued (Greenspan, Switzky, and Woods 2011) that developmental disorders, including but not limited to Mental Retardation (now termed "Intellectual Disability" or ID) should be considered a form of "Common Sense Deficit Disorder." This idea is fleshed out more fully in chapter 9, while the construct of common sense itself is explored extensively in chapter 13.

THREE

An Explanatory Model of Human Foolishness

Scholars writing about foolish behavior have identified four broad explanatory factors that can, in any instance, contribute to the kind of risk-exposing behavior that I am terming "foolish." My main contribution to this literature (aside from pointing out the centrality of risk) was to combine these explanatory factors into a comprehensive model, both in relation to my longstanding interest in people with disabilities (where risk-unawareness is particularly problematic) and then in the general population. Initially, this effort was in the service of exploration of gullibility (Greenspan, Loughlin, and Black 2001) and a decade later (Greenspan 2009b; Greenspan, Switzky, and Woods 2011) in relation to all three kinds of foolish behavior depicted earlier in figure 2.1. A description of the foolishness model, in both linear and dynamic forms follows in the remainder of this chapter, with a fuller discussion of the four factors following in chapter 4.

LINEAR MODEL OF FOOLISH ACTION

A linear additive model of foolish action is depicted in figure 3.1. In this model, foolish action is viewed as an outcome which occurs as the result of the intersection of four broad factors, which come together at a moment in time, and which in some combination cause a person to act foolishly (or, non-foolishly, for that matter). The four broad factors each can be subdivided further; the subfactors are described and illustrated in chapter 4 and in subsequent chapters. One factor (Situation) is external to the actor, while the other three factors (Cognition, Affect/State, and Peronality) are internal to the person. A hypothetical situation will be posed, to illustrate what is meant by these four factors.

Situation is the problem posed to the actor, that they have to deal with, either successfully or unsuccessfully. Situations vary in terms of their complexity, as does the extent to which they pull or push the actor towards or away from acting foolishly. As unawareness of obvious risk is central to my theory of foolish behavior, the situation must contain some degree of risk, although the degree of obviousness can of course vary from one situation to another. For illustrative purposes, let us say that the actor is a young man, barely eighteen years old, named "John." The Situation occurs when John is approached by two police detectives who tell him that they believe he might have information pertaining to a recent store robbery, and that they would like him to come down to the police station to answer some questions that might help them solve the crime. John did not commit the crime, and he does not understand that he is actually a suspect. But he wants to appear cooperative and to clear up any misunderstanding about his possible culpability. So he agrees to go with the detectives (who do not have an arrest warrant; thus, his cooperation is entirely voluntary, although John likely does not fully understand that).

The interview began around 9:00 p.m. and continued until late into the night. John's parents were out of town, his cell phone was not working, and, lacking any criminal history, he did not have an attorney whom he could call. An hour into the interview one of the detectives told him he was a suspect and read to him his Miranda Rights (to remain silent and to contact an attorney) but the young man signed off on the warning and agreed to continue talking. During the interview, the detectives presented a string of lies to John, along the lines of "we have an eyewitness who can identify you," "your fingerprints were found at the scene of the crime," "your friend who was involved in the robbery has already confessed and said you were involved," "if you do not cooperate, you will immediately go to jail and likely will get a sentence of ten or fifteen years, while if you do cooperate, we will let you go home and recommend to the prosecutor that you get probation," etc. The detectives also hooked the young man up to what they said was a lie detector but in fact was just

Linear Model of Foolish Action

Figure 3.1.   Linear Model of Foolish Action *Source: Chart by author.*

a bunch of wires not connected to anything. They told John that the lie detector showed conclusively that his denials were untruthful, and that in fact he was guilty of the crime.

After six hours, at around 3:00 a.m., John cracked and said that while he does not remember being involved, if the lie detector says he was, then maybe that was the case. (The detectives offered the explanation that he may have blacked out but the lie detector can tap into his unconscious; that of course is nonsense, as the theory of lie detectors is that they detect anxiety stemming from consciousness of guilt). The detectives basically dictated a confession and John agreed to sign it. He was in fact allowed to go home but was arrested the next day and charged with the serious felony of aggravated robbery. In fact, the only convincing evidence that the police possessed tying John to the crime was this psychologically coerced confession.

Cognition is the collection of general and specific knowledge, and thinking and language abilities that individuals bring to the risky situation and which enable them to fully recognize or evade the risks facing them. The situation facing John—agreeing to talk to police officers investigating his possible involvement in a crime—is inherently very risky. It is risky because effective interrogators are trained to use a playbook (the so-called Reid technique) that is highly effective in breaking down the will of people they are interrogating and getting them to confess, sometimes (as many overturned convictions attest) to crimes they never committed. Even if a suspect does not confess to a crime, the mere fact to talking to cops gives the interrogators an opportunity to testify to admissions or evasions that the suspect may or may not have made, unless of course the entire interrogation (including the opening act, where improper threats or promises may have been made) is recorded. There is a reason why police and prosecutors in the United States generally resist laws mandating audio or video recording of interrogations, and the reason is that it makes use of improper interrogation methods, not to mention lying on the stand, more difficult to carry out.

John had some cognitive limitations which placed him at very high risk in this dangerous situation. The first had to do with his young age as well as his lack of experience with the criminal justice system. Individuals with some experience with the criminal justice system are more likely to know that the best way to deal with a request to be interrogated is to utter the magic words "No, I will not cooperate with you" and run, not walk, as fast as one can away from the situation. An interrogation can be compared to a Piagetian Concrete Operations experiment, such as "conservation of mass." This is typically carried out with two balls of clay (a variant involves two beakers of water). The balls start out round and equal in appearance, and then one is rolled into a cigar shape that is thinner but longer. After initially confirming that the two balls have equal amounts of clay, the subject is asked, after the transformation, if the ball or the cigar has more clay or if they are the same. Obviously, the correct answer is "the same," but the outward change in appearance causes pre-operational children to focus on the domain that is more salient to them (usually the height of the ball, but sometimes the length of the cigar) and say that one or the other has more clay. In doing so, the pre-operational child demonstrates a failure to conserve the fact that the actual amount of clay has not changed.

In the case of a police interrogation, the thing to conserve is the fact that in spite of the police acting as one's friend and claiming that confessing is in the subject's best interest, the interrogator may actually be a malign presence who is trying to trick the subject into incriminating himself. While in most cases, police are helpful servants of the law to whom most law-abiding people (especially when young) have been taught to trust and to cooperate with, in the context of an interrogation, the intelligent thing to do is to conserve, in the face of various mystification efforts, that the interrogator is an enemy trying to put you in jail or worse, and is certainly not your friend. Furthermore, there is a natural desire to try and win the interrogators over, and to disbelieve that police officers would use deception as part of the interrogation process. In fact, after the US Supreme Court ruled in the 1969 case, *Frazier v. Cupp*, that deception is an acceptable police tactic, it is difficult to find any police interrogation that is not filled with several, sometimes dozens, of lies.

Of course, dealing with deceptive and psychologically coercive interrogation tactics is much easier to do if you do not agree to cooperate in the first place, or if you call off the interview as soon as you figure out that you are a suspect. The cognitive challenge in understanding what is actually going on, is exacerbated by the fact that most adults (such as a brilliant friend of mine with many accomplishments to his name) do not understand that they have a right to decline to be interviewed, or to exit the police presence, at any time. The young man in this case, John, along with my accomplished and fully-mature friend, lacked such background knowledge. John also lacked the verbal heuristic skills to know how to extricate himself from the situation once he became ensnared.

Personality refers to behavioral tendencies or needs that are relatively stable and that differentiate one person from another. Even if John had recognized and understood the danger of exposing himself to a coercive police interrogation, and even if he had truly understood his right to terminate the interview, it would still have required some degree of assertiveness and strength of will for John to have said "this interview is over, and I am out of here." But John was not a very assertive person, and was simply intimidated by the presence of two very persistent large adult authority figures. He might have prevailed if there was the presence of an advocate, such as a parent or an attorney, but without such an advocate he lacked the strength to survive the ordeal.

Affect/State refers to aspects of one's biological self-regulatory system. Affect involves emotions or feelings (such as fear or anger) while State refers to level of equilibrium or disequilibrium (such as exhaustion, intoxication, or sexual arousal). When self-regulatory processes are off, vulnerability to foolish action is increased, although affect and state work in somewhat different ways: high affect pushing one towards acting foolishly, "disequilibrated" state reducing one's ability to resist acting foolishly. In the case of John, the affect that pushed him towards signing off on a false confession was very high anxiety (he was literally scared out of his mind), while the state imbalance that lessened his ability to stick to his tale of innocence was physical exhaustion. There is a reason why police detectives often start their interrogation sessions late at night, as sleep-deprivation lessens the ability to assert one's will or, for that matter, to think straight.

In the preceding hypothetical example, involving John, all four factors were implicated in his foolish behavior: *Situation*, in the hidden nature of the risk and the coercive pressures that he faced; *Cognition*, in John's naïveté and lack of ability to see through the deceptive pressures placed on him; *Personality*, in John's non-assertiveness and passivity in the face of a manipulative situation; and *Affect/State* in John's being terrified by the prospect of a lengthy prison sentence, and the dulling of will power and of cognition associated with sleep deprivation. Given that all four factors were activated, and the forces were fairly strong, it is not surprising that he acted as foolishly as he did.

In most instances, fewer than four factors may be involved, and there may be some forces that are weak or even working in the opposite direction. In such a case, a foolish outcome is less predictable than it would be where all four factors are strong and all trending in the same direction. Of course, we generally do not know all of the factors operating on an individual at a given moment in time, and thus cannot adequately quantify these factors. At this point we can mainly use the model descriptively, to do *post-hoc* analyses of foolish acts. Such "foolishness autopsies," in fact, make up the bulk of this book.

PSYCHODYNAMIC ASPECTS OF THE MODEL

Although I do not consider myself a Freudian, and was not consciously influenced by psychoanalytic theory when devising the model, it has been pointed out to me (Shilkret 2009) that my model of foolish action bears some similarities to Sigmund Freud's "structural" (id, ego, super-ego) theory, as first described in his book *The Psychopathology of Everyday Life* (Freud 1901/1990a) and later elaborated on (Freud 1923/1990b) in *The Ego and the ID.*

Both the four-factor foolishness theory and Freud's structural theory are "psychodynamic," in that behavior is seen as resulting from the combination of various internal processes, in relation to an external reality. The comparison is portrayed in figure 3.2, with ego comparable to cognition, superego comparable to personality, and id comparable to affect/state. Situation does not have a counterpart in the structural theory, in that while external reality is implicit as something to be addressed in Freud's thinking, it did not really enter in as a separate motivational force. Two other differences are: (a) Freud mainly focused on *parapraxes* (verbal slips of the tongue) and memory lapses as outcome behaviors in his illustration of the structural theory and did not focus on overt conduct (although some foolish actions obviously involve verbal behavior); and (b) the unconscious was a major part of Freud's structural theory (even more so in his topological model), while it does not really play a part in my model (even though I recognize that some of the motivational forces which contribute to foolish behavior are outside of the conscious awareness of control of the actor) (Freud 1923/1990b).

The main contribution of a psychodynamic approach is that all action is seen as complexly determined, with the behavioral outcome in a given situation never completely predictable. It is not predictable for the simple reason that the strength of the motivational forces are never fully knowable. For Freud, ego (cognition in my model) is the moderator between the conflicting demands of superego (personality) and of id (affect/ state), as well as external reality (situation). In my model, ego/cognition is seen as a powerful part of the equation, but does not operate independently of the other forces.

A Comparison of Four-Factor and Freudian-Structural Models

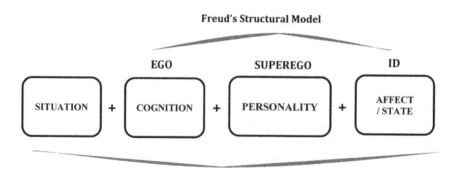

Figure 3.2.   A Comparison of Four-Factor and Freudian-Structural Models
Source: Chart by author.

A psychodynamic perspective can be described as a "systems" approach, in that it has some of the features of a hydraulic process, with forces interacting with each other in complex ways. Such a system can be described in linear terms (forces operating independently, but summed together to create an idea of their cumulative strength). However, a non-linear framework, in which forces interact with each other in complex feedback loops, may be preferable. For the most part, psychologists or other social scientists do not operate within a systems framework, and certainly not within a non-linear framework. An example of this non-systems bias can be found in Robert J. Sternberg's (2002a) afore-mentioned edited book on stupidity/foolishness, where virtually every chapter mentioned one or, at most, two variables, and did not attempt to offer a dynamic theory of foolish behavior. The one exception to this was a chapter by David N. Perkins (2002).

Perkins told the true story of a truck driver who at the end of a long day came to a railroad crossing just as the gate was coming down. He made the very foolish decision to drive around the gate and across the tracks, with the result that the train (a fast passenger train, not the slow freight train he likely expected) plowed into the body of the truck, killing several people in the process. Perkins explained this act as a failure of what he termed "self-organizing criticality," of which an important aspect is "emergent activity switching." This happens when forces in a system "increase in intensity, eventually reaching a tipping point that reorganizes the system into another pattern of activity" (Perkins 2002, 66). Emergent activity switching is seen by Perkins as a behavioral control system that generally "is a simple and serviceable way of guiding behavior in most circumstances" (66). However, it is not a perfect mechanism and for reasons that Perkins calls "mistuning," "entrenchment" and "undermanagement" (83), emergent activity switching can sometimes fail, resulting in foolish behavior.

The notion of defective self-management of activity switching, which is more likely to occur when such switching (in this case, from accelerating to stopping) needs to be made on the spur of the moment, is used by Perkins as an explanation for a wide range of foolish behaviors. In the case of the truck driver, what Perkins thinks happened is that the driver (who had a history of bad driving decisions) slowed when he saw the gate coming down, but he was eager to get where he was going and was already in a critical stage of impatience (and, probably, exhaustion). An impulse built up rapidly, which offered little time for self-management (Perkins 2002, 72). The result was an impulsive act that Perkins termed "emergent folly" (73).

One way of reframing Perkins' example, or foolishness in general, is as a sudden state change, from a state we can label as non-foolish (where extreme risk is not being challenged) to a state we can label foolish (where extreme risk is being challenged). Even in people with a history of repeated foolishness—such as, apparently this truck driver—foolish behavior is not an everyday occurrence (otherwise he would have been dead or in prison a long time ago). In what Perkins termed emergent folly, there is a sensitive balance, where the shift from non-foolishness (either doing nothing, or doing something safe) occurs suddenly, almost without warning. One mathematical theory that was invented to describe and to measure exactly such sudden state transformations (including phenomena as diverse as a dog going suddenly from passivity to biting, or the weather going suddenly from calm to stormy) has been termed the "cusp-catastrophe" model (Berecz 1992). (The term "catastrophe" is used to indicate a sudden bifurcated state change, and such changes obviously do not always involve how we normally use the word catastrophe, namely as some kind of terrible or disastrous event). In such a model, a slight change in one input variable (such as a stranger making a too-sudden move towards an already wary dog) can precipitate a violent change in the behavioral equilibrium.

In this model, alterations in one or more external or internal variables could explain a sudden "rubicon" shift, or bifurcation, from a usual state to a temporary very different state (Gollwitzer 1996). Such massive outcomes of what may be imperceptibly tiny inputs, make quantitative prediction difficult (for example, in psychoanalysis, the same explanations can be used for diametrically opposite behaviors) if not impossible. A complex non-linear model thus sheds light on the unpredictability of foolish action (although one could still predict a much greater frequency of foolish action for some people in general, even if not in a particular incident).

A trait model views foolish action somewhat circularly as emanating from the trait of foolishness, and one or both of its subtraits. Thus, someone who behaves foolishly does so because he is high on the trait of foolish cognition and/or foolish personality. An obvious limitation of such a meta-model is the absence of two factors, situation and affect/state, neither of which are mentioned by Sternberg (2002b) and Richard Wagner (2002), but both of which are needed if one is to be able to analyze why someone committed a specific foolish act.

NON-LINEAR IMPLICATIONS OF THE MODEL

While a trait model of foolishness helps to clarify the nature of the contributing factors, it is not really a theory of foolish behavior. That is because foolish people are not foolish all of the time. To be considered foolish it is only necessary to do something foolish on occasion, even on rare occasions. Only a dynamic model, which explains how various factors work together to produce a foolish act can provide such an explanation. Such a dynamic model was portrayed earlier in figure 3.1. It added two elements missing from the earlier static model: situations and state. Furthermore, instead of being presented vertically, the factors are now presented horizontally, with arrows indicating that a foolish act is an additive function, with four sets of variables—situation, cognition, state, and personality—contributing to an act that could be considered foolish (that is, resulting in an unwanted but relatively possible outcome).

A situation can be considered the stimulus, or "aliment" (to substitute the French word used by Piaget), out of which a foolish act emerges. Situations out of which foolish acts grow have some form of risk embedded in them, with the degree of obviousness of the risk varying. The less obvious the risk, the more likely one is to behave foolishly (but, paradoxically, the more one may be pardoned for acting foolishly). Situations vary on other relevant domains as well, including the extent to which they elicit affect (such as fear) or motives (such as greed), and in the extent to which they occur in settings in which other people are encouraging or discouraging a foolish act.

Under the "state" rubric, I am combining two factors that were addressed separately earlier: biological state and affect. Alterations in biological and affective state, triggered by a particular situation, can be considered the "motivating engine" which drives an individual to behave foolishly, even when the person possesses the cognitive resources to recognize the dangers inherent in the course of action.

The model of foolishness presented in figure 3.2 is similar to one by Greenspan, Loughlin, and Black (2001) that addressed the construct of gullibility (which I now define as a frequent form of induced social foolishness). That model was adapted from a similar model of motivated behavior developed by Martin Ford (1992).

A DYNAMIC NON-LINEAR VIEW OF FOOLISH ACTION

The problem with a linear additive model is that while foolish action may be determined by four sets of variables, such action is not always predictable and the weights to be attached to these predictor variables are not always the same across time or individuals. Furthermore, a small change in one variable can bring about a major shift in behavior. As an example, adding a very slight amount of foolishness "pull" to a situation, or slightly altering a subject's affective or biological state, can bring about a dramatic change in behavior, from a typical state of non-foolishness to a single act of foolishness that could have profound, and even fatal, consequences for the actor or others. Furthermore, a linear model of foolishness fails to take into account the role of the interaction and feedback between affect, cognition, and personality occurring idiosyncratically within the person. Such a dynamic "whole person" perspective is reflected in figure 3.3, which might be termed a "complexity model of foolish action." A key aspect of this model is that while a confluence of forces acting within and upon an individual creates a fertile condition for the initiation of a foolish act, acting non-foolishly is still a choice available to the individual. Thus, while foolish action may be explainable, it will never be entirely predictable.

As mentioned, the contributor to the Sternberg book who came closest to articulating such a non-linear dynamic systems view of foolish action was Perkins (2002), who discussed the case of the truck driver who tried to get his rig across the tracks before a train got there. I have already presented Perkins' attempt to describe this action as a failure in "activity switching." Perkins made distinctions between what he termed "true folly," "blind folly" and "plain folly" (Perkins 2002, 65). True folly occurs when someone has no awareness of the risk in a situation. In the case of the driver, this would involve not understanding the meaning of a closed railroad gate. Blind folly would involve recognizing risk but deceiving oneself as to its applicability in a given situation. In the case of the driver, this might involve concluding that he has more than enough time to make it across. Plain folly involves recognizing the risk, but mindlessly and impulsively ignoring it. Perkins believes, because it happened so quickly, that the train-racing behavior falls in this category, but it has some qualities of blind folly as well (71).

Perkins refers to a general systems phenomenon that he terms "self-organizing criticality" to explain the foolish behavior of the truck driver. An important aspect of this process is "emergent activity switching," which happens when forces in a system "increase in intensity, eventually reaching a tipping point that reorganizes the system into another pattern of activity" (Perkins 2002, 66). Emergent activity switching is seen by Perkins as a behavioral control system that generally "...is a simple and serviceable way of guiding behavior in most circumstances" (66). However, it is not a perfect mechanism and for reasons that Perkins calls "mistuning," "entrenchment" and "undermanagement" (66) emergent activity switching can sometimes fail, resulting in foolish behavior. The notion of defective self-management of activity switching is used by Perkins as an explanation for a wide range of self-deceptions and resulting socially foolish behaviors including, in addition to impulsiveness, procrastination and vacillation.

In the case of the truck driver, what Perkins thinks happened is that the driver slowed when he saw the gate come down, but he was eager to get where he was going and was already in a critical stage of impatience. An impulse built up rapidly, which offered little time for self-management. According to Perkins, this particular driver had a history of citations for reckless driving, and so "management of emergent activity switching may not have been his strength" (Perkins 2002, 72) anyway. The result was an impulsive act that Perkins terms "emergent folly." However, in line with the complexity model articulated in figure 3, it is very likely, indeed probable, that the same driver had been in nearly identical circumstances many times in the past and had dealt with the situation non-foolishly (either by not trying to get across or doing so but having a luckier result).

As discussed by several contributors to Sternberg's book, but most explicitly by Perkins (2002) and by Ozlem Ayduk and Walter Mischel (2002), foolish actions are discontinuous transformations in state, in which an individual goes from a condition of non-foolishness to a temporary condition of foolishness. An example would be Peter Reilly, described below. Peter was a naïve high school student who over a period of many hours professed innocence of his mother's murder and, then, in a moment of weakness said that perhaps he might have done it, a foolish statement (later recanted after some rest) which hugely complicated his life. Another example would be "Jeff," an intellectually challenged man to be profiled in chapter 10, who angrily ditched a not-yet-formally purchased vehicle after discovering a defect. A reflection of foolish thinking, to be sure, but one of only two or three occasions in this man's marginally-adjusted life when he did something foolish enough to get himself convicted of a crime. If the actors in either case had been able to discuss their problem with a wiser person, or been in a less impaired state (Peter from grief, terror, and exhaustion; Jeff from alcohol and anger), they might have continued on in their typical state of non-foolishness and not suffered the very serious consequences that ensued.

A foolish act—as opposed to, say, irrational thinking which in the right circumstance can predispose one to foolish action—is, thus, typically a sudden and infrequent behavior that represents a disequilibrium change which could be precipitated by the most minor and chance of happenings (for example, the railroad gate coming down when it did, rather than three seconds earlier). For such discontinuities, affected by so many variables, and with such not completely predictable outcomes, a different conceptual and methodological framework is required. Such an alternative worldview may possibly be found in two non-linear systems frameworks: "chaos theory" (sometimes referred to as "complexity theory") and "catastrophe theory" (sometimes referred to as "bifurcation theory").

Chaos theory is a deterministic theory that is "a reflection of the forces operating on (and within) the system" (Carver and Scheier 1998, 250), but in which predictability is not very good because: all of the influences on the system cannot be known totally or precisely; the influence of the forces may be non-linear, with feedback among and between the forces; or a very small increase in one force can have very major impact on the system. Thus, the behavior of the system, "though highly determined, can give the appearance of randomness" (251), in part because it involves oscillations in behavior that are highly irregular (as is the case with foolish acts, which typically occur irregularly). Another core aspect of chaos theory is the role of "attractors" (areas which a system approaches more frequently than others) and "repellers" (regions that seem to be actively avoided).

Catastrophe theory, although emerging from a different body of mathematical theorizing (specifically, topology, a modern branch of geometry), shares many similarities with chaos theory, in that it reflects a non-linear, dynamic systems worldview, and uses attractors as core concepts. A major difference is a focus on bifurcation, that is a sudden discontinuous state transformation (a shift from the dominance of one attractor and its replacement by the dominance of another attractor), with such a dramatic state change brought about by a small change in one or more control variables. Catastrophe theory would appear to be particularly applicable to understanding foolish action, as one can view non-foolishness as the typical equilibrium state of almost all adult humans (even those with high propensity to act foolishly), with a foolish act being a discontinuous shift to a new equilibrium brought about through the non-linear combining of four sets of variables—situation, cognition, affect, and personality—with a small variation in one or two of the variables making all the difference in determining whether or not an individual acts foolishly.

Catastrophe theory has been used increasingly in social and personality psychology, as in papers by Abraham Tesser (1980) and by Tesser and John Achee (1994), on dating and mating as resulting from the conflict between dispositions and social pressures; on impulsive "rubicon" actions (Gollwitzer 1996) brought about by an abrupt shift from a deliberative mode to an implemental mode; on the factors contributing to sudden shifts in attitudes (van der Maas, Kolstein, and van der Plight 2003) and on the relationship between attitudes and behavior (Flay 1978). Catastrophe theory has also been used to address clinically-relevant issues, such as child abuse (Tutzauer 1984) and adolescent alcohol use (Clair 1998).

There are several elementary catastrophe models, named after the shape of the resulting graph, with the most commonly-used model being the "cusp catastrophe," in which there are two control variables. Because the causative model of foolish action contains multiple variables, I shall not attempt to depict it, but just state that in such a model the three within-person factors of cognition, personality, and affect/state could be collapsed into the control variable "internal pull," while the "situation" factor could be labeled the control variable "external push."

High external push would be qualities of a situation that is, social or other attractors) that impel the person to act foolishly, while high internal pull would be those qualities of the person which also impel the person, in that situation, to act foolishly. The Behavior Surface" would be the third dimension in this model, and it is on this surface that relative foolishness would be depicted. The cusp is the point on the Behavior Surface at which the plane folds over onto itself in an overlapping fashion. The "Control Surface" is the bottom plane, on which the two control variables of internal pull and external push would be depicted. The "Bifurcation Set" is the shadow that the cusp on the Behavior Surface casts on the Control Surface below. It is in this zone, where the two control factors are in a relative equilibrium, that small changes in one of the control factors can, somewhat unpredictably, cause an individual to jump from non-foolish to foolish action, or vice versa.

At the top of the behavior surface, people are in a typical resting state of non-foolishness. In catastrophe theory terminology, internal push can be considered the "normal factor." That is because, in the absence of external forces, foolish action is likely a monotonic function solely of internal pull. Stated differently, people are likely to behave foolishly when internal push is high and unlikely to behave foolishly when internal push is low. An example would be someone who is highly intoxicated. In such a state, there is an elevated likelihood of foolish action, even in the absence of much external pull for such action.

In catastrophe theory terminology, external pull may be considered the "splitting factor," in that external pull alone (except perhaps in the most extreme of cases, such as torture) will not cause someone to behave foolishly (for example, against one's interests). Rather, at some point where external pull and internal push are in a rough balance, a slight increase in situational pressure will cause a bifurcation, in that some people will suddenly act foolishly while others will not. In catastrophe theory terminology, this region of precariousness is termed the "bifurcation set," which is the zone where the split occurs, with some people exposed to the same forces jumping suddenly from non-foolishness to foolishness, while others remain non-foolish.

The second control factor of internal push does not, obviously, remain constant, and even in a situation of relatively moderate external pull, a very strong internal push (for example, greed, fear, limited understanding, or a tendency towards compliance) can also cause someone to fall off the non-foolishness surface onto the foolishness surface. When external pull is low, then the relationship between internal push and foolishness likely remains monotonic. However, when external pull is moderate, then one can predict a bimodal distribution, where some people will respond to this pull with foolish action, while others will remain non-foolish.

When both internal push and external pull factors are weak, then a person is likely to remain non-foolish. Conversely, when both internal and external forces are strong, the likelihood is high that a person will behave foolishly. The catastrophe model, in which individuals can make sudden leaps from non-foolishness to foolishness, or back again, is most likely to apply when the forces are in the middle range, say when a moderate external pull towards foolish action is counter-balanced somewhat by moderate internal push forces that are resisting that pull. In such a state of affairs (depicted in Figure 3.3) it is difficult to predict which side of the equation the person will come down on.

An example of this can be found in a paper by Tesser (1980), cited earlier, in which he sought to explain sudden shifts in dating/ mating (D/ M) behavior as a function of love (internal push in our terms) and social pressure (external pull in our terms). Tesser was particularly interested in cases where someone who was disposed towards marrying someone was confronted by pressure, such as from parents, to break off the relationship, as well as the opposite case of someone who was disinclined to marry someone but who suddenly caved in to pressure to marry. In the middle ground where internal and external forces are in a state of balance, a slight increase in external pressure could (but not necessarily) cause someone to act suddenly against their internal inclination. The breaking point at which bimodality occurs is in the middle, known as the bifurcation set. Tesser (1980) noted that "bimodal distributions are predicted for each point in the bifurcation set and unimodal distributions for all other points on the control surface" (396). An example, profiled in Garth Sundem's 2010 *Brain Trust*, is a man who was on the fence but leaning against marrying his girlfriend, but who switched to the other side when he fell for a ploy by his mother regarding the great deal she was able to get on an engagement ring being sold cheaply by an elderly aunt.

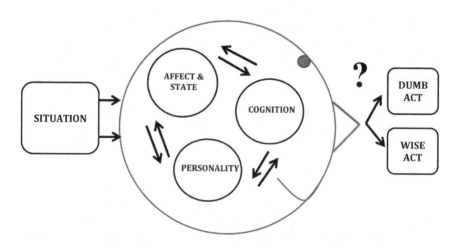

Figure 3.3. Dynamic Non-Linear Model of Foolish Action *Source: Chart by author.*

Tesser (1980) did not label such a contrary-to-inclination action as "foolish," but one can argue that it was, given that the man's misgivings were borne out and the marriage was not a happy one. The opposite example (deciding to break off very satisfying relationships) is reflected in works of art, such as the 1955 film *Marty* (Chayefsky 2000) and the 2004 play *Fat Pig* (LaBute 2004), depicting men who caved in to peer pressure to dump physically imperfect women they loved only to realize later what a mistake they had made.

The cusp catastrophe model can be used to explain many cases of foolish action, such as the false confession by an adolescent named Peter Reilly, on which the earlier fictional example of "John" was largely based. (An account of this notorious case of wrongful conviction can be found in Donald S. Connery's 1977 *Guilty Until Proven Innocent*). Reilly held out courageously for many hours in the face of outrageous interrogative pressure tactics (such as falsely telling him that a polygraph showed him to be his mother's killer). Finally, at some point, external pressures (such as when the interrogator threatened to seek the death penalty) pulled Reilly into the zone of a bifurcation set (and also, most likely, a dissociative fugue state), and he made an abrupt behavior shift, foolishly, but understandably, admitting that it was possible he could have been the killer. However, internal push factors must be entered into the equation as well, with these being: (a) cognition (a naïve young man, Reilly had no awareness that false statements are a standard part of interrogative practice; see Albert Joseph's 1995 *We Get Confessions*); (b) affect/state (Reilly was likely in an altered state resulting from exhaustion combined with grief and fear); and (c) personality (Reilly was a very compliant and trusting person who had difficulty asserting his will in the face of pressure from an authority figure). Given such a confluence of internal and external forces impelling Reilly to make a false confession, the wonder is not that he behaved foolishly but that he held out for as long as he did.

FOUR

Factors That Contribute to Foolish Action

The four-factor explanatory model of foolish action described in chapter 3 is fleshed out more fully in this chapter. For each of the four factors depicted earlier in figure 3.1, a number of sub-factors are listed, and examples are given for how each sub-factor might contribute to a risk-oblivious action. The reader should keep in mind that most foolish actions are brought about by some combination of factors, rather than from any single factor or sub-factor. One point of emphasis that needs to be stated is that the list of sub-factors under each of the four main factors is meant to be illustrative rather than all-inclusive. Thus, in the section on "personality," there are several sub-sections, each illustrating a different personality sub-factor, but other such sub-factors could have been discussed. The same is true of the other three main factors—"situation," "cognition," and "affect/state."

SITUATIONAL CONTRIBUTORS TO FOOLISH ACTION

Every foolish act occurs as a failure to solve some situational problem. In a sense, therefore, situations always contribute to foolish behavior. However, some situations pose much bigger challenges than others, and can thus be said to be major contributors to a foolish act, while other situations are so weak in their pull for foolishness, that the explanations must be found mainly in the person.

Obviously, even where the situational pull is strong, it cannot—in most cases—be solely responsible for the foolish act, as there will always be some people who resist the temptation to behave foolishly in that situation. In this chapter, I discuss a number of situational sub-factors

that should be considered when trying to understand why a person behaved foolishly. As in other chapters in this section, most of these brief
essays will contain an illustrative snippet based on a real or made-up case
example.

Time Pressure

Many foolish actions occur in situations (such as many sales pitches)
where a decision must be made very quickly and almost automatically,
with little time for reflection. Under such circumstances, one is much
more likely to behave foolishly. An example already addressed, by David
N. Perkins (2002), involving a truck driver who impulsively tried to beat
a train at a railroad crossing, was given at the end of the last chapter.

Situations requiring quick decision-making are especially problematic
for people who have low intelligence (that is one reason why they are
termed "slow"), but in fact, time pressure contributes to the likelihood of
bad decision-making in all people, including those of above-average intelligence. Thus, the best thing one can do when feeling pressured to
make an important decision quickly is to insist that one needs more time
(ignoring usually empty threats of the consequences of inaction), in this
way giving oneself an opportunity to consult others and to reflect on
one's action in a more deliberate manner. Daniel Kahneman (2013) made
a distinction between type 1 ("fast") and type 2 ("slow") cognitive processing. Without using the term foolishness, it is clear that Kahneman
believed that the second type of problem-solving was less likely to lead to
disaster.

An example involving me (in a younger and I like to think non-wise
phase) occurred when I made a Saturday morning appointment to have
my home gas furnace serviced. The technician came and quickly announced that he found a potentially serious problem and asked if he
could call his boss, who soon arrived along with another man in tow
identified as a representative of a furnace company who just happened to
be visiting. They told me that there was a defect in the furnace that could
cause me to die of carbon monoxide poisoning if I spent even one more
night in my home. They offered to install a new furnace, at a price described as very low (of course it turned out to be very high), but could
only offer it right then as the furnace manufacturer's representative was
about to return home. I succumbed to this time pressure and wrote a
check and told them to go ahead. They quickly dismantled and carted
away the old furnace (disposing the evidence of their fraud). When my
check came back endorsed to a race track, I contacted a lawyer who
quickly discovered that the heating company was a mob front with many
complaints against it. I allowed my fear (of dying in the night) exacerbated by time-pressure-induced greed to blind me to some obvious questions (such as "why would a manufacturer representative be visiting ear-

ly on a Saturday morning?"). Those factors, in combination with sleep deprivation, a highly trusting nature, and a lack of experience with the way fraudsters operate resulted in a failure to think of logical alternatives (such as calling the gas company, or spending a night in a friend's house) and to impulsively making a foolish decision. Fortunately, I had a good lawyer, Frank Monfredo, who managed to get some of my money back. He imparted an important principle (which I term "Monfredo's Law" in his honor), to wit: "never make an important decision without giving yourself at least one day to think about it, regardless of whatever pressures might be brought to bear."

Social Pressure

The above example involved time pressure but also involved social pressure (three men working in concert to encourage me to act). There is considerable research by social psychologists attesting to the role of social pressure in inducing people to do things that they do not want to do or that are not in their own best interest (Cialdini 1984). This research is focused typically on the deceptive and other tactics used by the persuader rather than on individual differences in the outcome, which can be considered foolish in that it is not typically something desired or beneficial. Social pressure can take numerous forms, ranging from sheer numbers (police interrogators, con artists, and other persuaders often work as a group), to various ploys, such as reciprocity tricks (do someone a small favor, such as a free dinner, and they will be much more likely to do a big one in return, such as buying a vacation home). Social pressure can have a more passive face, as in inhibiting autonomous behavior (often a requirement to act non-foolishly) as in the famous conformity studies of Solomon Asch (1956). In such studies, Asch found that in an experiment where the task was to judge which of two lines was longer, subjects would alter their own response to conform with the (incorrect) judgments of others, even when the correct answer was fairly obvious. An obvious practical application of such research is in jury functioning, where it is commonplace for one or more jurors in the minority to cave to a decision they disagree with. The task for a skilled defense lawyer is to instruct individual jurors before they deliberate to hold fast if they are unpersuaded by a majority calling for conviction.

While social pressure seems most relevant to explaining socially foolish action, it undoubtedly is a big contributor to practically foolish action as well. According to Lewis P. Lipsitt and Leonard L. Mitnick (1991) "more young people die of behavioral misadventure than of all diseases combined" (xiii), and many if not most of these behavioral misadventures take place with the active or passive encouragement of peers. The most prevalent of these fatal misadventures is, undoubtedly, car accidents. It is for a very good reason that many states prohibit newly-minted drivers from having other youths riding in their car, as reckless driving is much more likely to occur when a youth has an audience of peers urging them on to take risks.

Absence of Protective Persons

The social pressures discussed in the previous section are less likely to work—in inducing an actor to behave foolishly—if there are others, termed by anthropologist Robert Edgerton (1967) "benefactors"—to whom the actor can turn for advice or support. This is often the case with elderly people, particularly elderly women (who are more likely than elderly men to be widowed) who are easier to take advantage of, because their social isolation (dead spouse and dying-off friends, adult children who may live some distance away, etc.) make them more vulnerable to exploitation.

An example, discussed in my book *Annals of Gullibility*, involved "Jenny," a close friend of my late mother's. Her deceased husband was an insurance broker, who certainly would have warned her against an insurance scam, in which she was talked into lending her jewels (intended for her grandchildren) to a con artist who was going to have them appraised in order to get Jenny a lowered insurance rate. This example illustrates how this sub-factor (like most other sub-factors) can work both ways: as a force that when manifesting in one form (when benefactors are absent) can increase the likelihood of foolishness, or that when manifesting in another form (when benefactors are present) can decrease such a likelihood.

Novelty / Ambiguity

Diane F. Halpern (2002) addressed the contribution to foolish action of situations that appear on the surface to be familiar but that are changed in important ways. This causes the individual to rely automatically on a response that no longer is really suited to the subtly changed circumstances. A scholar who has addressed the mindlessly foolish misapplication of formerly successful schemas is Ray Hyman (1989), who explained why eminent scientists often fail miserably when they move outside their area of specific expertise. An example of this is the cold fusion fiasco, when two previously successful chemists at the University of Utah made fools of themselves when they made claims which, as non-physicists, they lacked the expertise or equipment to investigate properly.

Many foolish acts are attributable to cognitive "rigidity," that is in a tendency to rely on familiar schemas even when they no longer fit changed circumstances. An example of this can be found in the many examples of male college professors who for a long time got away with sexually harassing students, but who self-destructed when they continued such behavior into a new period where there was a shift towards seeing such behavior as unethical. Such a scenario likely describes Bill Clinton's foolishness regarding Monica Lewinsky, in that a history of getting away with philandering when Governor of Arkansas blinded the president to the greater dangers involved in continuing such a pattern in the restricted confines of the Oval Office, and to the greater scrutiny paid by the press and political enemies to occupants of the White House. Also, the president was now relying on the discretion of a woman barely in her 20s (who almost by definition was likely to blab), unlike the more tight-lipped older women he had shagged in the past. Even in France, where the sexual adventures of politicians have generally attracted little public interest, there is now a greater risk of exposure and ridicule stemming from the cell-phone camera revolution. This is illustrated by French president Francois Hollande, whose common law marriage ended when someone photographed him late at night heading away (on the back of a motor scooter) from the apartment of a woman with whom he was having an affair.

COGNITIVE CONTRIBUTORS TO FOOLISH ACTION

Johann Wolfgang von Goethe (1826), observed that "there is nothing more frightful than ignorance in action," an observation with which most critics of Donald Trump would concur. Previous scholarly efforts to describe foolishness have emphasized the cognitive piece of the puzzle, almost to the exclusion of everything else. That is understandable, given that foolishness has also been termed "stupidity" (Sternberg 2002a) and it is the "dumb" nature of the behavior that causes it to be seen as foolish. As in the preceding section on Situations, a number of cognitive sub-factors are discussed, with an illustrative case snippet provided for each discussion.

Deficient Knowledge

Ignorance, under the rubric of "tacit knowledge," is the major factor underlying foolish behavior in the writings of cognitive psychologist Robert J. Sternberg and his colleagues (Hedlund, Antonakis, and Sternberg 2002). Tacit knowledge (Polanyi 1966) refers to the procedural rules that govern success and (when violated) failure in various settings and that are typically unspoken and untaught, and it is therefore up to individuals within those settings to learn them on their own. A common example used by Sternberg is a junior faculty member at a major research university applying for tenure after a few years with almost no publications and then being shocked when tenure was denied. I knew one such person, who lamented to me that she believed the official university line that teaching is paramount (sorry to say, she was not a good teacher either), and that nobody had told her just how important publishing was to her ability to stay on there. But anyone who has spent time at a top-tier university knows of many indifferent teachers who have been promoted for their scholarly output, but few cases where the opposite proved true. Only a naïve or willfully blind person could fail to figure out going into, or after a short while within, such a setting, which of the two activities is valued the most.

It is limiting, however, to think that knowledge absence has to be tacit (untaught) to play a role in foolishness. There are many occasions where an individual could have avoided making a disastrous decision if they had possessed even basic acquired (non-tacit) knowledge relevant to the decision. Examples abound in the area of financial gullibility, as in the fraudulent scheme run by Allan Stanford, a Texan whose Caribbean-based Stanford Financial Group was charged in 2009 with running a multi-billion dollar Ponzi operation aimed mainly at Latin American investors. Aside from the fact that he had a very public checkered past which could easily have been uncovered, the 20 percent annual return on bank CD's that he promised was just so outlandish and anyone with even a basic understanding of banking and finance should have been able to see through it. In fact, the scheme was uncovered when an investor asked a journalist to check it out, and it took this finance- (and search-) savvy man a very short while to figure out that there was something very rotten in Antigua (Rushe 2012).

An even more unfortunate mass gullibility episode that could have been avoided had its victims possessed basic relevant content knowledge (in this case, about physics) can be found in the 1997 mass suicide in southern California of thirty-eight followers of Marshall Applewhite, the leader of a UFO religious cult known as "Heaven's Gate." The basic idea propounded by Applewhite was that the Hale-Bopp comet presaged the end of the world as predicted in Revelations, but that an alien spacecraft was waiting just behind the comet to pick them up after they exited the confines of their bodies. As noted by journalist Timothy Ferris (1997), two of the cult members had purchased a telescope to try and see the spacecraft (whose existence was fueled on the internet by a faulty digital image from an amateur astronomer in Texas) and seemed crushed when they could not find it. According to Ferris, "It's hard to avoid the reflection that the mass suicide might have been averted had just one of the observers declared, 'Gee, the evidence fails to support our belief. Maybe the belief is wrong!'"

Irrational Thinking Styles

Educational psychologist Keith Stanovich (1999) has disputed the idea that foolish decision-making is usually a function of low intelligence. (If this and my gullibility book show anything it is that having a high IQ is no protection against behaving stupidly.) Rather, according to Stanovich, the cognitive contributor to foolishness is an absence of "rationality," a construct which has less to do with the number of cognitive schemas one possesses (which is how Stanovich describes intelligence as typically measured) than with how effectively one applies those cognitive schemas when faced with real-life problems. It is well-established that much of what passes for thinking in our everyday life is just the automatic calling up of memory (Wason 1968). Even people with very high IQs are likely to rely on such heuristics when confronting everyday decisions or action. (This topic is addressed more fully in a discussion of "rationality" in chapter 13).

Perspective-Taking

An aspect of social cognition that at one time was a major focus of my research (Chandler and Greenspan 1972) is role-taking, also known as perspective-taking. This refers to the ability to put oneself in the shoes of other people and to see an event, or oneself, as others see it or you. Very often the risk of a practically foolish act lies less in its possible negative physical consequences than in its very probable social consequences, namely foreseeing how it will be viewed and valued by others. Such an absence of perspective-taking and social foresight can bring the actor very serious unintended grief.

An example occurred in early 2010 when a veteran air traffic controller, Glenn Duffy, took his nine-year-old son to work with him in the control tower at New York's JFK airport. He allowed the boy to give the clearance to a jet awaiting takeoff. This was such a positive experience for Duffy and his son (and the pilots who seemed to enjoy it) that the next night he repeated the stunt with his son's twin sister. Unfortunately for Duffy, and his supervisor, Shawn Simms, audio recordings of these episodes made in onto the national news shows and the blogosphere, and as a result, the two men were suspended, harshly condemned, and threatened with loss of their jobs. Being competent in one's private and professional life requires, in the era of the Internet, an ability to ask oneself "could this action become widely public and if so how would it be perceived?"

Absence of perspective-taking lies at the root of many foolish acts. Another alleged example, told to me by a former student, took place at the University of Connecticut during the 1990s when I was teaching there. A group of mostly white fraternity members, according to this story (which may be apocryphal) was walking on a path in the woods, singing the philosopher's beer drinking song from Monty Python. A group of football players, many of them African American, was passing in the opposite direction, just as the frat boys got to the lyric "Immanuel

Kant was a real puissant who was very rarely stable. Heidegger, Heidegger was a boozy beggar who could think you under the table" (Hardcastle, 2006). Mistaking "Heidegger, Heidegger" for "Hi N—er, Hi N—er," the athletes confronted the singers and were prepared to beat the crap out of them. While one might wish that the football players had some knowledge of German philosophy (not to mention alternative cinema), the frat boys may be faulted for failing to anticipate the possibility that African Americans would be offended by any word ending in "–gger." There have been several real-life cases and one fictional one (Philip Roth's 2000 *The Human Stain*) where politicians or teachers have been wrongly (but understandably) punished for uttering "niggardly," a word that means "stingy" or "miserly." When speaking, or singing, one needs to understand that certain innocently expressed words can be misinterpreted as slurs.

Social Foresight

A skill that is closely related to (and undoubtedly reflective of) perspective-taking is "social foresight." This has to do with the ability to anticipate social consequences of actions, including of course risky consequences. An example of this cropped up when I ran across an article by Paige Williams (2013) in the *New Yorker* magazine, about a commercial paleontologist in Florida named Eric Prokopi, who made a nice living acquiring, mounting, and selling fossils and other extremely old natural objects, including dinosaur bones. The story described how Mr. Prokopi got into serious legal and financial difficulty over a highly rare, completely intact large *Tarbosaurus bataar* dinosaur skeleton that he was able to smuggle out of Mongolia (where such exports are now forbidden). He likely would have gotten away with the crime had he followed the advice to keep a very low profile and arranged a quiet private sale to a museum or wealthy dinosaur collector. Instead, Mr. Prokopi put the skeleton up for public auction where it was described, along with a photo, in a widely disseminated catalog that attracted the attention of the news media and also the governments of Mongolia and the United States. As a result, Mr. Prokopi lost custody of the specimen, and lost out on the great deal of money he would have made from its private sale, suffered the shuttering of his business, and found himself facing the possibility of a lengthy prison sentence. Before the legal difficulties occurred (and even before the scheduled auction), the bone merchant had conversations with a number of commercial and professional paleontologists who all told him how foolish it was that the Florida man had brought attention to himself and his illegally obtained dinosaur exhibit by trying to sell it in a public auction. They all predicted the problems that would ensue from this foolish action, problems that likely would have been avoided had Mr. Prokopi possessed a modicum of social foresight or common sense.

PERSONALITY CONTRIBUTORS TO FOOLISH ACTION

The term "personality" refers to habitual dispositions, needs, traits, and intra-psychic tendencies that are peculiar to an individual, and that give their behavior a relative degree of self-definition and consistency over time. In terms of foolishness, this is summed up in *Proverbs* 26:11 (NRSV) thusly: "as a dog returns to his vomit, so a fool repeats his folly." Personality can be a major contributor to foolish action and thought processes. For example, there is research indicating that people high on the trait of "open-mindedness" are more likely to make smart decisions than are people with similar IQs who are low on that personality trait (Stanovich 1999). The reason for this is fairly evident: closed-minded people are less able to view the world as it really is as opposed to how they would like to think that it is.

A great many personality factors can contribute to a foolish act. In emphasizing the role of a particularly salient personality factor, it should not be forgotten that other personality factors may also play a contributing role, as well as the other three non-personality factors (cognition, situation, and affect/state) in the explanatory model. The list of subfactors described below is by no means all-inclusive, especially if one considers that the "Needs" approach which is addressed first can be broken into an almost unlimited number of needs, any one of which can be very motivating for a particular individual.

Personal Needs

One interesting view of human motivation, termed "sensitivity theory" and developed by an acquaintance of mine, the late psychologist Steven Reiss (2000; 2008b), attempts to explain human behavior, including those that get us in trouble, as resulting from the intersection and relative strength of sixteen basic human needs. All of us have these needs to some extent, but we differ widely according to our individual needs profiles, that is the relative strength that each of these needs plays in our lives. For example, for some people, power (the need to control or to exert influence over others) is a very strong need while for others (such as, I like to think, myself), the need for power exerts very little influence over behavior.

Reiss' sixteen needs (derived to some extent from Aristotle, but validated from surveys of thousands of people) are: Power, Curiosity, Independence, Status, Social Contact, Vengeance, Honor (traditional rule-following), Idealism, Physical Exercise, Romance (sex), Family, Order, Eating, Acceptance, Tranquility and Saving (Reiss 2000). A public opportunity for Reiss to illustrate his ideas came when the political career of former New York governor Eliot Spitzer came crashing down when he was caught foolishly using a wire transfer to pay for a prostitute while in

Washington on a planned business trip. Unlike psychoanalysts, who interpreted Spitzer's foolish behavior in terms of mental illness concepts, such as an unconscious Oedipal conflict with his father (who reportedly was pushing him to become the first Jewish president), Reiss (2008a) saw it as the inevitable behavior of someone with a very high need for sex combined with a very low need to behave honorably.

A limitation of Reiss' framework is that he (earlier known for important work in the field of Intellectual Disability) did not seem to have a place for everyday intelligence (social risk-recognition) in his formulation. Thus, at a conference on sex and politics (Greenspan 2009c), I raised the possibility that maybe Princeton grad Spitzer wasn't as smart or as knowledgeable (for example, about Federal monitoring of financial transactions with mob-operated prostitution rings) as he and everyone else assumed he was. Of course, one could argue that he was thinking with the head down below rather than the head up on top, in which case a needs-based explanation still holds some weight, while illustrating the importance of a multi-dimensional explanatory framework, in which the personality/personal needs domain is combined with information about cognition, self-regulatory state, and the situation itself.

Arrogance / Narcissism

Much foolish action occurs because of an individual's narcissism or arrogance, a term that refer to a quality of "unreasonable and inordinate self-esteem" (freedictionary.com). Arrogance and narcissism—defined variously as self-love, self-involvement, and egotism/selfishness—are closely related constructs, as many arrogant people are described as narcissistic and vice versa. While narcissism in extreme forms is characterized as a personality disorder, it is also a trait dimension on which people can be located according to the strength of their narcissistic tendencies. In its mild form, narcissism can have positive benefits, as it motivates people to address difficult tasks and achieve greatness in various spheres, such as science, business, and politics (there are very few people who have ever campaigned for high political office who could not be described as having some narcissistic qualities). At higher levels of intensity, it can be destructive, in that very narcissistic individuals bring harm to others through their manipulations, and to themselves through their failure to accurately assess the consequences of their own behavior (Ogrodniczuk 2013).

Narcissism can take various forms such as "conversational narcissism" (a tendency to monopolize conversations and steer them towards oneself) and "medical narcissism" (a concern about status which sometimes blinds physicians to essential information coming from nurses or medical residents). A form of narcissism which appears relevant to understanding celebrity screw-ups is "acquired situational narcissism," a term coined by the late psychiatrist Robert Millman (Sherrill, 2001). This term refers to very famous people, such as star athletes, movie actors, and political leaders, whose pre–fame narcissistic tendencies (which likely impelled them to become stars) become full-blown and exaggerated as a result of all of the adulation, attention, and coddling that now pervades their lives. It is easy, indeed almost inevitable, for such individuals to become insulated and detached from reality and from the constraints and consequences that most people have to deal with. Foolish behavior, often involving sexual misconduct, is a common consequence of such celebrity narcissism, as illustrated by Tiger Woods, the superstar golfer whose career, marriage, and public image became endangered when his secret life as a serial womanizer became public in late 2009. It has also been suggested that the delusional decision by George W. Bush in 2003 to invade Iraq in search of non-existent weapons of mass destruction resulted in part from the narcissistic certainty in his own infallibility (encouraged by advisers who preyed on his ignorance and religiosity) that developed after he became president.

Will Power

Character strength, also known as will power, refers to the extent to which one can maintain moral autonomy in the face of temptation. It has obvious implications for socially foolish action, given that manipulators appeal to motives, such as greed or fear, that test moral will power. Although not much emphasized by personality theorists in recent decades (Berrios and Gili 1995), the notion of conscious will has been making a comeback, particularly through the writings of the recently departed Walter Mischel and colleagues.

Ozlem Ayduk and Walter Mischel (2002) cite studies that demonstrate the importance of will power as an aspect of "emotional intelligence" with important implications for life success and for the avoidance of making foolish choices. Specifically, they argue that there are two forms of self-regulation, an emotional hot system and a cognitive cool system. People with weak will power, in their view, are more likely to rely on the emotional hot system and, thus, are more susceptible to foolish action.

Will power plays an important role in morality, which refers to the extent to which one is impelled to do the right thing when temptation, convenience, or social pressure would push one to do the wrong thing. Often, morality will be a brake against social foolishness, in that many manipulators appeal to selfish motives, such as greed, that a very moralistic person will disdain. Sometimes, however, a moral schema will make a person more foolish, as when a victim accommodates a manipulator because saying "no" violates their politeness or hospitality norms.

In using the term "morality," I am referring to an individual's notions of what is "good," "just," or "fair," and of the importance that those ideas hold as a motivating force affecting one's actions, especially in situations where one's self-interest might be better served by acting immorally. The study of personal ethics is complicated by the fact that moral principles are often in conflict, as is the case in dilemmas such as Lawrence Kohlberg's famous "Hans" story. Kohlberg (1981), conceptualized moral development on a continuum ending at the ability to identify, conserve, and abstractly opine about the one moral principle (for example, Han's wish to save a loved person's life) that is most relevant to a specific decision, in the face of one or more obfuscating countervailing moral principles (in this case, Hans' obligation to follow the law preventing breaking into a pharmacy to obtain a life-saving drug). In a similar vein, Willard Gaylin (2003) attributed the foolish decision by many US Catholic bishops to cover up evidence of sexual misconduct by priests to their inability to conserve the primacy of the moral obligation to protect children in the face of two obfuscating countervailing moral principles: (a) to forgive possibly mentally ill priests claiming to wish to repent their sins, and (b) to protect the reputation of the church. As in many other cases of foolish conduct, the bad decision made by any individual bishop was affected by social norm ("groupthink") pressures, namely that other bishops they were in contact with were making the same foolish decision.

Self-Efficacy

Another relevant personality domain is "self-efficacy," also known as "agency beliefs." This term refers to the extent to which one feels confident in one's ability to perform various tasks. As conceptualized by Alfred Bandura (1977) self-efficacy is not a general personality trait but is applied very narrowly to specific domains of competence, such as "interpersonal self-efficacy" (the belief that one can prevail in a stressful social interaction). This is a type of agency belief that would appear to be very predictive of foolishness, especially gullibility, as one is more likely to give in to a manipulator if one does not feel there is any chance of prevailing in such a contest. An example described by Carol S. Dweck (2002) is that children and adults with a history of poor academic performance tend to give up when faced with a challenging academic task. Such a resigned attitude guarantees failure and makes such individuals appear less capable than they really are.

Drivenness / Compulsion

An aspect of personality that likely contributes to much foolish behavior is "drivenness," a term used by David Shapiro (2000) that "implies a more or less continuous activity, activity for its own sake, that seems to be urged or pressed internally, and of an intensity that cannot be relaxed without discomfort" (93). The specific nature of the drivenness can vary.

Thus, people with obsessive-compulsive disorder (OCD) are driven to do a specific ritual, as a way of warding off anxiety associated with spontaneity, while people with hypomania are driven to do something highly spontaneous, as a way of warding off anxiety associated with being too disciplined. Hypomania, as in the behavior of psychopaths or in group rioting (a kind of mass euphoria fueled by non-psychopathic followers emulating psychopathic leaders) can result in very foolish (and, sometimes, evil) behavior. The rigidity associated with OCD, involves a deep-grained need to maintain one's autonomy, and a concomitant unwillingness to engage in any behavior that could be considered "giving in." Because this rigidity and autonomy-maintenance schema is activated in any and all situations, there is often some inevitable lack of fit with the demands of reality and with the needs of a situation.

Stalking behavior is an example of obsessional drivenness that causes many seemingly rational people into extremely risky, irrational and self-destructive conduct. An example involved Solomon Wachtler, a highly respected jurist who served from 1985 to 1993 as chief judge of New York State's highest court (Manegold 1992). A noted court reformer who authored several important legal decisions, and was the original source of the widely-cited quote (repeated in Tom Wolfe's 1987 *The Bonfire of the Vanities*) that "a grand jury would indict a ham sandwich, if that's what you wanted" (624). Wachtler's life started to unravel after a niece named Joy Silverman cut off an affair that started when Wachtler served as coexecutor of her step-father's estate. Unable to take this rejection, Wachtler began to harass Silverman in an unhinged fashion, even going so far as to threaten in writing to kidnap her daughter if she did not resume the affair. He was arrested in December of 1992 and pled guilty to criminal harassment, serving a little over a year in a Federal prison. Following his release, Wachtler (1997) wrote a memoir, *After the Madness*, and became an advocate for prison reform, particularly calling for improved services for mentally ill inmates. Wachtler eventually had his law license reinstated, and became a professor of law and psychiatry.

Interpersonal Trust

A personality trait that has been explored with respect to social-induced (gullible) foolishness is "interpersonal trust." Personality theorist Julian Rotter (1980), a late colleague of mine at the University of Connecticut, found that highly trusting people were somewhat more likely to be gullible, as measured in an experimental task where a confederate asked subjects to operate equipment that was throwing off sparks and seemed unsafe. However, there was a statistical interaction with intelligence, such that trusting people who were bright were no more gullible than people who were of lower intelligence. Thus, Rotter concluded that gullibility was not equivalent with trust, but rather was a form of naïve or "foolish" trust. An example can be found in the case of a psychotherapist (Zuckoff 2006) who wired $400,000 to an unknown internet scammer in Nigeria. The victim was described by his wife as one of the most trusting people on the planet, which is reflected in the fact that even after his life had been destroyed (he eventually went to jail for bank fraud) by this scam, he still expressed a belief that his correspondent existed and would come through and save the day for him. The lesson from such a story is *not* that it is bad to be trusting (most settings operate on trust, and it would be a grim world if that were not the case), but that social survival requires us to recognize and take seriously obvious red flags indicating when trust needs to be reined in.

Closed-Mindedness

A neighbor of mine in Colorado, "Bob Smith," was a wealthy man who owned his own airplane. He had a reputation for being a know-it-all who would dismiss any advice, on the ground that he knew better. A benign example of this occurred when Bob hired a photographer at a substantial fee to take a family portrait, and then informed her that she would only get the chance to shoot one picture. The photographer, also a neighbor, told me that she pleaded with Mr. Smith to let her take a few more shots, arguing that it would certainly make for a better result. But Bob stuck to his guns, telling the very experienced photographer that he doubted the truth of her assertion.

A less benign (to put it mildly) example of Bob Smith's closed-mindedness came when he took his twelve-year-old grandson and another adult up in his plane for a late afternoon flight over the Rockies. Coming back into a small airport south of Denver just after dark, Smith was told by the tower operator that he was coming in too low and needed to increase his altitude. He responded in his usual style, by rejecting the controller's warning, and flew his plane into a hill, killing himself and both of his passengers.

The story of how Bob Smith's arrogance led to his demise, and that of his grandson and a friend (who happened to be a psychologist) is one that would be quite familiar to readers of ancient Greek literature. In Athens, "hubris" (excessive self-regard), whether in dealing with Gods or other mortals, was considered a crime, and always characterized by authors as folly, by which they meant an action that would backfire with disastrous consequences. In other words, for the Greeks, as for us today, arrogance is offensive both on moral grounds, because it involves putting others down, but also on empirical grounds, because it blinds one to reality, including dangerous reality.

There is no shortage of examples from the everyday world of arrogance resulting in disaster. Often, this manifests when those in authority refuse to listen to warnings from people below them in a hierarchy when the underlings raise concerns. Medicine is a fertile field for the disastrous workings of hubris, given that folly can prove fatal and given that many physicians are reluctant to show weakness in the face of suggestions from nurses or more junior physicians (Wen and Kosowsky 2013). The first episode in June 2009 of the TV show "Nurse Jackie" gives a good example of this. A bicycle messenger was brought to the hospital after being hit by a car. Jackie Peyton, a very experienced emergency room nurse, tells a brand-new physician, Dr. Cooper, that she suspects the patient may have a brain bleed. Dr. Cooper lacks the experience to recognize the danger signs, but is too arrogant to admit that a nurse might know more than he does. So he dismisses Jackie's warning and the patient died. A fictional story, but one that plays itself out in hospitals around the world probably on a daily basis.

The military and business are two fields where catastrophic decisions are often made by people in charge who self-assuredly ignore warnings or suggestions from more experienced and knowledgeable underlings. A particularly catastrophic example can be found in the December 1941 Japanese raid on Pearl Harbor. Two US Army privates who were experienced radar operators were stationed on the northern tip of Oahu when they saw a very large blip on their radar screen, which they estimated to be around fifty planes. One of them contacted the radar office at Fort Shafter and communicated their concerns to the duty officer, a first lieutenant who was new to his position and who had received virtually no training. The officer, assuming it was a returning squadron of B-17s, did not appreciate the seriousness of the information, and uttered the words immortalized in *Tora! Tora! Tora!* (Forrester and Oguni 1970), and other films: "don't worry about it." The consequence of the officer's failure to understand the limits of his own ignorance was a likely greater loss of lives and ships than otherwise might have been the case.

While "hubristic" decisions in war and medicine can kill people, such decisions in the realm of business can kill companies. In the *American Prospect*, journalist David Dayen (2018) wrote about how hedge fund billionaire Eddie Lambert bought Sears Roebuck on the cheap and, by arrogantly believing he knew more about the retail business than the company's experienced executives, drove the historic company into bankruptcy. He bought the company as what is known as a "property play," meaning that if the company were liquidated, he could make money by selling off the valuable real estate that it owned (that tactic is being tested at the time these words are being penned). However, he believed that the company could be profitable, mainly by refusing to emulate competitors, such as Target, who he believed were foolishly spending too much capital on store renovations.

When company executives tried to tell Lambert that the stores badly needed refurbishing, he fired them and replaced them with executives inexperienced in retailing and, thus, less likely to challenge his views. As might have been predicted, the company started losing sales to competitors, because of the increasing shabbiness of its stores. Later, Lambert (whose net worth took a huge hit as Sears' stock value plummeted) was forced to close most (and eventually all) of its stores, thus putting in motion a test of his property play theory. While the eventual demise of such a storied company is a loss for the communities it serves, it is an even bigger tragedy for the 300,0000 Sears employees who ended up losing their livelihoods because of the hubris of a man who turned out to be far less brilliant than he told himself and others that he was. (This story reminds me of a folk tale told by my late father about a farmer who bragged that he could save a lot of money by feeding his horse half the amount of hay, and then a third the amount of hay and so on, until to his dismay one day the horse keeled over dead from starvation).

In terms of my four-factor explanatory model, "Personality" might be the most important here, given that arrogance is a personality trait and given that it was the major factor in explaining at least three of the stories: pilot Bob Smith, the fictional Doctor Cooper, and investor Edward Lambert. In the Pearl Harbor story, personality was implicated in another way: in the lieutenant's marked lack of curiosity or initiative in not asking for more information or following up with superiors. Situation, as usual, played some role as well, especially in the Pearl Harbor story, given that radar was in its infancy, the information conveyed to the lieutenant was not as emphatic or unambiguous as it could have been, and a very poor system of training and action protocols had been established.

AFFECT AND STATE CONTRIBUTORS TO FOOLISH ACTION

Alexander Pope, in his *An Essay on Criticism* (1711) wrote "fools rush in where angels fear to tread." That pretty well summarizes the role that *affect* and a dysregulated *state* play in foolish action, especially when impulsivity (the root of much foolishness) rears its head. Affect and state may be considered quasi-biological in nature, as they both involve some alteration or imbalance in an individual's homeostatic equilibrium. Both affective and state imbalances can contribute to foolish behavior, but they work in somewhat different ways: *affect* (for example, anger) by pushing the person in a foolish direction, *state* (for example, inebriation) by reducing one's inhibitions against acting foolishly. In this section, examples of both affective and state contributors to foolishness are discussed, with an example given for almost all sub-factors.

Exhaustion

Former President Bill Clinton—who is a notable night owl and who, when president, almost never went to bed at a reasonable hour—has said "every mistake I have ever made happened when I was tired" (Huffington, 2017). Exhaustion, including sleep deprivation, is a common contributor to foolish action, as it is an altered state which clouds one's judgment and powers of concentration. Roy Baumeister (2001) is the psychologist who has done the most to explore the link between tiredness and foolish action. In a number of studies, both with children and adults, Baumeister and colleagues have found a distinct lessening of perseverance and performance occurring on a variety of cognitive and behavioral tasks as one's energy becomes depleted. (see Baumeister and Tierney 2011, for the most evolved popular statement of the role of willpower in the face of exhaustion and temptation).

Even relatively small demands can result in what Baumeister terms "self-regulatory depletion." As stated by Baumeister (2001), "the exhaustion theory holds that once the self has become depleted, it lacks the resources necessary for further exertion of volition" (310). Baumeister (2001) argues that "the self has a single resource that resembles energy or strength . . . [and it] is used for a broad variety of seemingly quite different operations, including making choices, taking responsibility, exerting self-control, showing initiative, and avoiding passivity" (310). Clearly, according to this view, depleted energy, as through sleep deprivation, can contribute to the making of a foolish choice, as in the well-documented phenomenon of sleep-deprived individuals being more likely to cave in to coercive police or military interrogations (Blagrove 1996; Gudjonsson 1995).

Intoxication

A related aspect of state impairment that also often makes a significant contribution to foolish behavior is the reduction in judgment and inhibition that comes from alcohol or drug intoxication. This is seen in the fact that a very large percentage of the foolish behaviors that land people in jail or otherwise in trouble occur under the influence of alcohol or drugs (Newcomb and McGee 1989). There is some evidence in the scientific literature for the connection between intoxication and judgment impairment. For example, Rebecca D. Crean et al. (2011) have found that marijuana use impairs executive function, and other researchers (for example, Webster and Jackson 1997) have found a significant connection between alcohol use and highly impulsive behaviors, such as problem gambling. It is not a coincidence that casinos ply their customers with alcohol at the gaming tables, or that commercial galleries serve free wine at art show openings.

There are untold high-profile examples of generally competent people who commit professional *hara kiri* as a result of very foolish behavior committed while inebriated. One of these incidents occurred in 1997 when a TV baseball analyst for ESPN got drunk at a Cleveland nightclub and was arrested after allegedly urinating out a window onto two off-duty police officers standing outside. As if that was not bad enough, the man also allegedly resisted arrest. Not surprisingly, this alleged conduct led to the termination of his TV broadcasting job. Many other similar drunken incidents have led to termination of lucrative broadcasting careers by former professional athletes. One of these occurred to a football analyst (also at ESPN) who was fired after allegedly taking and sending out a photo of his penis while drinking at a Connecticut bar.

Similar incidents involving sports figures and broadcasters are plentiful not just because they tend to spend a lot of time in bars, but also because their celebrity causes their mess-ups to become widely known. But non-celebrities also do the most incredibly foolish things when they drink too much. One of the more bizarre such incidents involved the wealthy president of an investment firm, who allegedly became pathologically intoxicated during a long plane ride from Buenos Aires (where he was planning to donate funds to build an orphanage) to New York. After being cut off from being served more drinks, the man was accused of attempting to help himself from a liquor cart, verbally and physically assaulting flight attendants who tried to stop him, and punctuated his meltdown by pulling down his pants and defecating on the cart (allegedly wiping himself with linen napkins, rubbing his soiled hands on various surfaces, and then tracking his feces throughout the cabin) in full view of other passengers (who had their food service cut off by the pilot during the remaining four hours of the trip for fear of contamination). Not surprisingly, such extremely foolish conduct had severe legal (criminal as well as civil) and career consequences (Hester 1999). Most likely, the man had other contributing reasons besides being drunk for his reputation-killing conduct, but it is probable that he would not have behaved as he did if he had not been drunk.

Alcohol also is a major factor in precipitating violent behavior, whether in people who have a habitual tendency towards violence as well as in those who are generally non-violent. An example of this latter phenomenon occurred in April, 2003, when a 25-year-old Harvard graduate student named Alexander Pring-Wilson was walking back to his Cambridge-area apartment after an evening spent drinking with a visiting friend from his undergraduate days at Colorado College (Commonwealth of Massachusetts 2007). During that evening, Pring-Wilson had shown off to his friend a large pocket knife which he had recently purchased. Declining the offer of a shared cab ride, Pring-Wilson was staggering home when he passed a car containing two young men, one of whom made a sneering comment along the lines of "look at the drunk guy." Mistaking the comment for a request for directions, Pring-Wilson approached the car. Upon figuring out that he was being insulted, Pring-Wilson pulled open the car door and got into a fist fight with one of the young men, 18-year-old Michael Colono, a man with an arrest history but who was now working as a cook in a Boston hotel. During the fight, which lasted only seventy seconds, Pring-Wilson pulled out his knife and stabbed Colono in the chest and abdomen five times, fatally injuring the younger man. Upon reaching his home, Pring-Wilson, apparently overcome with remorse, called 911 from his home phone and gave a somewhat incoherent story about having been a bystander to the fight. Tracing the call, the police arrived, brought him in for questioning and, later, arrested him.

During a first trial, Pring-Wilson claim of self-defense was rejected by the jury, in part reflecting working class resentment against an advantaged Harvard student. Pring-Wilson's lengthy prison sentence was overturned due to the judge's refusal to allow testimony about violent episodes in Colono's past. A second trial resulted in a hung jury, and a third trial was avoided when Pring-Wilson pleaded guilty to a lesser offense, and received a sentence of two years, with credit for ten months for time already served. In addition to this incarceration, and enormous time and money spent on his defense, Pring-Wilson's plan to attend law school back in Colorado was obviously no longer an option.

If Pring-Wilson intended to get away with his violent act, then calling the police from a traceable phone was obviously very foolish. There is a good chance that he would never have been identified, had he not made the call. However, this was a young man without any history of criminal behavior, and his naïveté about covering his tracks was probably matched by a need to make amends and a failure to understand the importance of immediately seeking legal advice (which is interesting in that both his parents are lawyers and that was the career he eventually hoped to pursue). However, Pring-Wilson's main foolishness, and the one from which everything else flowed, was his responding to a minimal provocation from the victim by opening the car door and, even more so, by using the knife. If he had just walked away, or made a joking comment such as "you're right, I am drunk," or kept the knife in his pocket, his life would have continued on the success track that it was on and young Mr. Colono would not have died. This episode illustrates how alcohol intoxication can impair judgment, and relax inhibitions, enough to trigger the most foolish, and deadly, of actions in an intelligent person typically likely to keep his emotions in check.

Dopamine and Other Neurotransmitters

As a rule, psychologists and other mental health professionals tend to under-appreciate the explanatory role of hormonal or other brain-affecting biological factors in causing people to behave foolishly. The book *Behave: The Biology of Humans at Our Best and Worst*, by neurologist Robert M. Sapolsky (2017) is an attempt to counter that tendency by arguing that biology is the most important factor underlying the things that we do.

Dopamine is an especially good example of such a factor. It is a neurotransmitter that is associated with increased risk-taking, as part of the chemical's motivational role in activating pleasure-seeking behavior. Parkinson's Disease (PD) is a motor disorder that is caused by a dying off of dopamine receptors in the brain, particularly in a midbrain region known as the *substantia nigra*. As the primary drug treatment for PD involves L-DOPA (a chemical precursor of dopamine) or dopamine agonists (which activate dopamine receptors), it should not be surprising that people with PD who are being treated with dopamine drugs often (as many of 20 percent) develop very serious compulsive gambling behaviors, or other addictions (such as hyper-sexuality), which they did not have before they started on the dopamine regimen.

In a radio interview (Lehrer 2009), science writer Jonah Lehrer told the story of a woman named Ann Klinestiver, who was diagnosed with PD and put on a dopamine agonist drug. As mentioned, the purpose of these drugs is to increase the amount of dopamine in the brain to help compensate for the massive cell loss of dopamine neurons in the brain. Ms. Klinestiver lost her marriage and her life savings (over a quarter of a million dollars) playing slot machines (which are especially activating of the dopamine system) for fifteen or more hours at a time. Once she stopped taking the dopamine drug, her compulsive gambling behavior stopped. While Ms. Klinestiver did not have a gambling problem before starting the dopamine regimen, it can be assumed that her personality (which I know nothing about) played some role. As the majority of people with PD who are on dopamine drugs do not become compulsive gamblers, it is possible, indeed likely, that there was some underlying personality trait which caused her, and others like her, to behave in such a socially risky fashion. It should also be re-stated that gambling is not the only addictive behavior that people with PD begin to manifest, so it is possible that a large percentage of people with PD are at risk of developing other seriously foolish (risk-unaware) behavior patterns after being prescribed dopamine drugs.

Greed

The term "greed" refers to an abnormally strong desire to possess wealth for oneself far beyond what one needs to be comfortable, and sometimes beyond the bounds of what is legally or morally appropriate. Greed is typically considered a negative quality, as in Catholic theology where Thomas Aquinas termed it a sin against God. In some modern settings, however, greed is glorified, as in Oliver Stone's 1987 film *Wall Street*, where the main character, a corrupt investor named Gordon Gecko, exclaimed "greed is good" (Weiser, 2008). Stone's inspiration came from a real-life stock swindler named Ivan Boesky, who in a 1986 speech at the University of California, stated that "I think greed is healthy. You can be greedy and still feel good about yourself" (Meserve, 2012). The problem with greed, however, aside from being in very poor taste, is that it pushes individuals to go too far, as Boesky himself found out when he went to jail for insider trading.

One of the most extreme examples of greed causing very socially disastrous consequences can be found in the story of Leo Dennis Kozlowski, a former CEO of Tyco International, a major home security company. Kozlowski, who presided over a very prosperous period in the company's growth, was extremely well compensated, bringing home salary and bonuses in the vicinity of $100 million annually, plus perks such as a $30 million apartment paid for by the company with extravagances such as $6,000 shower curtains. His greed was so all-consuming, however, that he stole over $100 million more from the company in unauthorized bonuses, real estate, and other payments. The pinnacle of his excess came when he got the company to partially fund a $2 million fortieth birthday party for his wife on the island of Sardinia, featuring a private concert by Jimmy Buffet and an ice sculpture of Michelangelo's *David* urinating vodka. His excessive greed inevitably attracted the attention of prosecutors, who charged Kowalski with looting a public company (Hill and Michaels 2002). Although the legal case against Kowalski (which hinged on his supposedly not having his expenditures authorized) was considered shaky by some legal experts (because he never hid what he did, and so much of his reign of excess had been authorized by his company's well-compensated and thus conflicted Board of Directors), his excessive greed made such a bad public impression that he was given a lengthy prison sentence. In an interview, Kowalski himself admitted that he had been foolish, in not anticipating the public revulsion that his unrestrained self-aggrandizement would have on regulators, prosecutors, judges and jurors (Kaplan, 2015).

Fear

Fear can be defined as a feeling that one is in danger. As foolishness is defined as action that ignores risk or danger, fear can play an important role in helping people to act non-foolishly. This explains why fear is such a universal feeling, as it undoubtedly played an evolutionary function in keeping people safe and alive. Paradoxically, fear is also one of the most powerful motivating factors in causing people to act foolishly. That is especially the case when the fear is excessive or irrational, that is, is based more in imagination than in reality. It is for this reason that induction of fear has played an important role in influencing people to vote for a particular political candidate or party (the successful 2016 Presidential candidacy of Donald Trump is an example of a campaign based largely on fear-mongering), and also plays an important role in merchandising of products claiming to ward off threats to one's health or longevity.

The amygdala is a brain structure that plays a critical role in alerting individuals to danger, by mediating the development of memories of aversive situations or stimuli. Damage to the amygdala usually causes people to lose the ability to experience fear and, consequently, increases the likelihood that they will behave foolishly. An example of this has been much written about, involving an Iowa woman known as "SM" who had lost much of her amygdala due to a very rare chromosomal disorder: Urbach-Wiethe disease. Her inability to experience fear had put her in great jeopardy, both physically and socially. For example, she had to be protected from picking up poisonous snakes, as her curiosity put her in danger of being bitten, and her identity has been deliberately kept secret, as she has no ability to recognize danger in her dealings with people. When asked by a neuroscientist studying her if she can ever remember being afraid of anything, she responded that she could only remember one occasion in her life, over three decades earlier, when she was afraid of a catfish that her father had caught. When her children were small she was once walking to a store when a deranged man on a park bench called her over. The man put a knife to her throat and threatened to cut her. According to SM, after the man let her go unharmed (when she calmly told him to get lost), she did not call the police, as she did not experience the harrowing event as dangerous to herself or others. Post Traumatic Distress Disorder (PTSD) is a debilitating psychiatric condition in which actual past danger experiences (such as having been in very life-threatening military combat situations) keep coming back as recurring fears triggered by everyday noises or events. It has been suggested (Koenigs and Grafman 2009) that one treatment for PTSD might be the development of drugs that reduce the activity of the amygdala.

II

Forms of Foolishness

In the previous chapter, I gave separate examples of situational, cognitive, personality, and affective/ state factors that influence humans to behave foolishly (that is, to ignore fairly obvious risks to their social or physical well-being). However, even in those examples, where my intent was to highlight and describe distinct individual factors, it was difficult to focus on just a single factor, as the role of other factors usually could not be ignored. For example, when discussing the *situational* role of time pressure in getting me to buy an unneeded new furnace, I also had to mention the role of *affect* (my fear of dying from carbon monoxide), *state* (not having fully woken up), *cognition* (my youth-related ignorance of con men and how they operate) and *personality* (my tendency to be trusting).

In this section, there are three chapters, containing analyses of foolish behavior in three categories: Practical Foolishness, Noninduced-Social Foolishness, and Induced-Social Foolishness. In none of these analyses is only one explanatory factor emphasized, although the weight given to any factor varies according to the circumstances surrounding (as well as what is known about) each of the cases. For the fact is that foolishness is multiply determined, as most of the stories in the following three chapters (and the balance of the book) illustrate.

FIVE

Practical Foolishness

Practical foolishness occurs when someone acts without paying sufficient attention to a fairly obvious physical risk to life, limb, or property, one's own or another's. An example is found in Shakespeare when *Hamlet* (act 5, scene 2) utters these words of regret: "I have shot mine arrow o'er the house. And hurt my brother." In this chapter, a number of real-life incidents of practical foolishness are discussed, and the four-factor model is used to analyze each incident.

PEOPLE WHO JUMP INTO OLD FAITHFUL

The term "foolhardy" refers to behavior that is reckless and oblivious to danger, particularly when it puts one's very survival at risk. This definition is reflected in its inclusion in the subtitle of the book *Death in Yellowstone: Accidents and Foolhardiness in the First National Park*, by the park's unofficial historian, Lee Whittlesey (1995). The book describes the various ways in which people have died while visiting Yellowstone, often due to lack of awareness of the many dangers to be found in such a wild setting. A common example of such carelessness can be found in people who fall or intentionally jump into one of the park's many thermal hot springs, which reach temperatures ranging from a low of 220 to well over 300 degrees Fahrenheit. Over twenty people have died in this manner (I have seen estimates as high as forty), while many others have been seriously burned but survived.

As with any foolish act, there can be many causes. In a relatively recent fatal accident, curiosity and a contrarian need to go beyond the usual tourist experience seems to have been responsible. It occurred in June 2016, when a twenty-three-year-old Oregon man, Colin Nathaniel Scott, fell into a hot spring in the Norris Geyser basin, the hottest of all the

Yellowstone geyser areas, after he and his sister left the boardwalk and walked over two hundred yards beyond a sign that told them to venture no further. According to news reports, the ground in that area forms a thin crust and it is very easy to fall through what looks like firm land. Once Scott was in the water (which in that area could reach 400 degrees Fahrenheit), there was no saving him, as he likely died instantly. Furthermore, the water there has high acidity, which caused his remains to disappear and become unrecoverable (Whittlesey, 1995).

A recent college honors graduate who was planning to enter a PhD program in psychology, Mr. Scott was obviously someone with above-average IQ, but that did not prevent him from putting himself and his sister at great and very preventable risk. Nothing else is known to me about him other than he had a fair amount of wilderness experience. Nor do I know what transpired between the siblings when they hatched the tragically foolish scheme to wander off the marked boardwalk. I suspect that the fact that Mr. Scott had some wilderness experience may have been a factor in the decision to create a special experience for his sister not available to the general public. This reflects a common phenomenon: a smart person with some knowledge but who has a need to act like he is more of an expert than is actually the case.

Maybe the most common, and understandable, reason why people have jumped into one of Yellowstone's thermal springs has been to rescue a pet. Unfortunately, there have been many cases of dogs that escaped their leashes or car confinement, and then made a beeline for a thermal spring and jumped in, thinking it was a pond fit for splashing around in (animals, also, can be very oblivious to risk). When the dog quickly starts yelping in pain, the natural instinct of an animal lover is to dive in to pull it out. That is what happened on July 20, 1981 when a visitor from California, twenty-four-year-old Allen Kirwan, jumped into one of the hottest of Yellowstone's thermal springs in an attempt to rescue his traveling companion's dog Moosie. The friend tried to talk Kirwan out of going in, as did several onlookers, but Kirwan brushed their objections aside and dove headfirst into the pond. Kirwan actually reached the dog, but when he let go and became lifeless, the friend waded in and pulled him out, severely burning his feet in the process. Kirwan, blinded and with third degree burns over 100 percent of his body, said "that was really stupid" before succumbing to his injuries (as did Moosie).

A FOOLISH DOCTOR

According to the "Peter Principle" espoused by Laurence Peter and Raymond Hull (1969, 22), "in a hierarchy every employee tends to rise to his level of incompetence." We see this every time a good underling is promoted into becoming a disastrous leader. The principle applies in other settings beside organizations, and may be reframed in systems (and cautionary) terms to read: "people are tempted to aspire to roles for which they are unsuited or unready, but it is in their own interest to honestly weigh the risks and rewards before they take an upward leap." As in anything, the risk in taking on an unsuitable role can range from minor (unhappiness and failure) to major (catastrophe). The story of Dr. Conrad Murray, the physician whose behavior resulted in the death of pop icon Michael Jackson as well as his own career, is an illustration of the latter.

Jackson met Murray when the entertainer was in Las Vegas and the doctor was called on to treat one of Jackson's children. Murray was an internist and (non Board-certified) cardiologist, with offices in Nevada and Texas. Jackson apparently liked Murray and asked him to be his personal physician for the duration of a planned six months long show in London and during the several months of rehearsal leading up to that show. Murray, a man with seven children, a complicated love life and major debts, was teetering on the brink of (a second) bankruptcy. When approached by Jackson, he initially asked for a yearly salary of $5 million, but eventually settled for $1.8 million. Murray's major job was to help Jackson, a man with severe insomnia, to sleep. Jackson made clear to Murray that he wanted him to administer propofol, a powerful drug used by anesthesiologists to induce sedation in surgical settings. Jackson, who had previously been given propofol for cosmetic procedures (always by an anesthesiologist), had asked other medical personnel to administer it to help him sleep, but had been repeatedly turned down. Murray, a physician with no training in either anesthesiology or sleep disorders, apparently had no such reservations, and agreed to the request.

According to his recorded statement to police, Murray had been administering propofol to Jackson for over a month, using an injection followed by an IV-drip. On the night when Jackson died, Murray claims he initially resisted giving propofol, feeling the singer was becoming addicted, but he eventually relented. Leaving the singer's side to go in another room (he claimed it was a two-minute bathroom break, but cell phone records suggest it was much longer) he returned to find Jackson had stopped breathing. Instead of calling 911 immediately (he delayed that critical step by thiry minutes), he called in a security guard and ordered him to dispose of evidence, then made an inept (and counterproductive) attempt at chest compression, when the correct protocol called for pumping in oxygen (as the problem was not cardiac arrest but lack of oxygen getting to the heart). When paramedics arrived, Murray did not tell them he had administered propofol (suggesting consciousness of wrongdoing), and he also kept this critical information from the doctor treating Jackson in the emergency room. After the coroner found that Jackson had died from acute propofol intoxication, and in light of

Murray's admission to having administered the drug, the physician was charged with and convicted of involuntary manslaughter: essentially gross negligence reflecting disregard for life.

Murray received a sentence of four years in prison, but also exposed himself to significant financial liability and the loss of his license, career and reputation (Medina 2011). Although Murray's disposing of evidence makes some speculation necessary, the most likely explanation for what happened is that the propofol was being administered through an IV-drip without the use of a dose-regulating pump, and there was a malfunction or miscalculation resulting in way too much of the sedative getting into Jackson's bloodstream. This caused the patient to cross over the thin line between unconsciousness with, to unconsciousness without, breathing. The lack of monitoring or emergency equipment, coupled with the doctor's lack of knowledge or preparation in coping with the emergency situation, combined with his fear-driven delay in calling 911, all contributed to a probably preventable death.

In terms of the Peter Principle, an attractive upward status move (a sizeable salary and the prestige of attending to the world's most famous entertainer) resulted in the worst kind of failure imaginable for Murray. According to my causative theory of foolish behavior, such an act results from the intersection of four factors, one of them (situation) being external to the actor, and three of them (cognition, personality and affect/state) being internal (see figure 3.1). There were two action points in this story that involved foolishness: (a) the first was when Murray agreed to Jackson's request to administer propofol, (b) the second was his failure to use appropriate emergency procedures, including immediately calling 911. I will not consider Murray's incriminating statements about propofol administration to police as foolish (after first trying to cover it up in the hospital), as I believe full honesty in such a situation is an ethical requirement. However, as a general rule, it is usually a mistake for a criminal suspect or offender to agree to a police interview, as nothing good for the interviewee generally comes out of it.

In explaining Murray's first foolish act, agreeing to administer propofol, there were two situational pulls: being asked by Jackson to give the drug, and the fact that it had been used by Murray without mishap for several weeks. The first situational pull was relatively mild (other doctors and at least one nurse had no trouble saying "no") but the second one was relatively strong, as nothing bad happening at first can lull a person into underestimating the risks of something bad eventually happening later. Cognition clearly was a factor here, as Murray evidently did not appreciate the risks associated with giving such a powerful sedative, as reflected both in his agreeing to administer it and in his many deviations from standard procedure in the way it was administered. Personality entered in here in two ways: weakness in standing up to Jackson (who he saw as his employer and friend more than his patient) and in a seeming tendency towards self-delusion in over-estimating his own abilities. Probably the biggest factor here was affect: Murray was apparently in a very desperate state financially, and he saw the chance to pull in very big bucks (while getting to rub shoulders with a superstar) as too attractive to turn down. Affect (boredom from standing around watching what he thought of as non-risky sleep) also likely contributed to Murray making the fundamental error of abandoning his post to attend to his cell phone (a device that has contributed to untold numbers of foolish outcomes). Affect, in the form of fear (as he saw his life come crashing down) also explained Murray's unconscionable behavior after he noticed Jackson had stopped breathing, although cognition (profound ignorance of proper emergency procedures) undoubtedly was also a contributor.

The Conrad Murray story is interesting to me not only as an example of foolishness (risk-oblivious behavior), but also for the insights it gives into the role of competence in professional ethics. As a licensed physician, Murray was not committing a crime in purchasing or administering propofol, but he was acting unethically in going beyond his training and competence in doing so. It became a crime after it went wrong, but wisdom or common sense (awareness of medical and career risks), combined with a stronger or better character, would have caused him to avoid putting himself in that position in the first place. The fact is that every professional is given enough rope by his or her license to do things that are outside of their training or competence, but ethical codes require one to avoid doing so. That is because in going beyond one's competence a professional runs the risk of performing poorly and thus failing to meet his or her obligations to a client. I do not doubt that Murray was competent in other aspects of his medical practice, whether treating Jackson's child in Las Vegas or (reportedly) saving the life of a man with a heart condition in Houston. But as a sleep doctor and propofol pusher, Murray was a catastrophe waiting to happen. Physicians, and mental health professionals for that matter, sometimes find themselves faking it (usually in minor ways), such as opining on subjects where their knowledge is a little shaky. I saw my own former internist doing that from time to time, as when he spouted off on nutrition (a topic on which he, like most physicians, received almost no training), but I trusted that he had the sense not to try and perform heart surgery on me. It is tempting for physicians (who are smart and confident in their ability to solve problems) to overestimate their ability to quickly take on and master new challenges (it is not a coincidence that doctors and dentists are the pilots most likely to die in single engine plane crashes). Unfortunately for Conrad Murray, becoming Michael Jackson's sleep doctor was one challenge where faking it failed to make it.

RISKY CONDUCT IN THE WILDERNESS

The nonfiction book *Into the Wild*, by Jon Krakauer (1996) provides what might be considered a foolishness autopsy of a fatal case of practical foolishness by Christopher McCandless, a 1990 graduate of an elite college: Atlanta's Emory University. Right after receiving his diploma, the highly-idealistic young man liquidated his college fund and donated the money ($24,000) to the hunger charity Oxfam, and then set out on a journey of self-discovery, after a last communication with his parents back in Washington, DC: a brief note accompanying his college transcript. Abandoning his old Datsun after it was damaged in a flash flood (likely an early indicator of risk-obliviousness) in a desert in Nevada in July 1990, Chris (who began calling himself "Alex Supertramp"), put his belongings in a backpack and hiked across the Sierra Nevada Mountains to Idaho (where he was befriended by Jan Burres and her boyfriend Bob). He later went to Montana where he was befriended by Wayne Westerberg.

After working for a while in Montana, Chris set off again in late October 1990, reaching the California desert town of Needles, from which he made it to Arizona, where he purchased a used canoe. Traveling on the Colorado River, in December 1990 Chris reached a dam on the Mexican border and, a few days later abandoned his attempt to reach the Gulf of California by canoe when he encountered dangerous waterfalls. However, in a pattern repeated often in his wanderings, he was helped by sympathetic strangers—in this case a couple of duck hunters—who drove him and his canoe to that body of water. Encountering high winds, McCandless camped for several days in a cave he had found on the face of a bluff on Christmas Day 1990. Back in his canoe on January 11, 1991, the young man almost drowned when he was caught in a violent storm.

On January 16, he abandoned the canoe and started walking north to the border, where he was arrested by Immigration officers when he tried to cross into the United States. Released after a night in jail, Chris made it to Houston and later, Los Angeles, where he applied for a job in February 1991. Changing his mind about the job, Chris hit the road again, and made it to the bottom of the Grand Canyon, where he camped with a young German couple. He noted in his journal that he had lost twenty-five pounds. Burying his backpack toward the end of February, Chris hitchhiked to Las Vegas, where he spent about eight weeks. Leaving Las Vegas in May 1991, Chris apparently spent the summer in coastal Oregon (Jan Burres received a card in which he complained about the unending fog and rain). In October 1991, Chris made it to Bullhead City, Arizona where he worked in a McDonald's for two months and lived in an empty RV owned by an old man named Charlie. Wanting to see Jan and Bob, he mailed them an invitation to visit him in Bullhead City, but he quickly decided to visit them instead, and he arrived at their campground in the

Mojave Desert in mid-December 1991. A few weeks later, while hitch-hiking by California's Salton Sea, he made a new friend, Ronald Frantz, an 80-year-old ex-Marine, who became very attached to Chris, and even offered to adopt him. In February, Frantz dropped Chris off in San Diego, where he lived on the streets for a week, before arriving in Seattle in early March. In what might be termed a "neurotic cycle" (seeking to go some-where and then almost immediately changing his mind and returning to where he had just come from), Chris quickly reversed course and made it back to the Southern California desert. After a night with Ron Frantz, Chris was driven by him to Grand Junction, Colorado. From there, he made it to South Dakota, where he spent two weeks visiting and working for his Montana friend Wayne Westerberg, who now ran a grain elevator.

At the end of March 1992, Chris began his final journey when he took off for Alaska. He made it to Liard Hot Springs, British Columbia where he caught a ride north with a truck driver named Gaylord Stuckey. Hitch-hiking on the Alaskan Highway, Chris arrived in Fairbanks, where he spent three days near the University of Alaska campus, reading about edible plants, buying a rifle, and sending postcards (none to his desper-ately worried family, with whom he had not communicated in nearly two years). Starting out again, Chris hoped to reach the Stampede Trail and, after camping out on frozen ground, was picked up on April 28 by an electrician named Jim Gallien, who drove him the final three hours to that trail. Concerned that Chris (who took only ten pounds of rice and his rifle) was not equipped to survive in the frigid and wet Alaska wild, Gallien tried to talk him out of his plan and, when that did not succeed, gave him a pair of waterproof boots. Others had offered to buy him better clothes and equipment, but Chris had refused the offers.

Chris had thought of hiking to the coast, but the difficult and boggy terrain caused him to stay for an extended time in an old bus he found on May 1 beside the Sushana River. Chris survived on edible flowers and wild berries and by shooting various small animals (squirrels, grouse, even a porcupine) and a moose, which he had to abandon to the wolves after it became maggoty. In early July, besieged by flies and mosquitoes, and bothered by malnourishment and dental problems (a crown had fallen off a molar), Chris tried to hike the twenty miles back to the Stam-pede Highway. He had to turn back, when he discovered that what had been an easily fordable river in April was now a dangerously raging and impassable torrent.

Had Chris possessed an adequate map, he would have seen that he was but a short distance from a hand-operated tram, and a mile from a logging road, which could have carried him safely across the river. Less than a week after trying to escape, Chris made it back to the bus on July 8. Writing in his journal, Chris detailed his deteriorating condition, writing on July 30 "Extremely weak, fault of pot. seed. Much trouble just to stand up. Starving. Great jeopardy." According to Jon Krakauer, Chris' death, while undoubtedly due to starvation, was hastened by illness caused either by mistakenly eating a toxic plant or by wet seeds that had become moldy. (Both of these theories have been disputed). On August 12, he posted an S.O.S. note on the door of the bus and foraged for blueberries. His last journal entry read "beautiful blueberries." He died in his sleeping bag a week later. A short time after that, in September 1992, Chris McCandless' body was discovered by hunters.

A particularly poignant aspect of this (already poignant) story is that after seeking to discover the meaning of happiness by living a hermetic life in emulation of his hero Henry David Thoreau, Chris' last journal entries revealed the insight that he was a social animal and that true happiness for him could only come through having meaningful relations with others. Thus, his attempt to return from the wilderness was motivated not only by his dangerously deteriorating physical condition but by a need to reenter the world of people he cared about, including, one would hope, his family. In a memoir *The Wild Truth*, Carine McCandless (2014) stated that her brother had revealed to her in advance about his plan to separate from the family, an extreme move driven by severe resentment of his father.

With respect to emulation of Thoreau, I know something that Chris likely did not, which is that Thoreau (a great exaggerator) frequently attended fancy dinner parties at the nearby homes of friends, during the time when he was promoting the virtues of living alone in the woods. (Walden Pond is less than two miles from the bustling Concord, Massachusetts town center). Just reading about the many people who were drawn to Chris during his two years on the road, and about his cyclical attempts to reconnect with them, it is obvious that he was a very friendly person who liked people and who was liked, indeed loved, in return. Several of his new friends tried to talk him into abandoning his ceaseless wanderings and to putting down roots near them. Like Voltaire's 1759 novel *Candide* (or Dennis Hopper's 1969 film *Easy Rider*), Chris McCandless discovered, too late, the benefits of staying in one place, surrounded by caring others.

The practical foolishness exhibited by Chris McCandless had less to do with the incredibly aimless nature of his repetitive wanderings (which could be described as going in one big, but expanding, circle) and more to do with the physical risks that he took, apparently without sufficient understanding, preparation, or forethought. Judging by final journal entries documenting a desperate desire to survive, Chris likely did not have a death wish, but he risked death on two, and possibly three, occasions (Alaska, Gulf of California, and perhaps the desolate Mojave desert). It does not appear that he fully understood those risks or sought the information, skills, companionship, or provisions needed to reduce or eliminate those risks. Arrogance (which sometimes makes one stupid) likely entered into the mix, as reflected in Chris' unwillingness to take seriously the danger warnings he received from individuals (such as concerned Alaska residents) with more experience and knowledge than he possessed.

What would cause an obviously intelligent young person such as Chris McCandless to enter the Alaska wilderness so woefully lacking in supplies, information, and preparation? People in their twenties are not far removed from the impulsivity and poor judgment of adolescence, and highly intelligent young (or older) people often overestimate their ability to improvise and address problems when they arise. Personality was obviously also a factor contributing to Chris McCandless' demise, as he appears to have been a stubborn individual, who did not listen to warnings and who seemed to reject the idea that planning or preparation are desirable traits.

In his analysis, Jon Krakauer (1995) (who admits to identifying with McCandless as he believes he also took excessive risks when young), saw him as done in by an accident that could have befallen any young person, including himself. But I know Krakauer slightly personally. He and my wife Helen (who, like Thoreau, grew up in Concord) were classmates at Hampshire College, and did some notable climbs together in Alaska's Arrigetch Peaks. From what she tells me, Jon was—even as a young man—a meticulous planner, who rarely undertook an adventure he had not researched thoroughly, and who was very willing to alter a plan if unanticipated dangers arose.

One controversy around McCandless concerns the extent to which mental illness may have played a part in his story. Krakauer saw him as a generally adjusted and talented young person on a spiritual quest who naively exposed himself to dangers that Chris' other writer hero, Jack London (a tramp once out of necessity, but always very interested in making money) mainly wrote about. London's most acclaimed short story, "To Build a Fire" (1902; 1908) ironically dealt with a young man like Chris who was new to the far North, and who also foolishly ignored a warning not to travel alone. He died largely because of a failure to bring a sufficient supply of matches.

A contrary opinion about McCandless' mental health was expressed by an Alaska journalist, Craig Medred (2007), who described Chris as basically a nut-case, whose lack of practical intelligence were signs of a schizophrenic disorder. Medred's evidence is highly dubious, citing mainly two facts: (a) cutting off contact with his family (something mentally ill people sometimes do), and (b) an episode reported by Wayne Westerberg, in which Chris ignored a horrible smell in his apartment, caused by allowing grease to collect in the bottom of a microwave oven (Medred asserts that schizophrenics have an impaired sense of smell). But there are other more plausible explanations (being a confused and inexperienced young person for one), and surely if McCandless was psychotic he would not have made so many friends, none of whom commented on him being odd or disturbed.

Unlike people with schizophrenia, McCandless was not so impaired in practical intelligence as to be unable to function independently in the world; in fact, in general, he coped fairly well. Undoubtedly, Chris had emotional problems (as mentioned, he deeply resented what he saw as his father's abuse). But as with other stories in the current book, the foolish action in question—a poorly prepared solitary adventure in the unforgiving Alaska wilderness—is not something that can be explained by pointing to just one single factor.

FOOLISH DISEASE MANAGEMENT

There is a lot of Type-2 (adult-onset) diabetes in my family and it was thus not a complete surprise when a few years ago I developed the disease myself. I had several times seen for myself the devastating complications (blindness, heart disease, amputations, early death) stemming from chronically elevated blood glucose levels. Therefore, I immediately adopted the recommended regimen (pills, rigidly controlled diet, exercise, twice-daily glucose monitoring) and was able to bring my levels down into the normal range rather quickly. I also understand that this is a life-long challenge, and it will take a great deal of self-regulatory effort, adaptability and intellectual energy to maintain normal sugar levels (and, hopefully, good health) over my remaining years.

It was, therefore, somewhat of a surprise, when I mentioned my new diagnosis to a friend and he replied "I have diabetes too, but I don't take pills; I want to avoid the side effects of medication." I asked him what his blood glucose level was (which he finds out only when he goes to the doctor) and he gave me a number that I consider shockingly high. Update: my friend later had major heart surgery, as serious heart problems are one of the main complications of untreated diabetes. I have since spoken to several others who have Type-2 diabetes and who choose not to treat the disease aggressively or, for that matter, at all. To what extent this reflects poor medical advice as opposed to personal failings in the patients themselves I am not certain, but I think I am correct in believing that these people (some of whom are starting to experience complications of the disease) are putting their health and longevity at risk. In my view, the potential serious side effects of diabetes medication (which have a relatively low probability of occurring) are nothing in comparison to the severe complications (which assuredly will occur) from the lack of disciplined effort to maintain near-normal glucose levels over a number of years. Of course, understanding of probability is quite low in the general public, as reflected in the irrational fear of flying in so many people who think nothing of driving a car (thousands of times more likely to kill or maim than an airline flight) recklessly and at high speeds.

As a rule, passivity and misinformation about disease are more likely to be found in less-educated people, as reflected in a study published by the National Academy of Sciences (Goldman and Smith 2010) indicating that the poorer long-term health outcomes of persons from lower socioeconomic status (SES) groups are in part attributable to the bad job they do in managing their chronic diseases. Here is an anecdote that illustrates what I am talking about. I was testifying in a court case in downtown Newark, New Jersey (a city with a high rate of poverty) and I stopped for lunch at a restaurant where I was the only person wearing a suit. I noticed several patrons, most of them older overweight ladies, drinking iced tea and I asked for a glass, specifying "unsweetened." The waitress, who seemed to be the owner, told me they only served sweetened and, furthermore, that I was the first person she could remember ever asking for iced tea that was unsweetened. I replied by asking if I was the first diabetic person to eat at that restaurant, at which point four women at the next table (one of them confined to a wheelchair, and who I noticed having earlier added sugar to her already sweetened tea) all piped up with "I have diabetes." The owner then laughed and said "I guess you are the first diabetic to ever eat here who follows his doctor's advice."

However, affluent professionals (such as my friend profiled above) are also often prone to demonstrating poor "health intelligence" as well. In the case of diabetes this can be attributed in part to the fact that people with elevated blood sugar do not necessarily feel sick; in fact, because they are being nourished by the breakdown of their own tissue, they can feel excellent. Therefore, the risks associated with having poor blood glucose control are in the future and thus less salient, and it takes a certain kind of intelligence (as well as knowledge) to keep in mind that feeling or looking healthy is not the same as being healthy.

An even more blatant form of health stupidity occurs when one has a more immediately life-threatening disease such as cancer but chooses not to treat it or to treat it with questionable or unproven methods. Two young women I knew, both now dead, responded to their diagnosis of breast cancer by resisting surgery and related medical treatments, and instead chose to follow advice to put themselves in the hands of dubiously credentialed natural healers who prescribed alternative treatments. After these treatments failed to work, and the tumors spread to various other organs, they finally turned to regular doctors for help. Unfortunately, at that point, there was little that could be done to save them. In both cases, the *situational* factor was having friends who espoused ignorant ideas about illness and who vouched for the credentials and success of quack healers. The *cognitive* factor was naiveté about cancer and an inability to evaluate scientific or pseudo-scientific evidence. The *personality* factor was a too-trusting nature. The *affective* factor was a fear of disfiguring surgery and of the side-effects of radiation and chemotherapy. As is often the case, affect may have been the deciding factor which pushed these otherwise intelligent individuals into making tragically stupid decisions.

FOOLISHNESS INVOLVING WILD ANIMALS

As the story of Chris McCandless demonstrated, Alaska is a place where there are many risks to one's survival, especially if one is off in the wild. Here is another Alaska story of death resulting from poor awareness of natural risk, but this one took place in the state's largest city, Anchorage. In January of 1995, I found myself in Anchorage giving a talk, when a story unfolded that made the national nightly news. It was an unusually high-snowfall winter, which caused hundreds of moose to come into the city in search of shrubs that they were unable to reach in their usual habitat outside of town. This resulted in many more moose-human encounters than usual, with one common outcome being a higher than normal number of automobile-caused moose fatalities. The story that made the national news involved a seventy-year-old man, Myung Chin Ra, who was on his way to meet his wife at the gym on a college campus where a mother moose and her calf were hanging out. At the end of a day in which the adult moose had become agitated as a result of students throwing snowballs at her, Mr. Ra came upon the two moose standing in front of the gym's entrance. Impatient to get to his rendezvous, the man dashed in between the mother and the calf, which caused the adult moose to attack and trample him to death. (Associated Press 1995). A bystander captured the incident on videotape, and the shocking image of this attack was seen in households all across the United States.

Without exception, all of the Alaskans I talked to at the time of the incident considered the victim to have been very foolish, in failing to understand the very severe physical risk involved in coming between a mother moose and her offspring. An equally foolish (but non-lethal) mistake was witnessed by me when I was driving in the Rockies a couple of years ago. In Colorado, moose sightings are much less common than in Alaska, but they do occur on occasion. One day I saw a number of cars pulled off on the side of the road just above a pond. Guessing people had stopped to observe a moose, I also got out to have a look. Sure enough there were two adult moose and a newborn baby moose wading around in the pond (I knew it was newborn, because the placenta was still dangling from the mother). Most of the onlookers kept a healthy distance from the three moose, but one man lacked the sense to do so. Intent on getting a close-up video, he made his way to within maybe fifteen feet of the moose triad, and seemed to have no clue as to the severe danger to which he was exposing himself.

In terms of the four-factor model, the *situational* component was weaker in the first story (where the moose presented an obstacle) and stronger in the second (where the moose presented an opportunity). Still, the main explanations in both stories came from within the two men. *Cognition* obviously played an important role, as neither man apparently understood that moose (especially mothers close by their babies) are dangerous creatures which when riled can kill a human rather easily. In the case of the Alaska episode, Mr. Ra may have developed a false sense of security owing to the fact that moose that winter were ever-present and almost always would leave humans alone. In the Colorado case, the *cognitive* factor likely reflected a lack of experience with moose, and a mistaken impression that a moose is nothing but a large deer or elk. In both cases, *affect* played a major role, in the Alaska case, a strong wish to not be late for an appointment, and in the Colorado case, a strong wish to get a memorable video. As this story demonstrates, affect, when not tempered by wisdom and restraint, can often put one in serious danger.

FOOLISH RISKS IN AVALANCHE COUNTRY

Living in the world, outside of say a cloistered monastery, exposes all of us to a certain degree of physical risk. Driving a car on a busy highway, for example, is an activity that could end one's life at any moment. Some activities are inherently more dangerous than others, and skiing in avalanche country during the spring is one of those activities. While to some extent being killed in an avalanche can be considered an example of very bad luck, there are things that one can do to minimize that risk (Handwerk 2013).

In Colorado, where I lived until recently, every year brings new stories of skiers killed in avalanches, when descending or traversing outside of groomed resort areas. One such tragedy (the worst in fifty years) occurred in April 2013, when a party of six expert male skiers and boarders, most of them experienced in the backcountry and all with state-of-the-art avalanche equipment, were buried in a massive slide below Loveland Pass, killing five of the victims (Nath 2013). Such tragedies are particularly likely in the spring, after the resorts close, when significant snow accumulations pose an irresistible lure to diehard skiers who are willing to put in the extra work needed to access slopes that are not served by lifts. Another reason why avalanche fatalities are more likely to occur in the spring is because when heavy new snowfalls accumulate in warmer weather on top of older layers of frozen snow, they form large unstable slabs. When temperatures rise during the day well above freezing, these slabs can break loose either naturally or when triggered by human activity, and slide over the now water-lubricated older snow, careening down the hillsides in fast-moving deadly slides that can crush and bury every-thing (including trees and humans) in their path.

Most backcountry skiers are well aware of the possibility of ava-lanches and take various precautions, including: checking websites for updated avalanche forecasts, skiing with one or more buddies (who can dig each other out), purchasing equipment such as locator beacons, probes, and devices for breathing while buried (the key there is not so much providing oxygen as it is diverting from one's face fatal build-ups of carbon dioxide) and taking courses taught by experts on avalanche avoidance and detection. These instructors espouse various well-estab-lished principles, such as: avoid skiing later in the day and on north-facing slopes and slopes steeper than 20 degrees, and with big wind-aided snow build-ups. One important principle, which seems to have been violated in several major avalanche disasters, is to avoid doing back-country skiing in groups that are too large. The problem there is less that larger groups are more likely to trigger an avalanche as it is that a "groupthink" process can take place, where individual concerns about risk become submerged. In such a process, even people with avalanche expertise (one of the victims of the Loveland disaster taught an avalanche workshop taken by my wife) can behave foolishly.

As with most other physical or social foolishness incidents, avalanche tragedies can be fruitfully analyzed using the four-factor action model. I will apply the model to the Loveland tragedy and to another multi-victim incident, which took the lives of three skiers (also all men), near Stevens Pass Washington in February 2012 (Branch 2012). Both cases are similar in that all four of the causative elements in my model of foolish action— *Situation, Cognition, Affect/State, Personality*—apply and help to explain why very intelligent people can sometimes make very foolish decisions, even when dealing with matters where they have some expertise.

In both the Colorado and Washington tragedies, the main contribut-ing *situational* factor was the large size of the groups. It is well known that individuals who may harbor reservations about the safety of a proposed course of action are more likely to keep their reservations to themselves in a large group. A related phenomenon is that when a large group makes a decision, there is a tendency of members to assume that the others in the group know what they are doing. Thus, a large group tends to give a questionable decision a legitimacy it might otherwise lack. That is why during avalanche season, a backcountry ski outing should never involve as many people as was the case in the two tragedies.

Cognition enters in as taking an unsafe risk is obviously less likely if the victim understands the full extent and nature of the risk. In my own case, my natural caution when in risky terrain is reinforced by my under-standing that I totally lack any expertise that would enable me to inde-pendently appraise the extent of the risk. This would increase my suscep-tibility to bad advice, were I ever tempted to ski out of bounds (which in my case will never happen). Ironically, most of the participants in the two tragedies possessed some knowledge and expertise about avalanches. A common phenomenon, however, is that people with expertise are sometimes prone to over-confidence based on an over-estimation of the extent of their knowledge. A related factor is that avalanche prediction as it relates to specific locations and times is not an exact science, and avalanche warning websites often do not provide fully accurate, up-to-date, or sufficiently detailed information. The ambiguity of the information needed to fully appreciate risk is an obvious factor which may lull some individuals into minimizing or ignoring risks that may appear less serious than they actually are.

In terms of *personality*, people who are attracted to backcountry skiing tend to be physical risk-takers; for example, many of them have engaged in rock-climbing, mountaineering, and other activities where the possibility of death or serious injury is well above zero. That is true of many of the victims, some of whom were attracted to a lifestyle that involved a certain love of adventure. While this does not necessarily translate to a death wish (most of the victims were devoted family members), it suggests a willingness to take physical risks on occasion. Another relevant personality trait that is specific to decisions when in groups is independence. Some people possess the ability to say "no" when their own judgment tells them to resist group pressure, but many people (including myself) lack that quality.

Affect and *state* factors often play a role in avalanche tragedies, as in most foolishness outcomes. The Colorado victims were on their way to a big annual spring gathering, which gave the outing a celebratory quality, which they likely were very loath to miss. Also, a backcountry group ski outing in the spring is a tremendously appealing and exhilarating prospect, and this makes a cautionary decision to abort the activity, especially if it is a sunny and beautiful day (almost always the case in Colorado), very hard to make. When strongly motivated to carry out an activity when risk is not clear-cut, many people will put their reservations on the shelf.

WHY YOUNG CHILDREN SHOULD NOT BE BAT BOYS OR GIRLS

A baseball bat, when swung hard, has the potential to kill or seriously injure anyone unlucky enough to be struck by it. This dangerous truth was illustrated in August 2015 in a tragic accident in Kansas, when Kaiser Carlile, a nine-year-old bat boy for a Wichita adult amateur team, was fatally struck in the head when he ran into the follow-through phase of a practice swing taken by a team member. As a result of this accident, the league—the National Baseball Congress—temporarily suspended the use of bat boys. As my topic in this book is risk-unawareness, I shall analyze this incident in terms of three levels of potential risk-unawareness: (a) the child who died; (b) the young man who swung the bat; and (c) the adults in charge of the team and league. In undertaking this analysis it is not my intent to assign blame, but rather to shed light on why such a tragedy, albeit rare, was to some extent foreseeable and thus largely avoidable.

Risk-Unawareness of the Victim: A bat boy (or bat girl) can have several duties, but the main one (which gives the job its name) is picking up bats discarded by players and lying on the ground, after a batter takes off for first base or after he is done with an at-bat. This primary duty is relevant to understanding the nature of the accident that took the life of Kaiser Carlile.

Details about the exact nature of the accident, as well as the identity of the batter, are largely missing from news accounts. I initially assumed that Kaiser was standing behind and too close to the batter who was warming up, but an eyewitness account clarifies that what actually happened is that Kaiser had run onto the field to retrieve a bat that had been used in a previous at-bat, and while hustling back to the dugout ran right into the backswing of a player warming up in the batter's circle. This clarification is important to understanding the accident, as both Kaiser and the warming-up player would likely have been aware of the need to be cautious if Kaiser was initially anywhere near the occupied batter's circle (where on-deck hitters stand when they are warming up).

By all accounts, Kaiser was a very diligent bat boy, who worked hard at his craft and was motivated to proudly do his job well and quickly. It is understandable that he was so focused on picking up a discarded bat that he would fail to recognize that he was running into a danger zone where an on-deck batter was taking practice swings. Using my four-factor explanatory model of foolish (risk-unaware) action, *affect* (in this case, a strong motivational need to quickly do his main job well) would have caused Kaiser to lose track of other things occurring on the field. But *cognition* also played a critical role, as the ability to "conserve" (keep in mind) a less salient and relatively abstract consideration (here, staying safe by scanning the field when running with a discarded bat) in the face of a more salient and concrete consideration (here, a bat needing to be picked up and returned quickly) is a skill that develops in the primary years and likely is not fully achieved by age nine.

Risk-Unawareness of the Batter: If, as I initially assumed, the batter had been taking warm-up swings with Kaiser standing near him, then I would have faulted him for failing to look around sufficiently before swinging. But as Kaiser apparently ran into the swing, I will absolve the batter of any responsibility, as no on-deck batter could have anticipated such a thing happening.

Risk-Unawareness of Team or League Officials: I do not know if young child bat boys or bat girls are commonly used by other teams in the National Baseball Congress, but I do know that they were banned by

Major League Baseball (MLB) after an eerily similar incident (but one with a happier outcome) occurred during the 2002 World Series. In game five of that series, between the San Francisco Giants and the (then) Anaheim Angels, the bat boy for the Giants was Darren Baker, the three-and-a-half year old son of Dusty Baker, the Giants' manager. When his favorite player, Kenny Lofton, hit a triple, Darren excitedly ran onto the field to retrieve the bat, and ended up in the base path near home plate just as two runners were rounding third base and barreling down on him. The first runner, J. T. Snow, had the presence of mind to pick Darren up by his shirt collar and yank him to safety before he could be injured. After that incident, MLB announced that henceforth, no one younger than 14 years old could serve in a bat boy or bat girl capacity. However, there reportedly are some teams that went even further, and established 18 years old as the minimum required age.

Admittedly, employing a bat boy of three-years-old is a more egregious violation of common sense than employing a bat boy who is nine years old. One can only marvel at the risk-unawareness (and ignorance of child development) of Dusty Baker and team officials at allowing Darren to serve in an on-field role that requires a level of situational knowledge (that base runners could score), judgment (recognizing when a play is still ongoing), and self-regulation (subordinating excitement to a need to stay out of harm's way) that no three-year-old in recorded history has ever possessed. But nine-years-of-age is still too young, in the opinion of this developmental psychologist, for a person to serve in a role as potentially dangerous—given the dynamic, complex, unpredictable and excitement-laden nature of baseball games—as bat boy or bat girl.

I believe that there was a "cuteness factor" that underlay the use of Darren (he was adorable and loved by players and fans) and also was operating in Wichita with regard to Kaiser (a very endearing boy who was described by one player as "the little brother I never had"). In addition to this *affective* factor is a *cognitive* process that might be termed the base-rate effect. Simply put, this refers to the fact that when the probability (given reported past instances) of a bad incident is very low, there is a tendency to assume that the risk of such an incident is negligible and thus not worth taking seriously. But when we are talking about the well-being of children, even a tiny possibility of tragedy (and I would bet that a number of near-miss or non-tragic cases have gone unreported) requires the adults in charge to say "no" to the employment of children in a role where tragedy is foreseeable even if likely to occur only rarely.

DEATH BY SELFIE: FOOLISH TAKING OF SELF-PHOTOGRAPHS

A selfie is an individual or group self-portrait, taken on a smart phone (typically holding the phone at arm's length but sometimes using a selfie stick) and shared with others on Facebook or some other social media website. The smart phone technology making the taking of selfies possible dates to around 2003, but it began to be very widely used around 2009, reaching its current level of popularity around 2014, which was dubbed "the year of the selfie." Posting of unusual selfies has become something of a craze, especially among teenagers, with one result being that picture-takers will go to great lengths to shoot a notable selfie, sometimes putting their own safety at risk (Lovitt 2011). The term "death by selfie" refers to the dozens of reported fatalities that occur every year to people who die while pursuing the ultimate self-portrait. Common examples of selfie-caused fatalities include: a boat tipping over causing someone to drown; a hiker stepping backwards and falling off a cliff; standing on top of a train and being electrocuted; taking a photo of an approaching train over one's shoulder; and a car crash caused by taking a selfie while driving. Compendia of selfie accidents (available by Googling on the topic) show a wide geographic distribution, with India leading the way with over 40 percent of worldwide selfie fatalities. Reasons obviously differ by situation and victim, but the two biggest likely explanations are the *affective* excitement of anticipating recognition and approbation from peers, and the *cognitive* difficulty that some people have in assessing danger, such as from high voltage train wires.

SIX

Noninduced Social Foolishness

Noninduced social foolishness occurs when someone acts without paying sufficient attention to a fairly obvious risk to one's social interests (including wealth, freedom from incarceration, and employment status). By calling the foolishness "noninduced," I mean to indicate that there was little or no attempt by others to suck the person in, and the incident was motivated almost entirely from within the foolish actor themself. A number of real-life incidents are discussed, and the four-factor model (see figure 3.1) is used to analyze each incident.

THE SOCIAL DANGERS OF FACEBOOK

Until recently, I lived off a winding canyon road in the foothills west of Denver, and twice I assisted drivers who drove into a stream or ditch when checking a text or answering a phone call. The teenage daughter of a friend sailed through a red light and totaled her car while distracted by an incoming text message. Most tragically, I knew one person who had a fatal head-on collision while fiddling with his smart phone. I can understand the desire to always feel connected, but I cannot understand risking one's life in the pursuit of that end. There has of course been a lot of media attention paid to the physical risks, especially distracted driving of cars and trains, associated with device-addiction; however, there has not been nearly as much attention paid to the social risks. My self-assigned role over the years has been to correct such an ignoring of the social domain, as when I was one of the first to point out nearly a half-century ago that social intelligence may be more important for life success or failure than academic (IQ-related) intelligence. Certainly, one can make the case that social harm is much more likely to come to people who cannot control their networking compulsion than is physical harm (Osu-agwu 2009).

Three forms of social harm will be discussed briefly: (a) retaliation for device-driven rudeness; (b) contributing to and establishing evidence of professional negligence; and (c) posting things that could get one in job or legal difficulty. Although old age is not a barrier to any of these outcomes, they are more likely to afflict younger people, for two reasons: (a) compulsive use of social media seems to be more an addiction of the young, and (b) older people are more likely to have acquired some understanding of social conventions, and the possible consequences of ignoring them. There is, however, one major exception to this generalization about age, and that involves older politicians, some of whom are, shall we say, less than fully grown up.

It is bad enough to see people checking their hand-held devices when they are walking down the street, riding on a bus, or sitting in a public place (such as a Congressional hearing, which has been described as "almost like attending a computer convention"). But such behavior definitely crosses the line when one does while engaged in a conversation with others. Former New Jersey Governor and United States Senator Jon Corzine, has been characterized as a "CrackBerry," who would compulsively execute trades on his handheld device while having meetings with associates at the company he headed, MF Global (which he drove into bankruptcy in part because of impulsive trades made by him). Such offensive behavior is boorish when conducted in the presence of underlings, but it is foolish (that is, risky) when conducted in the presence of people whose good will you are trying to win (Mazo, Trautschold, and Michaluk 2010) .

Former French president Nicolas Sarkozy (a boorish man by many accounts) found this out when he so annoyed Pope Benedict XVI in 2007 by sneaking a peek at his smartphone that the Pontiff later refused to grant an audience to the Gallic leader and his girlfriend (and later wife) Carla Bruni, ostensibly because they were living in sin.

The classic morality tale of how poor smartphone etiquette can backfire big time came in 2008, shortly after the Democrats in the New York Senate won a two-vote majority after forty years of Republican dominance. Tom Golisano, the billionaire founder of New York's Independence Party, felt that he had helped the Democrats win that majority, and he met with the new Senate president, Malcolm Smith, to discuss his plan for budget reform. Smith could not be bothered to even pretend to be paying attention, and he spent much of the meeting looking at his phone. Golisano got his revenge shortly after that meeting when he persuaded two Democratic Senators (who were in legal difficulty) to defect to the other side, thus teaching the suddenly ex-Senate leader Smith an important lesson about the need to at least feign courtesy when meeting with someone possessing the power to derail your career plans.

Just as device addiction can cause physical harm to oneself if done while driving, it can cause grave physical harm to others—and grave social harm to one's reputation, finances, and freedom—if it is done while one is supposed to be attending to someone's medical needs. Certainly, that is one of the factors that contributed to the involuntary manslaughter conviction and four-year prison sentence (not to mention license loss and grave financial consequences) of physician Conrad Murray, who caused the death of superstar Michael Jackson when he was attending to his handheld device rather than his unconscious patient. (This story was discussed in more detail in chapter 5). According to a *New York Times* story by Matt Richtel (2014), there is growing concern within the medical profession about the problem of doctors and nurses using technology (such as iPads routinely given out for case management and research) for unintended purposes—such as email, buying items on Amazon, and checking the prices of plane tickets—even in the midst of surgery. In one Denver case which resulted in a large malpractice settlement, a patient became permanently paralyzed after his neurosurgeon, using a wireless headset, made no fewer than ten cell phone calls to family and business associates while the operation was going on. The article went on to blame the problem on the inability of many young medical professionals, who have grown up doing device-related activities, to put those activities on the shelf when full attention elsewhere is called for.

A third area where social networking can have major social consequences involves the thoughtless sending of Facebook or Twitter messages. Consequences can be relatively benign (a high school teacher of my youngest child was severely embarrassed when her Facebook message about how much she disliked her current crop of students was tacked by one of them on her classroom door), but they can also be relatively serious. Many corporations now warn their employees not to make any reference to their place of employment on Facebook or Twitter posts, after incidents such as one in which a Wall Street trader was fired for placing a warning letter from his employer on his Facebook profile (there now are websites with titles such as "How to Avoid Getting Fired by Facebook").

Foolish tweeting seems to be especially problematic for athletes or media celebrities, as was the case for comedian Gilbert Gottfried. He was dropped from his lucrative gig as the voice of the duck in commercials for the supplemental health insurer Aflac (which gets 75 percent of its revenue from Japan) after he tweeted many tasteless jokes (such as "I just split up with my girlfriend, but like the Japanese say 'There will be another one floating by any minute now.'") about victims of the tragic March 2011 tsunami in that country. Gottfried later apologized, lamenting that he was born without a censor on his mouth or "send" finger (N. Lee 2014).

In terms of the four-factor theory of foolish (risk-oblivious) behavior, all four factors can play a part in explaining any incident of electronic stupidity, with the weights depending on the incident and the individual. In terms of *Situations*, the most important consideration is the stimulus value of an incoming message or of the device itself. That can be a very powerful factor, as for many individuals these are things that cannot be ignored or resisted. *Personality* enters into the equation, as some people— especially those who grew up with handheld devices—are obviously much more electronically addicted than others. *Cognition* enters into the equation when one considers that there are people (again more likely to be young) who lack an understanding of professional norms, who forget (or never learned) that what one does on the internet is very likely to become publicly known, or who are poor perspective-takers and are naïve about social consequences.

Such an example of naïveté and consequence-ignoring can be seen in the case of Ilan Grapel, someone with joint US-Israeli citizenship. A recent graduate of Johns Hopkins University (my alma mater), Grapel was arrested as an Israeli spy after he entered Egypt during the Arab Spring uprising. The young man was born in Brooklyn but at one time made an Aliyah (immigration trial period) to Israel during which he served in the Israeli army. Grapel entered Egypt by claiming to be a journalist covering the political uprising, but most likely he was an idealist who wanted to participate in the historic events taking place in that country. What got Grapel into hot water was that his Facebook profile contained a photo of him wearing his Israeli army uniform, and also contained some articles expressing anti-Palestinian opinions. Probably, Grapel considered it improbable that anyone in Egypt would think it likely that an Israeli spy would be so open about his background, but if that was his thinking he was being very naïve, given the depth of anti-Israel sentiment pervading most segments of Egypt society, especially during the midst of a popular uprising against an unpopular dictator seen by many as too cozy with Israel.

In the case of Grapel, and in so many other instances of electronic foolishness, *Affect/State* is likely almost always involved. There is an exhilaration that comes to many people from their electronic communications, and for some Facebook becomes an alternative (and sometimes more satisfying) social reality. When in that realm of enjoyment, consequences in the other (less satisfying) realm can disappear from one's consciousness. Young people are so addicted to sharing everything they do through the social media, that the possibility that such sharing could get them in trouble probably does not even enter into their thought processes. Facebook use can become intoxicating and as with other forms of intoxication (such as the more usual high that comes from alcohol or drug use, sometimes also implicated in intemperate message-sending), good judgment can fly out the window. As with any addiction, reality requires one to maintain some degree of self-regulatory control, if one is to survive to tweet another day.

TWO BEACH HOUSE STORIES

Here is a true (but slightly altered) Hollywood story that never made the papers. It was told to me by a friend who does consulting work for a famous movie executive, whom I shall call "Richard Francis." The main Francis family residence is in Beverly Hills (both the name and the location have been altered) but they also own a beach house which they rarely use. To protect the unused property, Mr. Francis hired a young couple—at an attractive annual salary—to be live-in caretakers, and fitted out a nicely appointed basement apartment for their use. When the couple had their first child, the employer generously added a room to their quarters to accommodate their need for more space. Francis had only two rules which he communicated clearly when the couple was hired. The first rule was to stay out of the main (upstairs) part of the house and the second rule was to avoid using any of the personal items belonging to the owner and his family.

In addition to a planned brief annual family vacation at the beach house, Mr. Francis did occasionally visit the beach house when he was in the area, but he always phoned ahead to let the couple know he was coming. One day Francis happened to be in the vicinity for a meeting which ended around lunchtime, and he decided on impulse to stop by the house to fix himself a sandwich. Not wanting to bother the couple, he dropped in unannounced. To his, and their, surprise he found the couple lying on his and his wife's bed watching television while their child was on the floor playing with toys belonging to the Francis children. The next day, the couple received a visit from the producer's secretary, who gave them a generous severance check and instructed them to vacate the property promptly.

Aside from the immorality of not honoring a commitment, the behavior of the couple was foolish in that it undermined a very attractive deal that would probably have continued indefinitely. Knowing nothing about the *personality* of the two foolish actors, I can only talk about the other three explanatory factors in the model. The *situational* lure is that it was just too easy and appealing for them to walk upstairs and use the main house. *Affect* likely played a role, as the basement apartment—however comfortable—could not have compared to the owners' spacious living quarters, with their attractive views and furnishings. However, I believe the main factor here was *cognitive*, namely the base rate problem referred to in chapter 5 to explain the use of young children as bat boys and bat girls. When you have a potential undesirable event that has never happened—in this case the owner coming by without calling first—it is easy to delude yourself into believing that such an event will never happen. Thus, the couple likely believed that the risk of being caught hanging out upstairs was non-existent and that they could ignore it with impunity; in fact, this expectation was probably confirmed every day for as long as they had lived there. In taking this risk, perhaps they were also counting on the owner to forgive them if they were caught, as by all accounts he is a kind person. However, when the consequences of an action are potentially catastrophic, it is a mistake to run the risk of engaging in it, however low the bad outcome's probability might appear.

Here is another California beach house story, but with a different twist (Sarno, Hong, and Beale 2009). The foolish actor in this story was a thirty-nine-year-old senior vice president (her real name was published, but I shall call her "Ms. Smith") of Wells Fargo bank in Southern California, in which role she was responsible for maintaining the bank's high-end foreclosed properties. One of the foreclosed properties for which she was responsible was a 3,800 square foot beach house in the Malibu Colony (an exclusive enclave) that was valued at $12 million, and which was so spectacular that it could lease for many thousands of dollars per month. In May 2009, the bank took back the property, when its owners, who lost much of their wealth in the Bernard Madoff Ponzi scheme, no longer could make the hefty mortgage payments. The house was kept by the bank off the market under an agreement with the owners (who, presumably, were hoping to buy it back out of foreclosure). The bank official was fired from her well-paying job, after the *Los Angeles Times,* alerted by a tip from a neighbor, ran a story in September 2009 reporting that Ms. Smith, a seventeen-year veteran of the bank, used the house as if it were her own vacation property, and held parties there on many weekends. The parties caught the attention of neighbors, who were among the richest and most influential people in the Los Angeles business and entertainment communities.

Presumably, Ms. Smith could have gotten away with her use of the bank's house, in spite of it being a clear violation of company policy, if she had done so in a very quiet and low-key manner. The foolish action here was holding frequent parties, in an area where houses are close together and where such use was likely to attract the attention, and most likely the concern, of neighbors, most of whom knew who had owned the house and how to get their concerns publicized.

In terms of the explanatory model, one can imagine that several of the factors played a role. As someone with keys to, and responsibility for, the bank's properties, it was a *situational* slippery slope for Ms. Smith, from coming by to check on the house, to using it herself, to holding parties there. Obviously, there was a strong *affective* lure to holding such parties, as her friends and family members had to have been impressed by her ability to entertain them at such a luxurious place. I do not know anything about Ms. Smith's *personality,* but it is possible she had a need to impress and a willingness to take risks. The chief factor here most likely is also in the area of *cognition*, as one would have to be somewhat lacking in tacit knowledge to not understand the real possibility that neighbors would blow the whistle, especially when being disturbed by the noise from frequent parties.

WHEN HUMOR TURNS INTO FOOLISHNESS

Humor generally is an adaptive form of social interaction, but it has the potential to backfire when something offensive leaks out. An example occurred in March 2009 when President Barack Obama—usually very socially sure-footed—made an appearance on NBC's *Tonight Show*. Joking with host Jay Leno about his poor bowling skills, Mr. Obama indicated that he still was not happy with his game, describing his latest score of 129 thusly: "it was like the Special Olympics or something." Needless to say, the President had to do some major apologizing (such as to my former doctoral advisee, Special Olympics CEO Timothy Shriver) to repair the damage done by his off-the-cuff effort at humor.

An example of Presidential humor with more serious long-term consequences involved the first President Bush, a man known for his spontaneous wisecracking but also for being somewhat verbally dysfluent. When accepting the Republican nomination in 1988, Mr. Bush had placated the anti-tax wing of the Republican Party with his famous catchphrase "Read my lips: No new taxes." Facing large budget deficits, the president had to back off that pledge in order to get Congress to adopt a budget in 1990. While jogging in a park in St. Petersburg, Florida, the President was asked to explain why he changed his stance. Without breaking stride, Mr. Bush pointed to his backside and said "read my hips" (Goodgame 1990). This flippant comment (which likely got laughs when used with family and staff, but not with the public), even more than the policy flip-flop, was considered to be one of the factors that contributed to the dramatic fall-off in popularity that contributed to Bush's failure to be reelected in 1992.

Another example of very foolish use of humor, this time somewhat more premeditated, involved Rich Mitchell, the former superintendent of a suburban Chicago school district. At a back-to-school-workshop for high school teachers in August 2006, Mr. Mitchell gave a presentation on how to inject humor and laughter into the workplace. What he did was to take videotaped interviews with new teachers, and then edit them by inserting his own gag questions, in order to make the faculty look like they were endorsing such things as terrorism, drug use, and stripping. There were many in the audience who did not find this particularly funny, but Mr. Mitchell thought it was so hilarious that he actually posted the mock documentary on the district's website, where it came to the attention of the news media. The public's reaction was so intense that Mr. Mitchell lost his job as a result.

Wisecracking involving racial or gender stereotypes is a staple of television sports commentators (as it is of sports celebrities in general) but there are increasing career dangers that flow from such comments. Among the examples of this are: basketball great Rick Barry, whose career as a premier NBA analyst was severely damaged when he directed a watermelon joke at his visibly annoyed on-air African American partner, Bill Russell; football analyst Tom Brookshier, who was demoted and later fired as a TV broadcaster, by joking that the five (all Black) starters on the University of Louisville basketball team "had a collective I.Q. of about 40"; and TV baseball analyst Steve Lyons, who was fired for making a joke that appeared to be saying that people who speak Spanish are likely to steal one's wallet (apparently, Lyons had been warned previously to cut out the ethnic joking but was unable to do so).

Such behavior seems to be a staple of athletes and sports commentators, partly because racism and racially-tinged teasing may be endemic to that field, and partly because many people involved in sports may lack the sophistication to understand that racist comments tolerated in private are less likely to be tolerated in public, particularly given emerging changes in the public's racial attitudes. This failure to understand contextual (tolerated in private, not in public) or historical (once tolerated in society, now no longer tolerated) variables is a form of *cognitive* deficit that undoubtedly explains many foolish actions, including those having nothing to do with humor or race.

The role of *situations* enters in minimally, except that some situations (such as being on a television set with other bantering ex-jocks) seem to call forth an effort at humor more than others. *Affect* and *state* enter in, as public speaking produces anxiety in most people (even experienced public speakers) and humor is a way of masking or dealing with such anxiety. Extremely foolish uses of humor are more likely to occur when the speaker is very tired or inebriated (which is sometimes the case, as some speakers will take a drink to lessen their anxiety). *Personality*, however, is probably the biggest explanation of career-threatening humor, as habitual humor use is a behavioral schema that is so relied upon by some people that it almost takes on a life of its own. The need to be funny is a generally positive trait, except when it becomes a compulsion and causes consequences that are not so funny.

An example of career demise through racially insensitive needling in a politician (who also has a sports background, as the son of a famous football coach), involved former US Senator George Allen of Virginia. In the homestretch of a tight re-election campaign against his Democratic opponent James Webb, Allen was caught on videotape directing a highly demeaning racial comment at a twenty-year-old man of Indian descent in the crowd, calling him "macaca" (a racist term supposedly meaning monkey), saying "welcome to American and the real world of Virginia" and then making comments about terrorists. These comments were seen as funny by Allen's supporters but when a cell phone video of the incident became public, the general response was anything but amused. When it became known that the man being taunted as an immigrant and terrorist turned out to have been born and bred in Virginia, Allen's campaign, in a state that now has a much more ethnically diverse electorate than in the past, went down in flames (Tapper and Kuhlman 2006).

FOOLISH SEX

Whether or not one believes that French Socialist politician Dominique Strauss-Kahn coerced New York chambermaid Nafissatou Diallo into performing an unwanted sex act in May of 2011 (and I happen to believe he did), there is no doubting that what happened in the hotel room had disastrous consequences for the horny septuagenarian (Solomon 2012). Among these were having to resign from his powerful post as managing director of the International Monetary Fund, severe personal embarrassment (even given his wife's initial public claim of indifference towards where her husband put his penis), and the end to his dream of becoming the first Jewish president of France. It also eventually led to the end of his marriage, after Mr. Strauss-Kahn was charged with other acts of sexual misconduct, one involving a sex club he allegedly founded that held orgies in Washington and Europe, another involving a young female novelist and journalist who accused him of trying to sexually assault her.

Strauss-Kahn is obviously not the only example of a prominent male politician done in by his inability to keep it in his pants. Several examples from American politics come to mind, one of which is the case of Democratic Congressman Andrew Weiner, who gave up a promising political future in New York after it was revealed that the just-married man had sent unsolicited and for the most part unwelcome sexually explicit texts and photos to several females (Berkshire 2013). While the Weiner case is atypical, in that his gratification appeared to be mainly through masturbation (he apparently never had direct contact with any of the women who received his messages), disgraced New York Democratic governor Eliot Spitzer and almost-impeached former Democratic president Bill Clinton are examples of politicians who took a more traditional (but, unlike Strauss-Kahn, clearly encouraged) route to political/ sexual catastrophe. Spitzer, who had to resign his position after he was caught sending a large wire transfer to pay for a prostitute, had, like Strauss-Kahn to give up his (or more likely his family's) dream. Clinton managed to survive an impeachment attempt, but he put himself, the country, and his loved ones, through many months of grief, as a result of his risky dal-

liance in the Oval Office, with the college student intern Monica Lewinsky.

All four of the priapic politicians named thus far are on the progressive end of the political spectrum, but conservatives are equally likely to
commit "career suicide by sex." Examples are Larry Craig (the Republican Senator from Idaho who propositioned a cop in a Minneapolis airport
men's room), Mark Foley (the Republican congressman from Florida who
made advances to young Congressional pages), and Mark Sanford (the
Republican South Carolina governor who bizarrely disappeared for several days to romance his "soul mate" in Argentina). However, Sanford
later made a political comeback when he was elected to Congress. All of
the examples discussed thus far involve politicians who engaged in a
pattern of behavior that had (in hindsight) a very high likelihood of being
exposed, with severe unwanted consequences for their reputations and
careers.

All of these were men of at least average, and in most cases, well
above-average intelligence, which leads one to ask the obvious question
"how could such smart people have behaved so stupidly?" Cognitive
psychologist Robert Sternberg in fact used a variant of that question as
the title of his edited 2002 book, *Why Smart People Can Be So Stupid*, which
was an attempt to explain why people of average or above average intelligence do foolish things. As the book grew out of a conference held
around the time of the Clinton-Lewinsky mess, many of the authors,
including Sternberg himself, used the Clinton sex scandal as a case study.
A striking limitation of those chapters which attempted to explain the
sexually foolish behavior of former president Clinton (a man with an
extremely high IQ, to be sure), is that none of them addressed all of the
factors that contribute to his sexual misconduct. For example, there was
no place in Sternberg's analysis for biological (*state*) acontributors to Clinton's conduct, of which the most obvious is sexual arousal (how can you
discuss horny behavior in males without discussing what it is that makes
them horny?). Nor was there discussion of a second biological factor that
I consider even more germane to understanding Clinton, and that is his
chronic state of sleep-deprived exhaustion. Clinton has said that "every
mistake I have made occurred when I was tired" and it is possible he had
workplace BJ's in mind when he made that statement (it was late in the
evening when Monica famously snapped her thong). Exhaustion is a
factor that contributes to many dumb behaviors, as psychologist Roy
Baumeister (Baumeister and Tierney, 2011) explained in his co-authored
book on will-power and its diminution

Using the four-factor model of foolish action, here is my take on Dominique Strauss-Kahn. The *situational* factor was that a bird of prey (a female, and a relatively powerless one at that) was unfortunate enough to
come into his field of vision. If not for that he likely would have gone
ahead with whatever he was planning on doing when he was walked in

on minus his pants. *Cognition* probably played little role here, as Strauss-Kahn is obviously smart (although not as smart as everyone thinks; as a young man he flunked the entrance exam for the *ecole nationale d'administration*). As such, he likely knew that forcing one's attentions on women, even chambermaids, has inherent risks. On the other hand, he has apparently done this so many times with impunity that perhaps he had come to discount those risks. *Personality* is a biggie here, as jumping on women appears to be a deeply ingrained schema that Strauss-Kahn exercised quite frequently and that came to have almost a life of its own. Part of this personality constellation was his almost delusional belief that at 70 years old he was still a lothario, and that women were likely to find his advances irresistible. (Here, as in so many other examples, in this book, Strauss-Kahn's stupidity reflected a failure to understand that social mores, even in France, were changing, and that behavior once tolerated or even smiled at could now bring dire consequences.) Finally, there is the *Affect/State* factor, in this case reflecting that Strauss-Kahn obviously was in a sexually needy and aroused condition, perhaps (as some have suggested) because he had taken a little blue or yellow pill.

Politicians, like athletes, may have stronger sex drives than other men, as suggested by motivational psychologist Steven Reiss (2008a) in his (earlier-mentioned) analysis of the Eliot Spitzer fiasco. Most politicians also possess a strain of narcissism, as reflected in Nicolas Von Hoffman's humorous definition of a male politician as "someone who when he wakes up in the morning cannot remember if he had a good crowd or a good lay the night before." Whatever the explanation, dishonorable men such as Dominique Strauss-Kahn deserve whatever negative consequences their foolish behavior eventually brings them.

MARTHA STEWART'S MOST FOOLISH CONFECTION

A classic example of foolish (risk-oblivious) behavior by a very smart and successful businessperson can be found in the story of self-made food and lifestyle guru Martha Stewart. In 2001, the taking of her company Martha Stewart Omnimedia public had made Ms. Stewart a billionaire and one of the most famous and wealthy women in the United States. This was all put at risk when she ordered her broker to sell her shares in a start-up drug-manufacturing company called ImClone after the broker's assistant had given her a tip that the stock was about to decline due to an unfavorable ruling by the US Food and Drug Administration (FDA) on ImClone's application for a new cancer drug (J. B. Stewart, 2011).

By making the sale then, rather than waiting until the FDA ruling became public (and the company's stock declined by 16 percent), Ms. Stewart saved all of $45,000, but she wound up spending far more on legal fees and eventually going to jail for five months for insider trading (actually, as is often the case, for lying to investigators about what she had known). In addition, she was removed as CEO of her own company, lost a substantial portion of her wealth (much of which she has been able to regain), and suffered considerable humiliation (for example, the British government blocked her from traveling to England to give a talk at a design college). Even after her action had become known, she could have avoided a jail sentence if she had been willing to come clean about what she knew and when she knew it. She compounded her initial foolishness in making the sale (saving what was to her chump change) with additional foolishness in which she persisted in denying any wrong-doing.

In trying to understand why Martha Stewart behaved so foolishly, all four factors in the explanatory model come into play. The decision was made during the end-of-year holiday, while Ms. Stewart was taking her private plane to a vacation in Mexico. She learned of the ImClone problem during the plane's refueling stop, and she was unable to reach her broker, Peter Bacanovic, or her friend and ImClone CEO Sam Waksal (both of whom also eventually went to jail). Nor was she able to reach any of her legal and financial advisers, some of whom likely would have warned her of the risks of trading on this inside information. Thus, a *situational* element, often present when people make a foolish impromptu decision, was the lack of time to think about the decision and absence of access to protective others.

Cognition enters in when one considers the possibility that Ms. Stewart, for all of her brilliance, may have lacked the tacit knowledge that her action in selling the stock was improper. One fact which works against this hypothesis is that she had worked for a brief time as a stock broker on Wall Street earlier in her adult life. However, she resigned that position under a bit of a cloud, allegedly because of kick-backs to brokers for pushing a particular stock, so it is certainly possible that she was not as knowledgeable about securities law and ethics as one might think.

Personality played a major (perhaps the most important) role in explaining Martha Stewart's foolish action. She was reportedly, at least during that time period, a highly arrogant and imperious person, who was determined to get her way in all matters large and small. It is very possible, indeed likely, that Ms. Stewart had a sense of entitlement and felt that society's rules did not apply to her, especially a rule (banning insider trading) that she knew to be routinely flouted.

Affect clearly entered into the equation in two ways: (a) in the panic and greed that set in when she learned that her investment was in jeopardy, and (b) in her rigid unwillingness to consider making any admission of wrongdoing. Basically, Stewart was facing a classic dilemma, in which she had to weigh the relatively minor risk to her image and business of admitting guilt (most likely to a misdemeanor) against the relatively major risk to her image and business if she were to be convicted of a felony. She made what turned out to be a disastrously wrong choice. The foolishness of this choice inhered in the fact that the risks were both clear and potentially disastrous, and wisdom should have led her to an action which minimized the potential risk.

FOOLISH BLUNTNESS

When I was growing up in New York, the baseball Giants played at the no-longer-standing Polo Grounds which I could see from my bedroom window (for a while the football Giants did as well) when their manager, the feisty Leo Durocher, uttered the famous words: "nice guys finish last." That dictum may work in the world of athletics, but in life it is usually the other way around. Of course, when addressing matters of success or failure, one needs to ask "first or last in what?" We typically think of success in terms of wealth accumulation, but there are many other outcomes one could mention. One obvious place where nastiness does not buy success is in being loved.

An example can be found in the case of a relative of mine. He was a mean person who was known to bully and humiliate others (one of my earliest childhood memories was of being tormented by him when he was in his late twenties). After he died, very few mourners other than his wife and grown kids (and even they bad mouth him today) came to his funeral. Of course, you could say "he obviously did not care what others thought of him, otherwise he would not have been such an SOB, and besides dead people don't experience rejection." But I do not think he enjoyed being as socially isolated and disliked as he ended up being towards the end of his life, as reflected in the small number of people who visited him during his several lengthy hospital stays. He may have thought that the opinions of others did not matter, but at some point he may have come to understand that thinking only about oneself has its costs.

This brings up an important point, and that is that success usually is measured by attainment of wealth or status, but while my relative was fairly successful in attaining his monetary goals, he would probably have enjoyed his wealth more if he had been loved by others. Furthermore, I think his nastiness held him back in the business sphere as well, as he was the target of several expensive lawsuits and after a while people were reluctant to do business with him.

A very noticeable arena for illustrating why not-so-nice guys do not usually finish first is the world of organizations, whether social, corporate, or governmental. Here, there are many examples of talented people who rise fairly high in a hierarchy but are frustrated in their quest to grab a much-coveted top job by the fact that they made too many enemies or bruised too many egos along the way.

One notable case involved Susan Rice, at a time when she was the United States Ambassador to the United Nations. She had been talked about as a possible nominee to succeed Hillary Clinton when, as expected, she stepped down from her post as Secretary of State. Democrats compared her to another African American female diplomat, Condoleezza Rice, and had been known to say "Our Rice is better than your Rice," to which Republicans could counter "maybe, but our Rice is five times as nice." It seems that Ambassador Rice (later the National Security Adviser in the Obama administration) was known for being unusually blunt (with much use of salty language) in her dealings with others, including diplomats from other nations, several of whom were quoted (some by name) in saying that elevating her to Secretary of State would be a big mistake. This raised some feminist hackles, by those who argue that there is a double standard operating here, whereby females are punished for acting too much (such as being aggressive) like males. But one could bring up many examples of males who were similarly thwarted in their race to the top by their lack of sensitivity to the feelings of others.

Two such examples surfaced in the corporate world, and they both involved highly-placed male executives at two competing mega-corporations: Apple and Microsoft. Both individuals were highly talented techies who were responsible for things that contributed to what their firms were known for: product design at Apple, software development at Microsoft. At one time, both were mentioned as individuals destined to rise to the top level in their respective organizations. However, both were forced to resign, and in both cases news stories noted that the firings were largely attributable to their bluntness and relative lack of social skills in dealing with others.

My long-standing interest in social competence has been focused mainly on individuals with intellectual disabilities, where low general intelligence makes it more likely that "social intelligence," especially perspective-taking, is also limited. However, because people with very high IQ have their boorishness interpreted as eccentricity, it is sometime the case that very creative or high-status people are given more freedom to be jerks, while for intellectually limited people, social ineptness, attributed to low intelligence, is punished. Thus, paradoxically, we sometimes impose higher standards for what we determine is "normal" social behavior in people who one would think should be entitled to having us cut them some slack. Of course, part of the explanation is that people with Intellectual Disability often reside in congregate settings where others monitor and control them constantly, but a big reason for this double standard is that we so value the creativity and contributions of very talented people that we are willing to tolerate their boorishness as the price we have to pay for what they may contribute to some collective enterprise.

This generalization needs to be qualified, however, as obviously many very talented people have excellent social skills, and at some point a talented person's *enfant terrible* act can start to wear thin. There is a developmental process at work here, in which social boorishness can be overlooked when one is heavily involved in narrow activities such as development of a product, but as one rises in the management hierarchy with more general responsibilities, social boorishness will be resented and resisted. In part, that is because one is now dealing less with relatively low-status individuals (who may resent being abused but lack the power to do anything about it) and more with relatively high-status individuals who are themselves so valuable to the organization that their complaints and threats to leave are taken more seriously. Another developmental factor that likely is operating here is that the organization itself, including its leadership, may have undergone important changes. Thus, it is probably not a coincidence that the afore-mentioned Apple executive was pushed out of Apple only months after the death of Steve Jobs (not the most socially nice person either, but he was largely immune from consequences of his social ineptness during his second [but not during his first] stint as Apple CEO). It is very possible that Jobs may have been acting as a protector of the individual, someone whose specialty—product design—was especially dear to Jobs' heart.

In terms of my four-factor explanatory model of foolishness, one factor—*"personality"*—largely explains why overly blunt people behave as they do, and another factor—*"cognition"* (especially social intelligence)—largely explains why such behavior is ultimately foolish, in that it undermines the attainment of much-desired dreams and goals. There are many factors that contribute to a *personality* style marked by excessive bluntness, with such a style likely forged during an individual's early years in the crucible of his or her family life, as reflected for example in Adlerian notions of the drive for power. Ultimately, however, behaving offensively towards others is a choice that one makes, and which one can temper, or become better at controlling, if one is motivated to change. This is where social intelligence comes in, as recognition that one's behavior is putting one's basic interests at risk can cause someone to seek insight and help, such as through psychotherapy or coaching assistance. There are some, however, whose pattern of not-nice behavior is so entrenched that they refuse to recognize or acknowledge any need to change. Such individuals are very likely to self-destruct, if not in the short-run then certainly in the long-run. Whether we like it or not, most of us operate in settings where whether we are liked or disliked has a lot to do with whether we finish first or last. Anyone who fails to recognize or heed that reality is, in my opinion, eventually likely to act foolishly.

FOOLISH LYING: HOW BRIAN WILLIAMS DESTROYED HIS CAREER

In his philosophical book *Love and Lies*, Clancy Martin (2016) made a distinction between good lies and bad lies. Good lies (such as a man telling his wife she looks fine with an unflattering outfit or hairdo) will, according to the thrice-married philosopher, keep a relationship going, while bad lies (such as are told to facilitate philandering) will kill a relationship. But I prefer a different dichotomy: foolish lies versus non-foolish lies. A non-foolish lie has a low likelihood of being detected, is likely to facilitate some important interest of the liar's, and is unlikely to harm the liar seriously if it becomes exposed. A foolish lie has a significant potential for being exposed, does not materially advance an important interest (in other words, it is unnecessary) and has high potential for harming the liar if it is exposed. The career near-suicide of NBC nightly news anchor Brian Williams provides a sad example of the risks associated with telling foolish lies. After describing the lies briefly, I will use the four-factor explanatory model of foolish action to try and understand why someone as phenomenally successful as Mr. Williams would risk it all in such a blatantly dumb manner.

Brian Williams was born in 1959, and became the anchor and managing news director of the ratings-leading NBC nightly news broadcast in 2004. For this, he was highly paid, reportedly pulling down a salary of $10 million per year. As with other network news anchors, Mr. Williams occasionally went on assignment to help to cover a major breaking story. Two early examples, both of which contributed to his later difficulties, were the War in Iraq and Hurricane Katrina in New Orleans. The problem is that Williams had a tendency to embellish his news coverage, and subsequent stories he told in non-news venues (such as his frequent appearances on late-night talk shows), both to make the stories more dramatic and compelling, and to enhance his own role and importance in the events he was describing. Although his Katrina stories had long raised eyebrows, it was the Iraq coverage that landed him a six-month unpaid suspension from his job and a very dramatic reduction in role and salary, when he was allowed to return. One lesson here seems to be that some lies, involving sacred matters such as a war where real heroes are dying, are more likely to get one in trouble than others.

The Katrina lies were not directly cited as reasons for the suspension, but they likely played a role in it. Here are three such examples from his coverage of Katrina (for which he and his network received many awards): (a) Williams told a story (never confirmed by others) of seeing a dead body float by outside his hotel in the French Quarter (which was one of the city's few relatively dry neighborhoods); (b) he told a story, not confirmed by others, of seeing roving gangs of thugs roaming freely through his (heavily guarded) hotel; and (c) he gave a highly exaggerated account of rampant crimes, including rapes, that he saw or directly heard about in the Superdome, where refugees from the storm were being housed.

The Iraq lie, which is the only one cited for his suspension (although NBC hinted that New Orleans entered into the decision), involved a much-repeated story that Williams told about being in a helicopter that was hit by a rocket-propelled grenade and forced to make an emergency landing in the desert. The real truth is that his helicopter was in a convoy of four helicopters, one of which (not his) was hit, with Mr. Williams not coming on the scene until quite a while later. Although his first reporting of the event was more or less truthful, over time it evolved into something blatantly untruthful, with such added embellishments as the detail that he actually looked down the barrel of the launcher before the grenade was fired.

What led to the undoing of Mr. Williams is that on his news broadcast of February 2, 2015, the news anchor showed a segment which featured a retired US Army sergeant-major whom he took to a New York Rangers hockey game where the soldier was publicly honored for his role in leading a tank battalion that came to the rescue of Mr. Williams and others after their helicopter was shot down. A chief warrant officer (presumably a helicopter pilot, as that is a typical Army pilot rank) who knew the truth wrote a correcting comment on the Facebook page of NBC News, and that comment was noticed and reprinted in a story in the widely-disseminated military newspaper *Stars and Stripes* (access at stripes.com) along with a weak admission and apology from Mr. Williams. That story (which Williams did not tell his bosses at NBC about) attracted much public notice, and triggered an avalanche of criticism and ridicule directed at Williams and the network. He compounded the problem by giving a very weak on-air apology where, instead of saying "I lied," he blamed it on imperfect "misremembering" and a resultant "conflating" of elements of truth and untruth. As if that was not bad enough, he made it seem as if he (referring to himself as "managing editor") was in charge of his own punishment, which he described as a few days' leave (in fact it was a move imposed on him by the network, but in typical ego-serving style, he made it seem to be his alone). The network quickly corrected that misimpression, by announcing that they were suspending Mr. Williams without pay for six months for what they considered to be egregious misconduct (Shafer 2015).

Several psychologists and researchers on lying weighed in with their own commentary. Some of this commentary has hypothesized that Brian Williams actually came to believe the lie and, thus, was not as morally culpable as he would be if he was conscious of telling falsehoods. I have great respect for this line of research (by eminent scholars such as Elizabeth Loftus). However, while I think this dynamic may play a slight role (in that a much-repeated lie may become a core part of a liar's story arsenal, and thus is called upon automatically when needed), my own view is that Brian Williams had long been a serial liar who does what such people do, which is to knowingly tell a lie when the truth does not sufficiently serve their needs. To understand why I hold this belief, an analysis using the four-factor foolishness model may be useful.

A curious thing about the US network news anchors, in contrast to the United Kingdom where they are more accurately called "news readers" (implying correctly that they have little or no role in developing the stories they introduce on the air) is that they tend to become major celebrities, who are described by themselves and their bosses as serious and accomplished journalists. As such, they often are invited—and encouraged by their bosses—to accept or pursue opportunities to promote and expand their brand, by going on talk shows, writing books, giving speeches, etc. Mr. Williams, unlike other news anchors (many of whom have print journalism backgrounds), has never written a book (although he has talked about his love of books on the Oprah Winfrey show) but he is a gifted raconteur with a talent for comic banter, as reflected in frequent appearances on Jimmy Fallon's late night show, where they would slow jam the news together.

As a result of his story-telling talent on the celebrity TV circuit, Mr. Williams had a very high Recognition Quotient (he is probably the only network anchor who was known by name to virtually all US high school and college students, most of whom got their news from Jon Stewart (on whose show Williams was a frequent guest) rather than the NBC nightly news. The resulting fame of Mr. Williams undoubtedly contributed to the high ratings for his show, which made hundreds of millions of dollars for his network. The acclaim, and encouragement, that Mr. Williams received for his story-telling prowess was obviously reinforcing for him. This led him to make the fatal misstep of repeating and embellishing his Iraq story once again before 18,000 hockey fans, and a TV audience of millions, some of whom now have access to Facebook, a technological innovation that is a very good lie-correcting mechanism available to people who previously might not have known how to easily (and virally) get their concerns known.

To be a successful liar, one has to be able to: (a) know when you are lying, (b) calculate the risks of being exposed, (c) recognize when the consequence of exposure is so great as to make lying not worth it, and (d) keep current telling of the lie congruent with past versions. Doing this is not easy, which is one reason why truth telling is a better policy (it is easier to remember an event or action when it actually happened). As a general rule, lies should be used sparingly, and should align as closely as possible with the actual truth. In other words, embellishment is okay (or at least forgivable) when it is done infrequently, told before audiences unlikely to object, and does not stray too far from what actually happened. A smart person will figure out eventually that habitual lying comes with significant risks, and will come to scale back the lies, tell them more cautiously, or eliminate them altogether.

It is possible that Brian Williams is not as smart as everyone assumes he is. His academic history is one of the least distinguished of any major news anchor. He attended three colleges, starting with a community college, and he eventually dropped out after several years with a grand total of eighteen accumulated college credits. He likely started climbing the TV news ladder by having a very pretty face, along with a winning personality. I do not know the reasons for Williams' dramatically weak academic history, but typically lack of ability to do college level work is a contributing factor. Even if that is not the case here, it is highly likely that Brian Williams was embarrassed by his profound absence of academic training, and consequently felt the need to compensate for that by broadcasting scoops not obtained by peers who were more professionally qualified. Lying as a path to journalistic advancement is far from uncommon, as several scandals about made-up stories at newspapers and magazines in recent years have demonstrated.

Non-foolishness (that is, wisdom or common sense) involves recognizing and giving sufficient weight to relatively obvious risks. Telling lies about what Williams experienced first-hand when in New Orleans during Katrina was much easier to get away with, for the simple reason that no one could prove definitively what he did or did not see or hear, when looking outside his hotel room window or in other locations when not accompanied by others. Lying about an episode that occurred when you were on a helicopter with soldiers and colleagues (and not on the shot-down helicopter, where there also were soldiers) is much more difficult to permanently get away with, especially given that those soldiers likely had a strong motive to set the record straight (unlike Williams' co-workers, who likely had a strong disinclination to take on their powerful boss). For Williams to think he could keep telling the made-up Iraq story forever without being called on it by one of many witnesses to the truth is simply mind-boggling, a sign either of stupidity or psychopathology, or both.

I prefer to avoid using psychiatric labels such as narcissistic personality disorder, but TV and movie stars typically have strong narcissistic tendencies (both inherent and encouraged by sycophants), and Williams likely is no exception. An interesting clue to Williams' *personality* comes from the fact that when Jay Leno was in the process of finally stepping down as the host of NBC's The Tonight Show, Brian Williams is reported to have thrown his hat in the ring and asked the higher-ups at the network (who immediately scotched the idea) to consider him for the job. Obviously, Williams thought of himself as a major talent as a comedian and entertainer, a role he had perfected through appearances on Saturday Night Live (where he was a guest host), the Daily Show, David Letterman, and many similar venues. Telling entertaining stories (rather than real journalism) was his stock in trade, and it not surprising that he used that talent at every opportunity.

Personality is a term that refers to behavioral traits, tendencies, and needs that help to define a particular person. Telling lies about himself, for the purpose of making an entertaining story in which he appeared in a positive light, is a trait that certainly helps to define Brian Williams. Such tendencies go way back, as when he exaggerated his role as a rescuer of puppies when he was a volunteer fire fighter during his high school years in New Jersey. In his stories, Mr. Williams often portrayed himself in a quasi-heroic light, or at least as involved in dangerous situations where he associated with others who were heroic, as was certainly the case with his Iraq story. I am generally opposed to psychoanalyzing public figures who I do not personally know, so I will resist speculating about where this need for reflected or real glory came from, but I have little doubt that he has such a need. Brian Williams has, apparently, many positive qualities, as reflected in numerous charitable acts he has been credited with performing. Unfortunately, just being one of the most respected figures in TV journalism was not enough for him, and his need to continue telling tales about his fictitious brush with danger and heroism in Iraq led to his undoing.

SEVEN

Induced Social Foolishness

"Don't be so easily influenced by your friends."
—My late mother, giving me advice

Induced social foolishness (another name for gullibility), as with its non-induced variant, occurs when someone acts without paying sufficient attention to a fairly obvious risk to one's social interests (including wealth, freedom from incarceration, and employment status). But by calling the foolishness "induced," I mean to indicate that it happened as a direct result of one or more other people attempting (usually, but not always, deceptively) to suck the person into behaving foolishly. A number of real-life incidents are discussed and the four-factor model is used to analyze each incident.

HOW MADOFF MADE OFF WITH MY MONEY

As mentioned in the Preface, I was an indirect victim of Bernard Madoff. I never met Madoff, or for that matter even knew who he was. That is because I invested a chunk (thankfully, not all) of my retirement funds not in Madoff's firm (my assets were too puny for that) but in one of the so-called feeder hedge funds that, unbeknownst to me, turned all of their clients' money over to Madoff to manage. What happened is that during a vacation in Florida (where a large percentage of Madoff victims resided) I was talking to a friend of my family, a retired accountant, who told me of his second career as a financial consultant. What he did was to identify hedge funds that produced decent but very steady returns and then used his connections with these firms to allow clients of his to participate in those funds. His fee for this entrée, and for his continuing to monitor and oversee the investment, was an annual charge of approximately 1 percent of the accruing balance. That was in addition to the management fees (enormous, but which I never bothered to find out) charged by the hedge fund itself, and in addition to the fees (ridiculously small, which should have been a dead-giveaway) charged to the funds by Madoff himself. His reason for making the deal so attractive to the funds was because he needed a constant influx of new monies in order to pay off existing investors, a key to keeping the scheme afloat.

I went ahead and made the decision to put what to me was a great deal of money in the Madoff feeder fund, about a year before my adviser called me up and gave me the bad news that the whole thing was a sham. Naturally, I was pretty upset, but I immediately wrote an essay that used my foolish action framework to analyze the foolishness of Madoff victims, using myself as an illustrative case study. This essay was quickly published in the online version of *Skeptic* magazine (Greenspan 2008), where it was noticed by the Wall Street Journal, which invited me (less than a month after M-day) to publish a slightly expanded version (Greenspan 2009d). The essays attracted a great deal of reader comment, which fell in two camps; (a) hilarity over the irony of a gullibility expert being gulled, and (b) appreciation by those who applauded my willingness to self-disclose in the interest of educating the public, including investors (most of whom found my analysis convincing), about an important topic. What follows is a much scaled-down version of my essay, minus a substantial amount of material on other fraudulent or non-fraudulent investment crazes (for example, Tulipmania, Charles Ponzi, the Nigeria internet inheritance scam, etc.).

A Ponzi scheme, such as Bernard Madoff's, is a fraud where invested money is pocketed by the schemer and investors who wish to redeem their money are actually paid out of proceeds from newer investors (Lewis 2015). As long as new investments are expanding at a healthy rate, the schemer is able to keep the fraud going. Once investments begin to contract, as through a run on the company, then the house of cards quickly collapses. That is what happened with the Madoff scam when too many investors—needing cash because of the general world financial meltdown in late 2008—tried to redeem their funds. Madoff could not meet these demands and the scam was exposed.

The basic mechanism explaining the success of Ponzi schemes is the tendency of humans to model their actions (especially when dealing with matters they do not fully understand) on the behavior of other humans. This mechanism has been termed "irrational exuberance," a phrase attributed to former Federal Reserve chairman Alan Greenspan (no relation), but actually coined by another economist, Robert J. Shiller (2000), in a book with that title. Shiller employed a social psychological explanation that he termed the "feedback loop theory of investor bubbles." Simply stated, the fact that so many people seem to be making big profits on the investment, and telling others about their good fortune, makes the investment seem safe and too good to pass up. In Shiller's (2000) words, the fact "that others have made a lot of money appears to many people as the most persuasive evidence in support of the investment story associated with the Ponzi scheme [or, for that matter, non-fraudulent crazes, such as the dot.com bubble]—evidence that outweighs even the most carefully reasoned argument against the story."

While social feedback loops are an obvious contributor to understanding the success of Ponzi and other mass financial manias, one needs to also look at factors located in the dupes themselves that might help to explain why they fell prey to the social pressure while others did not. The four-factor explanatory model of foolish action helps, I believe, to shed light on why so many investors, including myself, were taken in.

Situation: Investing in the Madoff feeder fund, like every foolish act, involved taking on a risk that was perceived (and portrayed) as small, but in fact was enormous. Specifically, the above-mentioned Schiller social feedback loop was probably the most important factor explaining my throwing caution to the wind. The Madoff scam had social feedback pressures that were very strong, as reflected in a December 15, 2008 *New York Times* article (Feuer and Haughney 2008), which described how wealthy retirees in Florida joined Madoff's country club for the sole reason of having an opportunity to meet him socially and be invited to invest directly with him. Most of these investors (such as myself), as well as Madoff's sales representatives, were Jewish, and it appears that the Madoff scheme was seen as a safe haven for well-off Jews to park their nest eggs. The fact that Madoff was a prominent Jewish philanthropist was undoubtedly another situational contributor, as it likely was seen as highly unlikely that such a person would be scamming fellow Jews (which included many prominent Jewish charities, some of them forced to close their doors).

A non-social *situational* aspect that contributed to a gullible investment decision was, paradoxically, that Madoff promised modest rather than spectacular gains. Sophisticated investors would have been highly suspicious of a promise of gains as enormous as those promised almost one hundred years earlier by Charles Ponzi (Zuckoff 2005). Thus, a big part of Madoff's success came from his recognition that wealthy investors were looking for small but steady returns, high enough to be attractive but not so high as to arouse suspicion. This was certainly one of the things that attracted me to the Madoff scheme, as I was looking for a non-volatile investment that would enable me to preserve and gradually build wealth in down as well as up markets. Another *situational* factor that pulled me in was the fact that I, along with most Madoff investors (except for the super-rich), did not invest directly with Madoff but went through a large and respected family of financial firms. This created the strong impression that this investment had been well-researched and posed acceptable risks.

Cognition played an important role, as I was profoundly ignorant of finance, and had a somewhat lazy unwillingness to remedy that ignorance. To get around my lack of financial knowledge and my lazy cognitive style around finance, I had come up with the heuristic of identifying more financially knowledgeable advisers and trusting in their judgment and recommendations. This heuristic had worked for me in the past and I had no reason to doubt that it would work for me in this case.

The real mystery in the Madoff story is not how naïve individual investors such as myself would think the investment safe, but how the risks and warning signs could have been ignored by so many financially knowledgeable people, ranging from the adviser who sold me and my family member (and himself) on the investment, to the highly compensated executives who ran the various feeder funds that kept the Madoff ship afloat. The partial answer is that Madoff's investment algorithm (along with other aspects of his organization) was a closely guarded secret difficult to penetrate, and partly (as in all cases of gullibility) that strong affective and self-deception processes were at work. In other words, they had too good a thing going, for themselves and their clients, to entertain the idea that it might all be about to crumble.

Personality entered in through the fact that my strong tendency is to trust other people. Gullibility is sometimes equated with trust, but the truth is that not all highly trusting people are gullible (Rotter 1980). The key to survival in a world filled with fakers (Madoff) or unintended misleaders who were themselves gulls (my adviser and the managers of the feeder fund) is to know when to be trusting and when not to be. I happen to be a highly trusting person who also does not like to say "no" (such as to a sales person who had given me an hour or two of their time). The need to be a nice guy who always says "yes" is, unfortunately, not usually a good basis for making a decision that could jeopardize one's financial security. In my own case, trust and niceness were also accompanied by an occasional tendency towards risk-taking and impulsive decision-making, personality traits that can also get one in trouble.

Affect/State also played an important role here, as it generally does in most foolish acts. Emotion enters into virtually every gullible act. In the case of investment in a Ponzi scheme, the emotion that motivates gullible behavior is a strong wish to increase and protect one's wealth. In some individuals, this undoubtedly takes the form of greed, but I think that truly greedy individuals would likely not have been interested in the slow but steady returns posted by the Madoff-run funds. I know that in my case, I was excited not by the prospect of striking it rich but by the prospect of having found an investment that promised me the opportunity to build and maintain enough wealth to have a secure and happy retirement.

One reason why psychologists and other social scientists have avoided studying gullibility is because it is affected by so many factors, and is so microcontext dependent, that it is impossible to predict whether and under what circumstances a person will behave gullibly. A related problem is that the most catastrophic examples of gullibility (such as losing one's life savings in a scam) are low frequency behaviors that may only happen once in one's lifetime. While as a rule I tend to be a skeptic about claims that seem too good to be true, the chance to invest in a highly-touted fund was one case where a host of factors—situational, cognitive, personality, and affective—came together to cause me to put my critical faculties on the shelf.

AN INTERNET INHERITANCE VICTIM

There is a tendency to think that any act which fails is foolish, but that is not necessarily the case. The four-factor model can, I believe, help one to tell the difference between an act that was truly foolish and one that was less (or even not at all) foolish, in spite of its resulting in a bad outcome. The use of the model in this manner has proved to be useful on occasion in the aftermath of a fraud loss in which (as is often the case) a legitimate business such as a bank is being sued for having failed in its fiduciary duty to protect the victims from the consequences of their own naïve trust (Greenspan and Woods 2016). The question in such a case is whether the individual victim should bear the full brunt of their loss due to foolishness, or whether the fiduciary should bear some, or all, of the responsibility for giving assurances which reasonable (that is, non-foolish) people would have been justified in trusting.

As a result of notoriety stemming from my writings on gullibility, I occasionally am asked by an attorney to consult in a civil lawsuit where the gullibility of their client caused them to be a victim of a fraud. An example of such a case follows, but because the case settled just before the matter came to trial, potentially identifying details have been altered somewhat. The case involved what has become known as a "419 scam," after the number in the criminal code covering fraud in Nigeria, the country out of which many of these scams originate (Schoenmakers, de Vries, and van Wijk 2009). These 419-type scams have been around for a long time, and can take many forms (the classic "Spanish Prisoner" con game depicted in the David Mamet 1997 film of the same name is an example). It usually involves financially assisting some person (who may for example be depicted as a Nigerian prince) to obtain an inheritance out of which he has been cheated. In return for this assistance, the mark is promised a sizeable payment, such as 20 percent or 30 percent of the recovered loot. Part of the scam usually involves getting the mark to do something illegal (such as misrepresenting something to a bank) or helping the sender to do something illegal (such as evading taxes), on the assumption that victims will be reluctant to seek legal redress once they find they have been defrauded, because of fear of exposure (Zuckoff 2006).

Today, 419 scams invariably are carried out over the internet, and involve a victim receiving an email message from a stranger, who often describes himself as an attorney who is seeking the assistance of the message's recipient in return for substantial monetary compensation. Using automated message generation technology, millions of people can receive the same message with individualized features added. The vast majority of recipients are smart enough to ignore the message, but it only takes a very small number of extremely gullible people to get sucked in to make this a very lucrative business for the scammers.

In the case of the man, "James Smithson," on whose lawsuit I was asked by his lawyer to consult, the sender of the email (who claimed to be a London solicitor named "Daniel Okundo") asserted he was handling the estate of a recently deceased distant cousin of Smithson's wife, and she appeared to be the rightful beneficiary of two million dollars. In order for her to receive the money, the Smithsons would have to pay Okundo to clear up some problems. Mr. Smithson (termed by 419 scammers a *maga,* a Yoruba word for fool) was a formerly successful businessman in his early eighties, who had recently suffered a financial reverse. He was intrigued enough to call the phone number given in the message, telling his (very skeptical) wife "what do I have to lose by talking to him?" The answer, it turned out, was a very great deal.

As might be expected, the scammer, Daniel Okundo, was very charming, and Mr. Smithson—a religious man who had once been a missionary in a third world country—took to him immediately. His wife continued to try to warn him, but he ignored her, saying that this was the miracle he had been asking God to perform, to help him get back on his feet financially. Although Smithson's close friend was a prominent attorney, he refused to ask his advice as he knew that he would likely also tell him that his new friend Daniel was not to be trusted.

The scam started off on a small scale, with Smithson being asked on a few occasions to send several thousand dollars to clear up some legal complications. When the amount paid out reached $40,000, Smithson finally began to have some doubts, and he told Okundo "no more, until I start seeing some of the inherited money." Mr. Okundo replied a short time later and said that he had good news, bad news, and wonderful news. The good news was that the two million dollar inheritance was actually twelve million. The bad news was that there were some taxes that needed to be paid before Smithson's wife could claim that amount, and the taxes came to close to two million dollars. The wonderful news was that Okundo found an investor in Japan who would put up the entire sum in return for a sizeable interest payment, and Smithson would not have to pay one cent towards the taxes.

The arrangement that was worked out was that the two million from the Japanese investor was to be wired into Smithson's bank account and when he saw the money was there, he was to turn around and wire the two million to Okundo, who insisted that it go in and out of an account of Smithson's that was tied to a line of credit secured by his and his wife's largely paid-off luxury home. To accomplish this, Smithson had to increase the amount of the line of credit. The reason for this, not told to Smithson of course, is that banks are less likely to question sizeable checks as carefully when they are in a collateralized account.

While all of this was going on, there were frequent emails back and forth from well-known banks in various parts of the world. Virtually all of the emails would have aroused suspicion in a more worldly, savvy, and vigilant person than Mr. Smithson. For example, one bank's email had an s added to the end of the bank name in its email address, while the famous logo in the letterhead of another bank was noticeably off center. Mr. Smithson noted none of this, and his only cautionary action was to ask his "personal banker," a young man barely out of college, to tell him what he thought of the whole plan. He told Smithson he would check with his superiors, but obviously did not as 419 scams are well-known to bankers, and Smithson's bank was a local branch of one of the biggest banks in the country. Smithson checked his bank balance online several times a day, and his vigilance paid off when to his great glee the sum of two million dollars suddenly appeared in it, wired from an overseas bank. Smithson, being an honorable (as well as perhaps slightly greedy) person, again approached his wet-behind-the-ears personal banker and asked his assurance that the money was really in his account, and that he was free to send it off to Okundo. The banker got back to Smithson and told him the money was his and he was perfectly free to do with it as he wished. Smithson then dutifully wired the entire amount to an account of Okundo's as instructed.

A few days later, Mr. Smithson was contacted by his private banker, who gave him the bad news that the check wired from the overseas bank was no good, and he asked him to give back the two million dollars that the bank sent off as per his instructions. After (finally) consulting an attorney, Mr. Smithson refused this request, and the bank initiated proceedings to receive their lost funds by foreclosing on his house. Smithson's lawyer disputed that action, asserting that the bank should be held accountable for its own incompetence. A trial was scheduled, and I was engaged to address the gullibility issue, while an expert on bank procedures was hired to opine on several unprofessional actions by the bank, such as: (a) their initial failure to warn their client of the well-known dangers of internet inheritance schemes, (b) their rebuffing a warning from another bank (which tried to return the two million, saying they strongly suspected fraud), (c) the fact that the check from the supposed third-party investor had several things wrong with it, including the absence of a number to clear an automated bank verification machine, and (d) the fact that the check was written on a bank that was known to have problems.

In a deposition that occurred just before the case was settled, my position was that the forty thousand, sent before Smithson brought his bank into the drama, was his problem, while the two million was the bank's. While I do not know the details of the confidential settlement, indications are that the bank ended up eating much of the loss. My reasoning was that while Mr. Smithson's gullibility certainly played a role in his sending the two million on to an unknown scammer, trusting the assurances of one's banker at a major financial institution, after repeated requests for such assurance, is reasonable and something that even generally non-gullible people might have done. For the purposes of illustrating the analytic utility of my foolishness model, and explaining why I opined as I did, I shall divide the case into two separate episodes, which I shall label pre-bank and post-bank.

Pre–Bank Analysis

Situation. The situational pull in this 419 scam—an email from an unknown lawyer saying that Smithson's wife had inherited a fortune from a cousin she had never heard of—was incredibly weak, as reflected in the fact that 99.9 percent of the millions who receive such messages laugh them off. Furthermore, it lacked the important element that drives most scams, which is the persuasion skills that come from a face to face interaction with a skilled con artist. Of course, that equation shifted in the scammer's favor when Smithson made the fatal mistake of picking up the phone and calling him. That is because once one develops a personal relationship with someone, it becomes much more difficult to break off the relationship (Cialdini 1984), especially if one is as kind and morally agreeable a person as Smithson appears to be.

Cognition. As someone in his eighties, it is likely that Mr. Smithson had begun to show some signs of cognitive decline. One common tendency in frail elderly people (or people with brain impairment generally) is to cover up their limitations by agreeing with things said or suggested by others (Denburg et al. 2007). Regardless, Mr. Smithson showed remarkable innocence and ignorance by being one of the few email users in that time who had never heard of internet fraud. His naiveté in this regard was probably a sign in part of his age and lack of experience.

Personality. Mr. Smithson is a remarkably trusting and agreeable man. He had no meanness in his heart and had great difficulty believing others could be evil. Even after his life had been turned upside down by the disappearance of the two million dollars, Smithson continued to believe that Okundo was really who he said he was, and would come forward to clear up what was obviously a terrible misunderstanding. Smithson also obviously had a strong moral sense, in that he turned around and sent the two million forward, while many others would have kept it. Alongside these positive qualities was a very stubborn and willful streak, as reflected in his refusal to listen to the pleas and warnings of his wife, or his unwillingness to even listen to what his long-time friend and attorney might have had to say about the scheme. He was convinced the scheme was legitimate, and would not even consider the possibility he might be mistaken.

State. A big motivator that drove Mr. Smithson's gullibility was his deep religious faith, a faith which convinced him that Okundo was a messenger from God who was sent down from Heaven to answer his prayers and reward him for his faithfulness. An equally big motivator, which explained Smithson's need for a miracle, is that he had made some risky business decisions and was now in trouble financially. Thus, the inheritance promised his wife by Okundo seemed to him to be particularly timely and necessary, and increased his otherwise high degree of gullibility to something totally off the charts.

Post–Bank Analysis

The same factors that explain Mr. Smithson's gullibility pre–bank were also operative post–bank, so I shall keep my analysis of the post-bank phase brief. The one major difference is that the *situational* force went from very weak (Okundo's email would have convinced virtually no one to take the next step) to very strong (the money showing up in your online bank statement and being told by a bank officer that it is yours to spend would likely have convinced most people). In fact, this is the main reason why I was prepared to testify that the pre–bank ($40,000) loss was on Smithson (because it came almost entirely from his own foolishness), while the post–bank ($2 million) loss was on the bank, because he would not have wired the money to the fictional Okundo if the bank had not passively, and to some extent actively, essentially said "go ahead, send the money overseas."

Situation. As mentioned, the bank (by vouching for the reality of the unreal $2 million) played a huge role in Smithson's post–bank gullibility, but the key component of the scam (sending a phony $2 million into a collateralized account in the hope it would show up at least temporarily in the victim's account) was extremely clever. People fall for confidence tricks because the scammers are knowledgeable about human psychology and are able to contrive scenarios that are convincing and which play on the risk-unawareness and emotional needs—such as greed—of their victims. In this case, the appearance in his online bank statement of the $2 million loan from the Japanese investor was overwhelming evidence to Smithson that Okundo was telling the truth and was to be trusted.

Cognition. The average person lacks anything approaching a sophisticated understanding of how banks process and verify the legitimacy of
ordinary checks, let alone international wire transfers. Only a banking
expert would understand that banks can and do make mistakes, and the
reasons for such mistakes. Therefore, while Smithson would have been
much wiser to have waited a few days (and sought alternative assurances
from higher-ups at the bank) before taking the word of a very junior local
branch officer, it is very understandable, given his lack of banking expertise, his tendency to trust everyone, and his eagerness to get the full $12
million, that he would have gone ahead and wired the $2 million to
Okundo.

Personality. Smithson is a very honorable man, whose sense of religious duty requires him to keep his word. This explains why he did not
think twice about sending the Japanese investor's money to Okundo, as
he did not consider the money to be his, but rather saw it as a vehicle for
facilitating the processing of his wife's inheritance. Smithson likely also
was not a reflective man, and his need to immediately act on the last
stage of the process showed a certain impulsivity.

State. The haste with which Smithson sent on the money to Okundo
also reflected the great deal of excitement that he felt as the process for
receiving the supposed inheritance seemed to be nearing a successful
conclusion. Again, the motor that drove this train was Smithson's desper-
ation about feeling suddenly poorer than had previously been the case,
and his great desire to rectify that problem, through God's apparent
intermediary: Daniel Okundo.

GULLIBLE LAWYERS

The story of Scott Rothstein, a now-disbarred and imprisoned Fort Lauderdale attorney, is interesting in that it involves two levels of victim-
hood: the over 250 individuals, hedge funds, and charities that were
hoodwinked (to the tune of $1.5 billion) in Rothstein's Madoff-like Ponzi
scheme, and the dozens of generally well-respected attorneys in Rothstein's law firm, who were unwittingly lured by very high salaries, fi-
nanced by the scam, into joining the firm. The two scams were joined in
another way, as the investors were lured by the fact that the scheme's
profits supposedly came from lawsuits filed by the law firm. I shall here
focus more on the law firm rather than the investors, as an illustration of
the "Emperor's New Clothes" phenomenon operating within an organization made up mostly of people with above-average intelligence and
who, but for self-delusion, should have been able to know that something
very fishy was going on.

The scheme (Urbina 2008), as described to investors, involved large
structured financial settlements made by deep-pocket defendants in civil

lawsuits, mostly involving alleged sexual harassment or gender employment discrimination (labor law was the main specialty of Rothstein's firm). The individuals who were the recipients of these settlements agreed to sell their interest in these structured settlements in return for deeply discounted up-front payments.

In and of itself, this is a legal activity: firms offering to buy structured settlements advertise freely on television, although I am unaware of their then turning around and bundling those settlements to other investors. Also, apparently in some cases, these were described by Rothstein as imminent future settlements, while legitimate firms deal solely in already-ratified settlements. What made this particular scheme illegal is the fact that these were wholly fabricated settlements mostly involving lawsuits that either never happened or in which Rothstein had no ownership interest. With the help of one or more assistants (for example, Caputi 2015), Rothstein prepared phony promissory notes and settlement documents, with names of litigants redacted supposedly because of court-mandated confidentiality requirements.

As with the Madoff scam, Rothstein dealt both directly with very rich individual investors and with a few so-called feeder hedge funds that served as intermediaries between Rothstein and the somewhat smaller-scale investors in the funds (smaller being a relative term meaning a minimum investment of a million dollars, although some fund investors lost much more than that). In the case of the feeder fund investors, it is likely that most of them never knew who their money was being invested with (as was true in my own case, in which I do not recall hearing Madoff's name mentioned by the fund intermediary I dealt with) or how much of the returns were being pocketed by the fund managers.

Investors in the feeder funds were promised annual returns from a low of 15 percent (in the same ballpark as the Madoff feeder fund returns) to as high as 30 percent, while those who invested directly with Rothstein were promised even higher returns, sometimes over only a few months. These returns are comparable to those of Charles Ponzi (who told naïve investors they could get 50 percent returns in four months) and constitute a huge red flag which makes Rothstein victims (investors and fund intermediaries) seem more gullible to me than Madoff's. The genius of the Madoff scam was that the returns were modest but steady, thus deluding investors into thinking his was the equivalent of a safe but exceptional bond fund. As with all Ponzi schemes, there were no actual investments by Rothstein, who used newly obtained funds to pay off existing investors and to support a very lavish lifestyle.

Unlike most Ponzi schemers, Rothstein managed to flee to Morocco, a country with no extradition treaty with either the United States or Israel (where Rothstein also broke the law) with millions of dollars of wire-transferred money just before he could be arrested. But then he improbably returned (with his cash) to face the music, allegedly to deal with threats against his family from Russian mafia confederates. Master con man that he was, Rothstein cooperated with the FBI in getting the Russians arrested for money laundering, before he was sent to prison essentially for the rest of his life.

As mentioned, a notable element in the Rothstein saga is that the Ponzi scheme was embedded within a large and respected Fort Lauderdale law firm—Rothstein, Rosenfeldt, and Adler—which essentially served as a front for the illegal activities. Rothstein built this from a five-member firm into one of the largest firms in South Florida in a little over four years, by offering huge salaries and bonuses. For example, second named partner Stuart Rosenfeldt was given, among other bonuses, a Ferrari, $1 million in reimbursed personal credit card debt and a fifty-four-foot yacht, and was given a check for $500,000 to cover taxes on these and other gifts on the same day that Rothstein absconded. Rothstein appeared to do almost no real legal work within the firm and the little bit he did do was incompetent. In this respect, he differed from another fraudulent lawyer, Marc Dreier, who also used illegally obtained funds to operate his huge New York law firm, in that Dreier was, by all accounts, a talented attorney (Burrough 2009).

There is no evidence that Rothstein's lawyer colleagues knew about or participated in the investment scam, but proceeds from the scam were used by him to pay them their large salaries and bonuses. Rothstein, as managing shareholder, chairman, and CEO, ran the firm and its finances in an unusually solo and secretive manner (he was described by one senior partner as a "benevolent dictator"), with internal security and bodyguard protections that to my knowledge are almost unheard of in large law firms. Rothstein claimed it was because of the murder of an associate, allegedly by the estranged husband of his assistant (a woman with whom he had many business and personal ties). The real reason for all of this security was to keep other attorneys in the firm from acquiring an understanding of the firm's complicated and shady financial picture. In one disclosed document, Rothstein directed the firm's accountant not to allow any firm member to examine the firm's financial papers. Because of the merged nature of its legitimate and crooked revenue streams, collapse of the Ponzi led inevitably to the collapse of the law firm.

Because his law partners and associates would probably have quickly figured out the bogus nature of the scam, and (one would hope) blown the whistle on it, it was essential for Rothstein to keep the investment scheme a secret from the other lawyers in the firm. Attorney colleagues were curious, but apparently not too curious, about where Rothstein obtained the funds to pay them compensation at least double what they had been earning previously. Nor did the firm members seem too eager to look into the fact that the company's expenses (including enormous sums for advertising) were at least twice what the firm could be expected to bring in from client billings.

Rothstein's need for secrecy (which was shared by Madoff mainly with regard to the details of his investment strategy) severely limited his ability to market the scam publicly and to bring in sufficient new investors. However, some non-attorneys in the firm apparently helped Rothstein prepare phony legal settlement documents and investor payout statements. This was similar to the Bernard Madoff scam, where the illegitimate operation was kept separate from the legitimate larger firm, and he was assisted mainly by high-school educated co-conspirators who lacked the sophistication at first to spot illegalities and whose continued participation in the corrupt scheme was assured by extremely high compensation and, possibly, fear for their own legal jeopardy in facilitating the scam.

Aside from possible tax and civil liability from profiting indirectly from Rothstein's stolen monies, some attorneys have been accused of illegal conduct in making political contributions at Rothstein's direction, for which they were later improperly repaid through bonuses. In fact, this is one of the major reasons cited by the Justice department in (for its first time ever) charging a law firm as a conspiracy under the 1970 Federal *RICO* (*Racketeer Influenced and Corrupt Organizations*) Act.

As with many other scams, it should not have taken a potential investor with even minimal internet search skills more than a few minutes to see some red flags. Here is an example: one of Rothstein's reported deals involved his claim that he "represented 450 people who were due $2 million each in wrongful death cases against the fruit company Chiquita Brands International." This was a real lawsuit that was filed in a Federal Court in South Florida and which involved allegations that the company had exposed banana workers to a highly toxic pesticide. It should not have taken an approached potential investor very long, however, to have figured out (or paid someone to figure out) that neither Rothstein nor his firm represented anyone in that lawsuit and that the case was still unresolved. Yet, very few people approached with such a deal possessed the information (or the inclination to obtain the information) needed to see the fishiness of the proposition.

Such a lazy stance towards verifying a deal with the potential for bringing one to the brink of financial ruin may, however, be more a matter of one's *personality* style than of one's *cognitive* ability. Similarly, most investors—even those with some expertise in finance—lacked the ability or inclination to analyze or even understand complex schemes such as Rothstein's, especially given that the details (supposedly because of confidentiality agreements) were often sketchy. Certainly, media interviews with some of Rothstein's victims, including feeder fund managers, gives a picture of individuals who were operating more on the basis of blind trust than on the basis of in-depth knowledge or understanding.

In terms of the lawyers who agreed to work for Rothstein's corrupt firm, it is fair to say that *affect/ state* played a major role. The most obvious affective consideration was greed, activated by the prospect of getting greatly increased compensation. Greed was a positive motivator, drawing dupes to their downfall, but it also caused a need to suppress any doubts that might have arisen. Thus, affect contributed to self-deception (wishing for something to be true makes one think that it is) and self-deception often plays a part in gullibility (Trivers 2011). *Affect* also contributes to gullibility in one other way and that is in the positive feelings one may have, or come to develop, for the duper, who in this case was incredibly generous, both with money and continual expressions of praise and affection. Stuart Rosenfeldt, the second named partner in Rothstein's firm, for example, said "I loved Scott, he couldn't do wrong in my eyes" (Malkus 2013). This affective infatuation was in line with Rosenfeldt's personality, which he described in the same interview as follows: "my primary mistake was naïveté and trust. . . . I've always been a [overly] trusting person" a trait that he attributes to having grown up with a mother with multiple sclerosis, and being told to never create any disagreement that might upset her.

Rosenfeldt revealed that he did not always feel this love for Rothstein. In fact, his initial reaction, upon first meeting Rothstein (long before they ever worked together), was one of instant dislike. Rosenfeld found Rothstein to be very arrogant and he was really turned off by his personality. In hindsight, Rosenfeldt now wishes he had stuck with his initial gut reaction and not allowed himself to be charmed and won over.

Staying with one's gut reaction, when encountering a seductive schemer, is one of the keys to remaining non-gullible, as there are almost always warning signs. An illustration of this can be found in the account told by a female attorney who was courted by Rothstein, but who had the sense to turn him down. She said (Malkus 2013) that "Rothstein recruited me and during the 'interview' he did almost all the talking. At the conclusion of his 'pitch,' he only had one question: 'how much annual salary is it going to take in order to bring you into the firm?" Upon thinking for a minute, she responded: "I'll consider joining your firm for 400 thousand dollars." Rothstein replied "done." Then, she let him know that currently she was part of a practice group with two additional attorneys. "How much will these attorneys need to make to come over?" asked Rothstein. "Each of them would need to make 150 thousand dollars a year," she said. Again, Rothstein replied "done." The attorney told Rothstein that conversations would need to take place with her two team members. Upon leaving Rothstein's office, the attorney realized that not only had he not asked about her current clients, he did not even inquire as to the "book" that her associates had. Her gut feeling was that no law firm CEO would move forward with hires without knowing how much business they could generate for the firm. She said that in spite of the substantial salary being offered by Rothstein, it was an easy decision to turn down the offer to join his firm.

III

Implications of Foolishness

Foolishness is a concept with many types of applications. Three special applications, each deserving of book-length treatment, are explored in this section. The first has to do with the fact that collections of people (groups, organizations, nations) often behave foolishly. The second has to do with the fact that some people (young, old, special needs) are particularly vulnerable to behaving foolishly. The third has to with foolish acts that qualify as crimes. Illustrative examples are explored within each of these three categories.

EIGHT

Foolishness in Collectivities

In the second century BCE, the Roman statesman Cicero noted that "all places are filled with fools" (Stone, 2013). While the main focus of this book is on foolish actions by individuals, one can also speak about foolish actions taken by organizations or other groups as well. This happens when a business, a government, an educational organization, or a group such as a youth gang, engages in a course of action that is so foolish (that is, fraught with risk) that it endangers the health or even the survival of the collective entity or its members. In this chapter, several examples of collective foolishness are examined, using the same four-factor explanatory framework used to analyze the foolishness of individuals, although one of the factors, "personality," cannot always be used to describe a collectivity consisting of individual group members who differ widely in that domain. In cases of collective foolishness, however, one or more leaders (whose personalities can be described) typically play a dominant role in convincing others that an obviously flawed course of action is worth pursuing.

FOOLISHNESS IN A STARBUCKS

On April 12, 2018, two twenty-three-year-old African American budding entrepreneurs, Rashon Nelson and Donte Robinson, entered a Starbucks in Philadelphia's center city to meet with someone to discuss a real estate deal they had been working on for months. Mr. Nelson asked the white female manager to use the restroom and was told by her that they were reserved for paying customers. He joined his colleague at a table, where they sat waiting without ordering anything, even after the manager came over and asked if they planned to make a purchase. The manager asked the young men to leave, and then called the police when they did not comply. Several squad cars responded, the men were handcuffed (they wisely did not resist) and were taken away. As they were being taken away, the third person (who is white) they had been waiting for showed up and pleaded for their release. His pleas were ignored and the two men were arrested without explanation or any attempt to discuss the matter. The incident (which lasted only a few minutes) was recorded on a cell phone and received millions of views, sparking yet one more debate about race in America. After the store refused to press charges, the two men were released, with the explanation that no crime was committed, and that it was never the company's intent to have them arrested. The company later apologized, announced a day of racial sensitivity training for all employees, and offered to pay to help Nelson and Robinson complete college.

The incident has had significant consequences for the manager (who appears to have been fired), the police (the commissioner has deeply apologized), and the company (Starbucks was widely criticized, and its founder, known for his political liberalism, scheduled a day when thousands of stores were closed—at incalculable expense—for racial sensitivity training for all workers). The incident has been widely discussed (E. Stewart 2018), but not from the standpoint of a foolishness analysis. I shall proceed to do such an analysis, focusing on three sets of actors: (a) the store manager, (b) the police, and (c) the arrested men. By including "c," I am in no way absolving or excusing the implicit racism revealed by the actions of "a" and "b." First, I wish to discuss a relevant contextual matter, namely the implicit dual tacit functions of Starbucks as both "America's meeting place" and "America's bathroom" (and possibly also "America's place for getting good free WiFi when working on a laptop").

Ironically (and coincidentally—my home WiFi was down), I wrote most of this essay at a Starbucks in my former lily-white Denver suburb. I first went into the restroom (nobody stopped me) and then sat down at a table with my laptop for a couple of minutes before buying the least expensive drink (water—I was already over-caffeinated) on the menu. Every table was taken by a single white person (or at most two white people), almost all looking at a laptop, and sitting there undisturbed for long periods of time. When making my modest purchase, I asked the Barista if she or a coworker had ever asked anyone at a table to place an order, or had ever told someone they could not use the restroom unless they ordered. The answer to both questions was "no" and she then added "Starbucks is a great place for a customer to work, so why would I bother someone, even if they did not order something?"

I am old enough to remember the days before Starbucks and even before McDonald's when finding a public bathroom (let alone a clean one) could be a real challenge. It is possible that Sigmund Freud's strong dislike of the United States can be traced to the fact that he famously peed in his pants when walking with almost equally famed Swiss psychiatrist

Carl Jung in a park near New York's Columbia University on his only trip to the US. Sociologists have noted that institutions have both manifest (official) and latent (unofficial) functions with the latter often being more important than the former. The manifest function of Starbucks is to sell coffee and related products to customers, while the latent function is to provide the public a decent place to hang out and, when needed, relieve themselves. While the company would likely prefer to emphasize the manifest function (which produces revenue), they do implicitly understand that the (free of charge) latent function contributes to the bottom line. In fact, they advertise themselves as "America's meeting place." Their understanding of this was demonstrated when they once backed off (after customer protest) from an attempt to set time limits for internet use.

In fact, most people understand that paying an exorbitant amount of money for a cup of Starbucks coffee is the hidden price for using the facility as a nice place to pass the time. Ernest Hemingway made a similar observation about cafés in post-World War I Paris with his 1933 short story titled "A Clean Well-Lighted Place." It dealt with an elderly impoverished man who would spend hours sitting unimpeded in his neighborhood bistro while nursing a drink all day, and was allowed to do so by the empathetic waiters. Along those lines, I once saw the manager of a Starbucks (in the college town of Davis, California) give a free coffee and pastry to a homeless man who lived on the nearby streets. Presumably, the recipient of this kindness honored a reciprocal understanding that he would not over-use this privilege and would avoid bothering (such as by panhandling) other customers.

In the several decades that I have been using Starbucks (or my second choice, McDonald's) for emergency bathroom access, I have run into push-back only once, when I found I needed to ask for a key to access the restroom in a very run-down McDonald's in a dilapidated neighborhood near downtown Detroit. I assume that the reason was related to the extensive homelessness problem that I had noticed in the neighborhood. As a rule, Starbucks (unlike McDonalds) stores are not located in the very poorest neighborhoods, in part because they require either a car to get there or substantial cash to buy something. (The one exception would be a store in a center city area like Philadelphia's, where one can see a mix of wealthy young professionals and poor street people such as those the manager mistakenly assumed Nelson and Robinson—casually but conventionally dressed—to be). I have not seen a racial breakdown, but it appears that black people generally make up only a small percentage of Starbucks clients. Thus, the implicit racial bias of the manager was likely influenced by the fact that relatively few of the store's customers were black, and a higher percentage of the latter may have been people she assumed were penniless. This is not to excuse her apparent racial bias, but only to raise the possibility that fully understanding the incident requires more information about the history of this store and of the employee's past behavior.

I do not know for certain, but I suspect that asking a non-paying customer to leave was not unknown in this store, or by this manager. Most likely people asked to leave were perceived to be poor or homeless. A mistake made by this manager was being unable to see that she was here dealing with customers very similar, but for skin color, to the many young white customers who were camping out for varying periods of time in her clean and well-lighted place. Likely, most people asked to leave would comply without complaint (homeless people tend to be diffident) and police would not be called. Thus, she would be unused to being told "no," was certainly unused to having her behavior recorded and put on social media, and likely lacked the skills, training, or personal inclination to treat this passive defiance as something not requiring police intervention. One part of the manager's foolishness was in not understanding that when police are called, things can develop in unanticipated, unwanted, and, fortunately not in this case, violent directions. Thus, the foolishness of the store manager was not anticipating that by this single act she might not only lose her job but could open herself up to considerable opprobrium.

When analyzing a conflict situation between two or more people, it helps to know on a precise micro level all aspects of the context, including the words, intonation, and body language of all of the actors. Unfortunately, the recording did not start early enough for those facts to be known. What was the manager's tone of voice and attitude? Ditto for the arrested men. I have no reason to think that was a significant factor here, but in most cases of a conflict, words, tone, and attitude explain most of the variance.

It must have been a slow crime day in Philadelphia for multiple squad cars to show up to deal with such a minor problem. Presumably, the arrest reflected the "broken windows" policing philosophy in which the idea is that showing zero tolerance for minor infractions (such as jumping subway turnstiles) is a way to catch and prevent more serious crimes and criminals. The most upsetting thing about police behavior here is not the extreme action (shooting, beating) that has spurred the Black Lives Matter movement (that could have been different if the men had put up a fight), but the routine demeaning behavior of hassling young black men for something close to no reason. If the arresting officers had made any effort to talk the situation over calmly with Nelson and Robinson (who the officers would quickly come to understand had no criminal intent), there is little doubt the standoff could have been resolved peacefully. The police chief (himself a black man) initially was somewhat defensive, criticizing Starbucks for not letting the police know that it advertises itself as a meeting place. He quickly responded to criticism, however, by apologizing for what he described as a personal failure, and vowed to revamp his department's policies and procedures (such as by emphasizing negotiation skills for resolving minor disputes).

Every place has its own cultural norms, and I have had enough experience with Starbucks to know its norms and how to fly under the radar when visiting one of their stores. What I am saying is that I always try to anticipate and follow (or pretend to be following) institutional expectations for Starbucks or any other public place. With regard to Starbucks, one norm (and I have rarely seen it not followed) is to buy a coffee or some other modest item before sitting down. I also have never asked permission to use the bathroom, even when just walking in and back out of the store when on a road trip. It is possible, as a white (and older) person that there would be no negative consequences if I ever violated those norms, but I have never been inclined to find out. It is possible that Rashon and Donte had little or no experience with Starbucks and, thus, lacked the opportunity to learn those behavioral norms. I would like the chance to ask them why they blew off the manager's (admittedly biased) request, and if they made any attempt at explanation (such as "we will order something once our business meeting starts"). Also, I would like to ask them why they did not just accede to her request. Were they planning on leaving once their friend showed up? Was the supposed policy (later changed by the company nationwide as a result of this incident) communicated disrespectfully? Were they trying to make some rights-related point? Or (relevant to risk-recognition) did they consider that the manager might drop a dime on them for trespassing? I realize (having some risk-awareness) that I am opening myself up to attack by suggesting that these victims of racial bias could or should have behaved differently, but in this as with most other bad outcomes, the truth is multi-faceted. From a decency standpoint, however, I wish some empathy and flexibility had been followed by the store manager and by the cops. Fortunately, Starbucks has wisely responded to this event by providing better staff training and by announcing that anyone can use store bathrooms, whether they make a purchase or not.

WHEN TRADE UNION MEMBERS COMMITTED MASS SUICIDE

Collective work stoppages were given the English word "strikes" in 1768 when sailors in London who were sympathetic to labor protestors "struck" (lowered) the topgallant portion of square-rigged sails of merchant ships in port, to immobilize them. In the nineteenth- and twentieth-centuries work stoppages conducted through labor unions were used in the United States and other countries to create a more level playing field when workers were seeking to address abusive pay and working conditions. Desperate workers at the end of their rope went into these strikes knowing they were facing physical (being beaten by goons) and social (arrest, loss of jobs) risks, but considered those risks worth taking. In fact, many strikes achieved the workers' goals, when companies caved, usually when the damage to the company was serious and especially when the workers won widespread public sympathy.

Working conditions in industrialized countries have improved dramatically compared to a century ago, largely as a result of the pressures imposed by organized labor unions willing to strike. Thus, there is nothing inherently foolish about strikes, even when a successful outcome in a particular case is far from guaranteed. But a strike can be considered foolish when the circumstances are such that it is almost guaranteed to fail, sometime with dire consequences for the union's members and, as in the case described below, the labor movement generally.

That is what happened on August 3, 1981 when over 12,000 of the 13,000 members of the Professional Air Traffic Controllers Organization (PATCO) in the United States went on strike against their employer, the Federal Aviation Association (FAA), a unit of the federal government. They struck in spite of a law (which workers swore an oath upon being hired to honor) making it illegal for federal workers to strike (McCartin 2011). Just before the strike began, President Ronald Reagan made a strong pronouncement vowing to fire workers who did not return to work within forty-eight hours. What made the strike foolish was not just the outcome—over 11,000 workers (1,000 went back to work) who permanently lost their jobs (many subsequently falling into poverty) and being prevented from further employment in other federal agencies (a provision later relaxed), decertification of the PATCO union, and a significant undermining of union power even in private industries. A reflection of the latter is that the frequency of union-led work stoppages in the United States is now well under 10 percent of what it was before 1981.

The fact is that the failure of the PATCO strike could have been predicted by almost any objective and knowledgeable observer. (I remember as a forty-year-old with some life experience, watching on TV as the union's members were gleefully shouting "strike, strike, strike, strike" after a vote ratifying their decision to walk out and thinking "these poor shnooks are loudly celebrating their own stupidity"). Labor historians refer to the disastrously foolish PATCO strike as having played a significant role in the declining power of the labor movement in the United States.

Situational Factors. Sociologists divide US labor unions into two broad categories: (a) craft (or guild) unions, whose members have a valued and generally well-remunerated skill and can work semi-independently for various organizations (examples are electricians, plumbers, screenwriters), and (b) industrial unions, whose members tend to be less skilled, much less well-paid and who typically work for a single large company (such as an auto manufacturer or steel plant). Strikes have been more common, and more contentious in industrial unions due to two factors:

(a) the greater alienation and sense of powerlessness of industrial workers, and consequentially, (b) a sense of identification with the earlier combative labor union movement, often reflecting family histories of poverty, oppression, and struggle.

Although members of PATCO had a valued skill and (by national standards) were very well paid (after several earlier victories, stemming from two "sickouts" that went unchallenged by earlier presidents), most controllers came from working class backgrounds, were relatively poorly educated (except through FAA-run training programs) and felt themselves aggrieved by having two demands partly rejected by the FAA: (a) a significant reduction in working hours to relieve high degrees of work stress, and (b) a further increase in pay (which had risen significantly in recent years) to the same level as airline pilots, who the controllers questionably considered their equals in terms of training and level of responsibility. Thus, while being a controller afforded semi-professional guild status, PATCO and its members functioned more like a radicalized trade union, in terms of its demonizing of employers and its willingness to declare war.

A *situational* factor that should not be underestimated is that the union President, starting in 1980, was a long-time former controller, Robert Poli, who was elected because he was considered much more aggressive than his predecessor in articulating and addressing the union members' grievances. Poli was a very charismatic man, and he exuded great certainty in assuring the membership that they would prevail. His certainty was based in part on the fact that Ronald Reagan, who became president of the United States in January 1981, was a lifelong member of the AFL-CIO, and had led his union, the Screen Actors Guild, to its first ever strike when he was its president. Reagan had sought and received the union's endorsement when he was running, by assuring Poli that he supported the union's goal of upgrading the infrastructure and safety of the overtaxed air traffic control system.

Affective Factors. In collective foolishness actions, individual emotionality becomes reinforced and multiplied by the emotionality of the total group. This makes it difficult for the group to turn back or to act rationality. In the case of PATCO, members had a strong sense of grievance aimed at their employer, the FAA. This sense of grievance was, as mentioned, encouraged, rather than modulated, by the chief strike proponent, the union's president, Robert Poli.

Cognitive Factors. Cognition played a significant role in this as in most other collective acts of foolishness. Here the main cognitive feature was a failure to understand that while Reagan was supportive of strikes in private industry and was supportive of collective bargaining by unions representing government workers, he was dead-set in his opposition to strikes by public sector unions. He saw the strike as a threat to public safety, and gave the union a warning before the onset of the strike that he would go after the union aggressively (firing of all strikers, criminal indictments of leaders, enormous fines against the union's strike fund) if they challenged his determination to enforce the federal law prohibiting public sector strikes. Poli made a big mistake in underestimating Reagan's resolve, and essentially daring him to keep his word.

A related mistake by Poli was in overestimating the size of the threat that a strike posed to the air transportation system, and underestimating the ability of the government to keep air traffic going. Plans had been drawn up to bring on military controllers, to reduce some flights, to use supervisors, and to fast-track the training of replacements. These actions, in combination with the 2,000 PATCO controllers who stayed on the job, made it possible for the air system (at a time when passenger volume was much lighter than it is today) to continue safely and with minimal disruption. Another mistake was in assuming there would be substantial support from the trade union movement, and from the general public.

Poli's decision to strike was based on a (to me) cynical calculation that it would shut down the country's airline system, thus creating so much disruption that the government would have no choice but to give in to the union's demands. But it backfired, both because the FAA did rise to the challenge, but also because the strike completely alienated the flying public and undermined support from other unions. The strike was very unpopular with the public, who saw the already relatively well-paid controllers as irresponsible and reckless in turning down an offer that was not insubstantial, and the AFL-CIO resented Poli for keeping them in the dark about the strike plan.

In sum, PATCO was quickly crushed and its individual members found themselves unemployed and permanently barred from pursuing the profession that had been, for many of them, their only ticket to a middle-class lifestyle. In my view, all of this could have been avoided if the union had shown some risk-awareness, and the members had been able to bring under control their reason-undermining collective anger. While Reagan was faulted by some as inhumane for not allowing the rehiring of repentant PATCO members after the union ceased to exist, his effective handling of this major crisis so soon after assuming office was cited as important in causing him to be viewed as a strong and decisive leader.

FOOLISH COVER-UP AT PENN STATE

Joe Paterno (affectionately nicknamed "Joe Pa") had the most wins ever of any major college football coach and was someone who, until November 2011, had a reputation for always behaving ethically. That reputation was shared by his institution, Pennsylvania State University (PSU), which was known for running a clean athletic program that always played by the rules in recruiting, academics, and enforcing of behavior expectations for students and supporters. Joe Pa, who continued coaching until eighty-four years old, had every reason to expect that he could retire on his own terms. Instead, he was dismissed summarily, along with the President and other administrators, and PSU will be forever remembered as an example of how an institution can lose its moral compass (Moushey and Dvorchak 2011).

The road to perdition for Paterno and his bosses started in March 2002, when a graduate assistant named Mike McQueary claimed that he observed retired defensive coordinator Jerry Sandusky in a locker room shower engaged in the anal rape of a ten-year-old boy who was served by a youth foundation that Sandusky had founded. McQueary did not immediately intervene but instead ran out and called his father, who counseled his son to report the incident to Paterno, which the young man did the next day. Paterno, who claims he did not get all of the lurid details (a claim disputed by McQueary), told athletic director Tim Curley a day later that Sandusky had been observed "fondling or doing something of a sexual nature to a young boy." Some days later, McQueary was called in to a meeting with Curley and senior vice president Gary Schultz (whose portfolio included the campus police) to tell them directly what he had seen. Around March 27, McQueary was told by Curley that the youth foundation had been notified, that Sandusky was ordered to turn in his locker room keys, and that he was prohibited from bringing children into the athletic facility. McQueary was never contacted or interviewed by the police to whom, apparently, the incident was never reported. It is alleged that PSU president Graham Spanier (a noted authority on family therapy) knew about and approved the action that was taken, although Spanier--later indicted and convicted of a crime (recently overturned for tehnical reasons)—along with the two other administrators--denied knowing exactly what supposedly occurred in the locker room shower.

It turns out that this was not the first, or last, time that Jerry Sandusky appeared to have sexual contact with a minor. In 1998, the mother of an eleven-year-old boy reported Sandusky to the police after he came home with his hair wet after showering with the coach. In a conversation with the boy's mother that was surreptitiously monitored by detectives, Sandusky admitted to showering naked with other boys and stated "I wish I was dead." The case was closed after the Centre County DA Ray Gricar (who, bizarrely, has since disappeared) decided not to prosecute. Later that year, Sandusky retired from coaching at fifty-four years old (young for a top assistant at the height of his success) after Joe Pa informed him he would not be succeeding him as head coach. (A big mystery is whether Paterno knew about the 1998 incident and its investigation; many people suspect that he did).

Sandusky continued to have a presence on campus with his foundation, the Second Mile Foundation that began as a home for young boys, an activity which won him considerable local and national recognition. In the Fall of 2000, a janitor named James Calhoun claimed that he observed Sandusky in a locker room shower performing oral sex on a pre-adolescent boy. Calhoun, a temporary employee, immediately reported the incident to his supervisor, Jay Witherite, who told Calhoun how to go about reporting the incident. Calhoun decided not to follow up, and neither he nor Witherite contacted the police. Things finally began to unravel for Sandusky in the Spring of 2008, when the mother of a high school freshman informed his school that her son had been molested by Sandusky. The school barred Sandusky and reported the charges to authorities as mandated by law.

In early 2009, the Pennsylvania Attorney General Tom Corbett (he later became governor) began an investigation after a teen-age boy reported numerous instances of inappropriate touching over a four-year period. One assumes the state's attorney general became involved because of concern that the university and county law enforcement agencies could not be trusted to do the right thing. In 2010, Sandusky withdrew from any role at the youth foundation and on November 5, 2011, he was arrested and arraigned on forty criminal counts (he has since been convicted and given a sentence that will keep him incarcerated for the remainder of his life). On November 7, Curley (who resigned) and Schultz (who was suspended) were indicted (and later convicted) for lying to the grand jury that investigated the matter. A new Pennsylvania attorney general said that Paterno was not suspected of committing a crime, but she refused to rule out the possibility that the university's president would be indicted (he later was). The next day, an additional victim, the ninth known so far, contacted the state police. On November 9, expressing regret over failing to do more to protect additional children from exploitation by Sandusky, Joe Paterno announced that he planned to retire at the end of the football season, but later that same day, after receiving a report indicating that the coach had been more active in suppressing action against Sandusky than he had admitted, the PSU Board announced the immediate ouster of both him and Spanier. Only two months later, the previously adulated coach died of cancer after his statue was removed from a place of prominence on the campus. The interim president of PSU acceded to the NCAA action in voiding a large number of football victories during Paterno's tenure, but they later reversed that action when a lawsuit was filed which claimed that punishing a school for non-sports infractions were outside the mandate of the organization.

There has, not surprisingly, been considerable criticism of PSU, with most of the criticism focusing on the way in which the 2002 Sandusky incident (and earlier incidents later uncovered) was swept under the rug. Certainly, if it had been reported to the police and competently investigated, it is very likely that Sandusky would have been prevented from continuing his predatory conduct towards children. The university and its football program would have suffered some temporary embarrassment, but it would have come out of it with its reputation for ethical conduct largely intact. Instead, the reputation of PSU, and its storied football coach and program, will forever be muddied. In addition, the university and the four dismissed individuals are likely facing years of civil litigation from the abuse victims and their families. If all of this is not an example of foolish (that is, risk-oblivious) behavior by an institution and its highly paid leaders, I do not know what is.

PSU's collective behavior was foolish because avoidance of short-term negative consequences (embarrassment for the institution, worse for their admired and probably pitied colleague Sandusky) opened the possibility—if not likelihood—of far worse consequences for the institution, for all of the actors, including Sandusky (who will now spend the rest of his life in prison, and was denied the opportunity to get needed help earlier), and of course for the children whose lives most likely will be permanently scarred. To describe the university's collective handing of this situation as "foolish" does not, however, lessen one's right to label it as "immoral." In fact, I believe my four-factor explanatory theory of foolish action has utility in explaining both why generally smart people sometimes act foolishly and also why generally good people sometimes fail to act in accord with moral dictates.

The moral dictate in this case, as in all cases of suspected pedophilia, is to immediately make an oral or written report to the police or to a child protection hotline. Agencies or professionals that routinely have contact with children understand that they are "mandated reporters," which means that they are under a legal obligation to report suspected abuse, and that failure to do so is actually a crime. Where it gets sticky is that while a licensed professional is obligated to report abuse, an employee of a government agency (such as a school teacher) can report it to her supervisor (such as a principal) who then is the person mandated to make the report. What makes it problematic is that the evidence of abuse is sometimes ambiguous (say when a child tells a teacher that her father beats her with a hair brush) and then the agency head may be tempted to deny the credibility of the allegation and fail to take necessary action. (In the case of reported anal rape of a minor, any claim of ambiguity about the seriousness of the incident is obviously not credible, even though some of the PSU actors denied that they knew the details). It is because professionals or agencies have shown over the years that they cannot be trusted to deal with such allegations responsibly that mandatory reporting laws were enacted in the first place, and reporters—who often have a conflict of interest—are discouraged from handling such matters in-house and are encouraged to always err on the side of protecting children. In the case of PSU, determining which professionals and units are mandated reporters is not entirely clear, given that the relevant Pennsylvania statute refers to "staff members of a medical or other public or private institution, school, facility or agency, and who, in the course of their employment, occupation or practice of their profession, come into contact with children" (PA Statute: § 47.52. Suspected Child Abuse—Mandated Reporting Requirements).

University athletic programs and football coaches deal of course during the season entirely with young adults rather than children, but the facilities are routinely used by kids, such as in summer sports camps (which head coaches get big bucks to nominally run). So, my guess is that all of the people who have been suspended or fired were covered by the mandated reporters law, whether they knew it or not. Because PSU runs day care centers, health services, and other child-oriented programs, I believe the university president was certainly covered by the law and also, as a long-time mental health professional (whose papers on family dynamics are well-known to me) he could not claim ignorance of the law's requirements. At any rate, the question here is not the letter of the law but rather its spirit, which can be paraphrased as: "When child abuse is alleged, responsible institutions and professionals have one overriding moral obligation, and that is to report it immediately." All other considerations, including concern over the welfare of the institution or of the suspected perpetrator, should play absolutely no role in one's determination of the proper course of action. While we likely will never completely know all of the details concerning the deliberations that went into the 2002 decision process, one thing is crystal clear, and that is that the action taken was profoundly misguided.

In terms of the four-factor explanatory model, the first factor—*Situations*—comes into play in the dispersing of responsibility which comes about as the result of group decision-making in a hierarchical bureaucracy. McQueary felt he had discharged his responsibility by reporting the incident to Paterno, and Joe Pa felt he had "done what I was supposed to do" by reporting the incident to his nominal boss, Curley. In a limited sense, they are both correct in that in a hierarchy that is what one does. For that reason, McQueary and Paterno are probably the least morally culpable of the actors in this drama, even though it is hard to understand how Paterno could have felt comfortable with Sandusky's being allowed to continue interacting with children, even if no longer on his turf. The most culpable of the actors in my view are Curley and Schmidt, followed by Spanier who presumably was briefed on the situation and the proposed course of (in)action. By coming up with a collective resolution of the matter, these actors deluded themselves into thinking that they knew what they were doing.

I believe the second factor—*Cognition*—came into play in two ways: (a) ignorance of how to handle such a situation, and (b) confusion about the alleged incident. With regard to ignorance of how to proceed, one must keep in mind that child abuse is not something that Paterno or the others likely had any experience dealing with, and one should not assume that they had ever given much thought to (or received any training in) their legal or moral obligations in such a matter. With regard to confusion about the incident, one can only speculate at this point, but there is certainly the possibility that the specifics of the anal rape report—likely an embarrassing and distasteful topic, both to McQueary and Paterno—became soft-soaped (no pun intended) in the telling and retelling of the story, as it made its way up the hierarchy. In this way, it is possible that the actors other than McQueary deluded themselves into thinking they were dealing only with "groping" and "inappropriate contact."

The third factor—*Personality*—likely does not play much of a role here, except that none of the actors in this story showed much strength of character, and with stronger character they might have acted differently. The playwright Arthur Miller (1987) once opined that a man's character is defined both by the challenges he takes on and by the ones he walks away from (he was probably thinking here of how he abandoned a son born with Down syndrome). In the case of Paterno, he was willing to take on the familiar challenge of running a clean football program but he was unwilling to take on the unfamiliar challenge of seeing that children were protected from a pedophile. In this, Paterno is rightly pointed to as a moral man who failed the biggest morality test of his life, an opinion with which the coach appeared to agree.

The final factor—*Affect/State*—clearly does play a role here, as it does in other cases (such as the obvious parallel of priest pedophiles) where a bureaucracy is motivated to protect its own and its brand. This came into play here in two kinds of concern about the impact of reporting Sandusky to the police: (a) besmirching the university's reputation, and (b) destroying of the life of a respected (and undoubtedly sick) colleague. These considerations are certainly ones that all of the actors likely thought about, but in allowing them to surface (as I am certain they did) and play a role in their deliberations, they broke God's law even if not the state of Pennsylvania's.

FOOLISH CORPORATIONS: THE RISK OF STANDING PAT

When I began working in Rochester, New York in the mid-1960s, I asked my new colleagues how it was possible that our secretary Eleanor drove a new luxury car every year and showed other trappings of wealth. It was explained to me that Eleanor was one of many Rochesterians who had become millionaires almost overnight as a result of owning shares in a family-run printing company then known as the Haloid Corporation. Haloid changed its name to Xerox when (after giant cross-town rival Eastman Kodak turned down the opportunity) it purchased the rights to a revolutionary dry copying process known as xerography. Xerox quickly came to dominate the paper copying market, and its signature product—

the Xerox 914—was considered a technological marvel that became the single most-purchased business machine of all time. The iconic nature of the company is reflected in its becoming a widely-used verb, as in "I am going to the copy place to xerox something."

A hugely profitable company with widely admired research capabilities, Xerox had every reason to believe that it would continue to prosper and grow indefinitely. Yet, in February 2018, less than six decades after it produced the world's first dry-process copier, and after many years of financial difficulties, Xerox announced that it had ceased to exist as an independent company. It now was poised to function as a unit of Fuji Film Holdings, the Japanese company that ironically had played a role years earlier in knocking the other Rochester behemoth, Eastman Kodak, off its perch as a virtual monopoly in the film, camera, and film developing business. (Update: an outcry by some major shareholders appears to have put the acquisition by Fuji on hold, and an effort was initiated to try and keep Xerox independent. My larger point still stands, however, namely that years of bad decisions have brought an iconic company to the brink of dissolution.)

The main explanation for the decline of Xerox is what can be termed the "competency trap," namely when a company is very successful at one task, it lacks sufficient motivation to undertake necessary evolution (Deutsch 2000). Ironically, while the spectacular growth of Xerox was due to its recognition of an evolutionary shift in the technical processing of words, it was a failure to recognize and implement further such evolution that led to its downfall. I am referring of course to the digital revolution and the resulting move away not only from paper but from locating production of documents in centralized business settings. Ironically, many of the elements of the desktop publishing revolution (for example, the mouse, the graphic user interface, cut and paste dragging, icons, Ethernet, laser printing [also resisted by Xerox's board as impractical]) were developed at the legendary Silicon Valley Palo Alto Research Center (PARC), wholly owned by Xerox. But the board and executive leadership of the company showed an utter lack of interest in the accomplishments of PARC. Steve Jobs, who based the Macintosh computer almost entirely on ideas (and some personnel) snagged from PARC, famously asserted that he was blown away both by what he saw there and by the failure of Xerox to understand what they had. Interestingly, Jobs later sued Microsoft for basing its Windows-based PC computers on the Mac, but its case collapsed when the court ruled that the technology in question had first been stolen by Apple from Xerox.

Although my four-factor explanatory model of foolish action is an imperfect fit when applied to an organization rather than an individual, it may still provide a useful framework for reflecting on the foolishness that led to the demise of Xerox. In the following paragraphs, I attempt to do that. Where appropriate, I give examples of how two other meteorically risen companies—Apple and Microsoft—showed considerably greater adaptive competence, when anticipating that, and how, they needed to evolve.

As mentioned, the main *Situational* factor contributing to the Xerox corporation's lack of risk recognition was, ironically, the phenomenal success it had with its initial line of products, and the fact that for a long while, it had no real competition in the document copying business. In line with the competence trap phenomenon, the leadership of Xerox was lulled into underestimating the dangers coming from changed circumstances. Interestingly, even before the existential threat to Xerox from the changed nature of personal computing and document production technology, there was competition coming to the core copying business, caused by legal challenges to Xerox's patents and, later from the expiration of those patents. Some of this change reflected the move away from mammoth machines that were Xerox's specialty to smaller machines obtainable by individuals. This presaged the even more substantial challenge to Xerox caused by its failure to get on the personal computing bandwagon that it had (through PARC) done much to bring about.

As is often the case, the main cause of Xerox's foolishness can be found in the realm of *Cognition*. Steve Jobs had been quoted as saying that he followed the hockey great Wayne Gretzky's dictum "I skate to where the puck is going to be, not where it has been." If Jobs had taken the path of Xerox, Apple would have stayed with the Apple-II, or maybe the Mac, but not branched off into such other lucrative products as the iPod, iPhone, and iPad. Similarly, there were many who wondered why Bill Gates moved into the cloud computing and storage business at a time when Microsoft dominated the market in software sold and activated by disk. But that proved to be a very prescient move, given that most new computers are sold today without even a disk drive. (Today, software is sold mainly through the cloud, Microsoft lags only behind Amazon in providing cloud storage, and it is a very important contributor to Microsoft continuing to be a very profitable company). After the untimely death of its visionary early leader Joe Wilson, Xerox lacked leaders with an ability to forecast the future. This is illustrated even within its primary photocopying business, as Xerox pioneered the development of color copiers, but then sat on that invention for years, allowing Kodak to take the lead, because of short-sighted concern that color copiers would hurt Xerox's lead in black and white copiers. It is not unfair, I believe, to assert that the demise of Xerox was hastened by many poor decisions over a period of years.

The third explanatory factor, *Personality*, is more difficult to apply to an organization, but if a personality style could be used to describe Xerox (and other companies that fail to adapt), it probably would be "rigidity," followed by "complacency." The main manifestation of Xerox's rigidity was an inability to move away from the idea that the principal market for the company's products would continue to be institutions, such as businesses, schools, and government agencies. This likely played a role in Xerox's failure to exploit its technical breakthroughs in personal computing, as such exploitation would require an understanding that most of the purchasers of such technology would turn out to be individuals. An example of this is that when the Alto—the small Xerox PC that Apple copied—was first offered for sale, the company priced it at $16,000, way too high for individual purchase today, let alone in 1973.

The fourth foolishness explanatory factor, *Affect/State*, is even more difficult to apply to an organization, but I would argue that collective "fear" is a suitable candidate. This might seem a strange choice, as risk-unawareness/foolishness is generally thought of as a lack of necessary caution. But adaptive functioning in the world requires not only knowing when to hold back from acting but also knowing when action is required. Companies that built on initial success, such as Microsoft and Apple, were led by people willing to take major risks, while the great misfortune of Xerox was that it stayed too long in its comfort zone, not understanding that eventually a comfort zone can become a danger zone.

NINE

Foolishness in Vulnerable Populations

While all human beings, even very bright ones, are capable of acting foolishly, there are some people who—because of cognitive, emotional, or experience factors—have a higher than average likelihood of behaving foolishly. Some case examples are presented, illustrating three such risk groups: children/adolescents; people with cognitive disabilities; and people with mental illness. A fourth vulnerable group, the frail elderly, is not addressed, but several of the stories analyzed throughout this book involve individuals with dementia or other conditions associated with advanced age. The factors within the explanatory model that are particularly relevant to at-risk groups (for example, *cognition* for people with Intellectual Disability or *affect* for people with mental illness), will be emphasized in explaining specific foolish actions. But these factors always operate in combination with one or more other factors, just as they do with anyone who engages in a foolish act regardless of their vulnerability status.

TEENS DOING DUMB THINGS

Until March 2010, many Walmart stores allowed customers access to a microphone, for reasons that are obscure. In that month, a sixteen-year-old boy in a Walmart in Washington Township, New Jersey (near Atlantic City) activated the microphone with the announcement "Attention, Walmart customers: All black people, leave the store now" (CNN 2010). Apparently, this was the third similar incident in that New Jersey store in a several-month period. The offending youth quickly exited the store but his image, along with another youth and that youth's mother, were captured on security cameras hurrying out of the store immediately after the prank. Investigators were able to nail down the youth's identity by scouring Facebook postings, until they found entries bragging about the episode. The youth found out that his stunt was not so funny when he was arrested and charged with harassment and bias intimidation, and was facing the possibility of up to a year in jail. His friend and the friend's mother were also being investigated for possible complicity in the crime.

Given what a company spokesperson accurately called the "backward" nature of the stunt, I imagine the offending youth (whose name was not divulged) was neither bright nor sophisticated. Probably, he never imagined that he was committing a crime, let alone one that carried a possible one-year sentence. Nor could he have imagined that he would be held up to such widespread scorn and criticism. Presumably, he thought he could get away with it, even if he had noticed the store's security cameras. But then he could not resist the temptation (which seems to be universal among young people) to advertise his stupidity on the internet. So, two of the explanatory model's four factors)—cognition and situation—came into play: *cognition* because of the failure to understand the legal risks to which he exposed himself, and *situations* because of the reinforcement he expected and likely received from peers. Another aspect of *situations* was the temptation of having an open mike lying around, a policy that Walmart has since wisely ended. Undoubtedly, *personality* also entered into the equation as well, but we cannot know that given the protection of the juvenile's identity and the lack of specific detail provided about the young man and his motives.

Sometimes, pranks played by teenagers, often in cahoots with friends, have tragic consequences for the perpetrators. That is what happened in Little Rock, Arkansas in February 2014, when a group of teen girls thought it would be fun to punctuate a high school celebration by covering a stranger's car with a mix of toilet paper, eggs, mayonnaise, and leaves (Lynch 2015). Unfortunately, the car's owner, forty-eight-year-old Willie Noble, did not find the stunt particularly funny and he fired into the group of students, fatally striking one of them, a fifteen-year-old cheerleader named Adrian DeeJay Broadway in the head. Mr. Noble received a thirty-year sentence, as such a reaction was clearly excessive, given that he himself was under no physical danger and firing randomly into a group of people, even after they vandalized your property, is unjustifiably reckless.

An earlier Arkansas shooting of a young prankster, in Ouachita County, was, however, found by the authorities (in a very pro-gun part of the United States) to be justifiable, as the shooter felt that his life was in danger. In that incident, which occurred in November 1994 the killed person was also a young girl, fourteen-year-old Matilda Kaye Crabtree (Nossiter 1994). Telling her parents that she would be spending the night at a friend's house, Matilda and the friend hid in a closet in Matilda's house, with the intention of jumping out and startling the unsuspecting parents when they returned at 1:00 a.m. from an outing. Hearing a noise in a darkened room, Matilda's father, a fifty-three-year-old truck driver named Bobby Crabtree, went to get his handgun. When the closet opened, and the girls jumped out and screamed "Boo," Mr. Crabtree fired his gun, striking his daughter fatally in the neck. While the inconsolable father, crying "I shot my baby," held his dying daughter in his arms, Matilda uttered her final words: "I love you Daddy." The father's reckless action was clearly foolish, but understandable given that he believed his home had been invaded. But hiding in the closet in a dark house to scare her gun-packing father revealed a tragic degree of risk-ignoring on Matilda's part that reflected her age-related social-*cognitive* limitations, exacerbated by excitement (*affect*) over a stunt encouraged by her equally foolish friend.

Socially (and physically) risky stunts by teenagers are by no means limited to unsophisticated youths residing in semi-rural areas in the South (or South Jersey). Laurence Steinberg, a prominent adolescence researcher, was motivated to turn his attention to youth crime when his highly gifted teenage son was arrested for participating in a stunt in an affluent area of Philadelphia, not far actually from South Jersey. With some friends, the younger Steinberg was caught at night sneaking around the outside of a girl's house and allegedly attempting to climb in her bedroom window. Steinberg later asked his son if had thought about the possibility that his behavior would be reported as an illegal home invasion to police who would be responding with guns drawn, and his son said that the possibility had never entered his head.

This is the time for me to confess that in my adolescent years, I participated in two stunts similar to the one reported by Steinberg regarding his son; one of them resulted in a severe reprimand by a homeowner who told me I was lucky he did not shoot me, and the second resulted in my arrest. In both of these episodes, a big part of my motivation was that other youths (one of them today a much-honored medical researcher who has been nominated for a Nobel prize as one of the main founders of immunotherapy) participated alongside me. In considering why teenagers as bright as his son (not to mention me and my Nobel-nominated friend) would behave so foolishly, Steinberg emphasized not so much tacit knowledge (although that likely played a role) as he did the research indicating that the ability of teenagers to reflect on their behavior is not yet fully mature because the frontal cortex of the brain is still developing at sixteen and seventeen years old (and in many cases, beyond). His writings (as later described in Scott and Steinberg 2008) on the topic were in fact cited by the United States Supreme Court in its 2005 *Roper v. Simmons* decision as a basis for outlawing application of the death penalty to anyone who commits murder before the age of eighteen years (raising it from sixteen years old). However, Steinberg and others have argued that as the frontal lobe is still maturing past eighteen years old, the death penalty age ceiling should be raised even higher, to twenty-two or twenty-five years old.

NAÏVE MAIDENS EASILY SEDUCED

The Decameron (Boccaccio 1353/2003) is a comic narrative masterpiece, written in the vernacular Italian, and completed by its author, Giovanni Boccaccio, in 1353. It tells the tale of ten young people, seven females and three males, who escaped to a monastery outside Florence for a two-week period, during which the plague killed a majority of the Florentine population. To entertain themselves, the young people—spurred on by one of them serving as king or queen for the day—told a story each on every one of ten days (they took two days off each week). Many of these one hundred stories were of a bawdy nature and involved dissolute priests and religious figures. This made *The Decameron* a controversial work, which was banned at times in many countries, including England and the United States. One can understand why after reading about the following story, which was told by Dioneo as the tenth, and last, story on day three.

The heroine of the story was Alibech, the fourteen-year-old daughter of a rich man. Wanting to learn how to serve God, she set out from her North African town of Gafsa into the wilderness where she stumbled upon the hut of a young hermit named Rustico. Wanting to prove that he had a will of iron, Rustico allowed Alibech to sleep in a corner of his hut. After a few days, Rustico lost his battle of will, and upon determining that the girl had never been intimate with a man, he told her that the best way she could serve God was to put the devil back in Hell. Asking him what he meant, Rustico showed Alibech his stiff member and said that it was the devil tormenting him, but that she could save his soul from damnation by putting the devil in Hell. Placing the girl on the bed, the monk initiated her in putting the devil back in Hell. This became a regular event and after a while Alibech came to enjoy the sport and began to approach Rustico by saying "Father, I came here to serve God, not to idle away my time. Let's go and put the devil back in Hell."

Alibech's stay in the wilderness ended when a young man named Neerbal came looking for her to say that her family had all been killed in a fire and she was now a rich woman. Alibech eventually agreed to marry Neerbal, but before the ceremony the women of the town asked her what she had learned in the wilderness. She said that she had learned to put the devil back in Hell and that Neerbal had committed a sin by stopping her from doing that. After they stopped laughing hysterically, the women told Alibech "Don't let it worry you, my dear. People do the job every bit as well here in Gafsa, and Neerbal will give you plenty of help in serving the Lord." The story was repeated over the years, and a proverbial saying developed in Italy to the effect that "if you stand in need of God's grace, see that you learn to put the devil back in Hell" (Shmoop Editorial Team, 2008).

Although a fictional character, Alibech illustrates many of the qualities that make real-life young people vulnerable to being seduced, that is, naively allowing themselves to be unknowingly or unwillingly initiated into a sexual relationship. This is certainly what has happened in the case of many children who have been serially raped in the United States and many other countries, by priests who used a variety of seduction lines as described around 1500 (this is not a new phenomenon) in stories written by a French merchant named Philippe de Vigneulles, and collected in a book by Armine Avakian Kotin (2015), *The Narrative Imagination*.

But the seduction process also involves inducement into non-sexual forms of deviant behavior. For example, a common seduction narrative in late medieval (fourteenth through fifteenth centuries) and early modern (sixteenth through eighteenth centuries), mainly in Europe (but also in the United States, most notably in the Salem Witch Trials of 1692–1693) involved the initiation of young girls by maternal figures into the practice of witchcraft. Three witch trials in seventeenth-century Cologne (Elrod 2014) relied on the testimony of children who admitted to becoming witches at the urging of their mothers, or other women, many of who were executed as a result. Obviously, this testimony was obtained, at a time when hysteria over witches was all-pervasive, by interrogators who were able to prey on the suggestibility of children who, we now known, can be easily made to believe in the reality of false memories implanted by adults (Loftus and Ketchum 1994).

TOWN FOOLS

Court fools, discussed in chapter 1, simulated, or in some cases actually exhibited, symptoms of what today would be called Intellectual Disability (formerly known as mental retardation). The term "fool," therefore, was at one time used to refer to people with significant cognitive impairments. Before there was such a thing as an intelligence test, every community had intellectually lower-functioning individuals who were known to one and all because of their obvious behavioral (and often physical) abnormalities. The term "town fool" (or, more pejoratively, "village idiot"), was often used to refer to individuals who, before the development of human service agencies or formal intelligence testing, were known to have intellectual limitations, and depended for their survival on support from family and neighbors for protection and even survival.

One such individual was Millard Fillmore Hathaway, an intellectually disabled man born in 1858 and who lived in a small New England coastal village, where, in adulthood, he was a wanderer known to walk a circuit

from home to home requesting temporary shelter. Hathaway was pro-
filed by anthropologist Nora Groce (1992) in a paper titled "The Town
Fool: An Oral History of a Mentally Retarded Individual in Small Town
Society." Groce told many stories about the foolish behaviors that caused
Hathaway to remain a legendary character in this community many
decades after he died, at sixty-two years of age.

Almost all of the stories Groce recorded about Hathaway's foolishness
illustrated his inability to pick up on social cues or to understand social
norms (both examples of his limited *cognition*). Examples included: entering houses without permission, being tricked into doing work for no pay
(usually by Summer visitors who did not understand kindnesses shown
Hathaway by townspeople), being the butt of practical jokes, being very
indiscreet when gossiping about people who had given him temporary
shelter, and being overly blunt in his comments (such as when he was too
honest when a woman asked him how he liked the free meal she had
cooked for him). But Hathaway demonstrated foolishness in the practical
domain as well, as illustrated in his freezing to death due to a failure to
recognize the danger posed by spending several days residing in an un-
heated chicken coop during a very severe Winter cold spell. Thus, unawareness of risk (social, but more seriously physical) is central to the
intellectual disability phenomenon and is one of the main reasons why
protective supports (group homes, guardianship, living with relatives,
etc.) are put in place.

WHEN A DISABLED PERSON'S INCOMPETENCE IS PART OF SYSTEMIC INCOMPETENCE

Social incompetence, as in foolish action, is a defining feature of people
with Intellectual Disability (ID) and also of those who have severe mental
illness. Foolish action is typically thought of as residing in a particular
person (or corporate entity as in the previous chapter). But sometimes it
occurs as a result of the intersection of incompetent decisions made by
one or more persons or entities. The case described below, which resulted
in the tragic death in January 2013 of a man with a significant disability,
is an example of this latter phenomenon, although most of the public
uproar has understandably been directed at the police officers whose
foolish use of excessive physical force turned out to be the proximal cause
of the man's demise (McCormack 2013).

The incident involved Robert Ethan Saylor (known as Ethan), who at
five foot six inches tall and weighing nearly 300 pounds, was a twenty-
six-year-old man with Down Syndrome (DS), a chromosomal disorder
which is a major cause of ID, until recently known as Mental Retardation,
or MR. People with DS typically have IQs in the 50s or low 60s (the usual
ceiling for defining ID is 70–75), but Ethan's IQ reportedly was around

40. This means that he likely was even more cognitively impaired than the average person with DS. As with all people with DS, Ethan had a recognizable pattern of facial features, a pattern which in earlier and crueler times caused people with DS to be termed "Mongoloid." Unlike the popular (but over-stated) stereotype of people with DS as uniformly placid, cheerful, and compliant, Ethan was described by his family as very friendly but also stubborn and prone to angry outbursts. However, like all people with DS (and for that matter, all people with ID), Ethan lacked the judgment to know what to do (and to recognize the risks) in a novel social situation such as the one that occurred in January 2013 in Frederick, Maryland, a city of 65,000 people located about fifty miles west of Baltimore and an equal distance northwest of Washington, DC.

All of the facts of the incident have not been publicly divulged, because of legal actions, and there are conflicting reports on some details. The basic story goes as follows. Ethan lived with his family, but he received supportive services including being taken on outings by aides. One day an eighteen-year-old female personal care worker who had been working with Ethan for three months accompanied him to the Regal cinema, located in the Westview Promenade shopping center. The film they watched was Zero Dark Thirty , about the pursuit and capture in Pakistan of Osama Bin Laden. I would have thought such a movie beyond the comprehension level of someone with Ethan's IQ level, but presumably he enjoyed the non-stop nature of the action. Ethan (who reportedly always sat in the same seat in that theater) liked the film so much that he wanted to stay for another showing.

Here reports differ somewhat but it appears that Ethan (who had already had at least one other angry outburst that day) announced outside the theater that he did not want to leave. The worker was unable to get him to change his mind, so she apparently made two calls asking for advice, with Ethan's mother telling her to wait him out while her agency supervisor gave the (to my mind, questionable) advice to leave him waiting outside the theater while she went to get the car. While the aide was away, Ethan re-entered the theater, intending to see the film again.

What happened next is that the theater manager told Ethan that he needed to either leave or purchase another ticket (variously described as costing $10 or $12). Ethan did not have any money on him, but Ethan's mom Patti indicated in a speech that he tried making a cell phone call in an effort to figure out how to raise the cash. At some point, the theater manager called in mall security guards to eject Ethan from the theater. Three officers responded, all of them moonlighting Sheriff Deputies (one of them a lieutenant), who were not wearing their police uniforms. (Ethan idolized cops and would sometimes call 911 in an effort to chat). The young aide was not allowed back into the theater but she was overheard screaming that Ethan had DS and that he hated to be touched. An officer apparently put his hands on Ethan and he responded by resisting both physically and verbally.

The autopsy noted various injuries on Ethan's body, suggesting that substantial force was used. Among these were marks on his wrists, a result of his being cuffed behind his back (three linked sets of cuffs were used, apparently because of his obesity). A witness reported that Ethan was lying on the ground on his stomach while an officer was seen putting his knee on the young man's back. Ethan was heard calling out words along the lines of "I want my mommy." A fractured cartilage in Ethan's larynx is an unusual injury that strongly indicates that a choke hold had been used. Rather quickly, Ethan stopped breathing and when this fact was pointed out by a bystander, the deputies initiated CPR and called paramedics. According to a report by the office of the Maryland Medical Examiner, the death was classified a homicide (defined as a death that would not have occurred but for the action of one or more people) and the cause of death was asphyxiation, with Ethan's obesity and an undiagnosed cardiac condition likely contributing to the quickness with which he expired.

Not surprisingly, this incident received intense news coverage in Maryland, but also became a cause célèbre nationally among disability advocates, and especially within the DS parent community. An ensuing internal police investigation cleared the officers of wrongdoing and a grand jury chose not to indict them for any crime. The US Justice Department announced it was investigating to see if Ethan's civil rights had been violated. Ethan's family filed a civil wrongful death lawsuit against the theater, the three officers, and the county. (It was eventually settled for $1.9 million dollars).

The family asserted that the main motivation behind their lawsuit was to force the full facts of the incident to be divulged. Daniel Karp, an attorney in Baltimore who was representing the defendants, described the lawsuit as "the familiar hyperbole of a plaintiff that is suing for money." I suspect that Mr. Karp may have learned that attacking the bereaved parents of a man with DS, who would still be alive but for the actions of his clients, was not a wise public relations move.

The Governor of Maryland, Martin O'Malley, met with Ethan's parents and expressed deep concern about the incident, although he resisted their request for an independent state investigation. However, he did announce the appointment of a Commission for Effective Community Inclusion of Individuals with Intellectual and Developmental Disabilities, to be chaired by Dr. Timothy Shriver, a Maryland resident who is CEO of Special Olympics International. In spite of the broad title for this Commission, the Governor indicated that his main reason for establishing it was to bring about uniform training for police officers and other first responders regarding how to deal effectively in the future with challenging situations involving individuals with developmental disabilities.

At first glance, the Commission's task seemed pretty straightforward, but on closer examination, the task was not so simple. To me there are three levels of complexity here: (a) how and when a responder is supposed to determine whether someone qualifies as a person with a developmental disability, (b) where one draws the line between offenses when potentially dangerous force is justified, regardless of whether someone has an apparent disability, and (c) whether training (and what kind of training) should also be offered to caregivers who sometimes are faced with similar situations or who, as in this case, might have been able to prevent the police becoming involved in the first place.

One thing that is particularly shocking about the Ethan Saylor incident is that with his obvious facial features and clearly impaired speech, behavior, and intellect, he might as well have been wearing a sign around his neck saying "I have Down Syndrome and have ID, so please handle me with kindness." It is difficult to believe that the deputies (not to mention the theater manager who called them in) did not know that Mr. Saylor had DS or that they did not possess some rudimentary understanding of what that meant, but I suppose it is possible. In most cases, I believe that people with DS who are acting out will be treated more compassionately by first responders than is true of people with ID who are not as immediately identifiable as are people with DS. I do not know of any research to support that belief, but I am not aware of any other instance where someone with DS died as a result of excessive police force. Such outcomes happen routinely (usually without attracting much media interest), however, where the target of the police response has a more hidden form of impairment.

There is a natural tendency within disability advocacy groups to focus on individuals who possess the same disability label as their family member or clients and that was the case here. Thus, the Down Syndrome Congress (a parent group) and the Down Syndrome Society (a professional group), not to mention Ethan's family, all issued public calls to action to ensure that no person with DS ever again suffered the same fate as Ethan. The problem, of course, is that DS makes up less than 5 percent of the population of people with ID (which has several hundred known possible causes), and in the vast majority of cases of ID there are no obvious external signs of disability and it usually takes a little time (certainly longer than one has in a police confrontation, where it is not uncommon for "normal" people to be agitated) before an individual's limitations become apparent.

A recent trend in the ID field has been to expand the estimated size of the affected population, by increasing the IQ ceiling from 70 (the bottom 2 percent of the population) to 75 (the bottom 5 percent of the population) and by giving more diagnostic weight to "adaptive behavior" (how people actually function in the world). Furthermore, in most states, ID is part of a broader category of Developmental Disabilities (DD), which includes other forms of impairment such as Autism Spectrum Disorder (ASD), 60 percent of whom do not have IQs low enough to qualify as ID. Individuals within the broader DD population who do not quite qualify as having ID (such as the majority of individuals with ASD) have social incompetence tendencies which could make them almost as socially risk-unaware as Ethan Saylor. However, unlike Ethan, they do not have the outward signs of disability which might (but in his case did not) cause responders to adopt a non-coercive approach. What I am suggesting is that the Governor's Commission needed to focus its efforts not on particular disability labels but on behaviors and behavior signs that are found in a much broader population of vulnerable people (including the mentally ill as well as intoxicated young people) who have a higher likelihood of behaving in a non-compliant or challenging manner towards first responders.

A frequent question asked by critics of the police action in this case, is "how can one justify using deadly force over a measly movie ticket?" There are two implied preferred actions which go along with such a comment. The first implied preferred action, which assumes that Ethan's disability was recognized and taken into account, is that he should have been allowed to stay put at least temporarily, until a parent or caregiver showed up to resolve the problem. The second implied preferred action, which assumes neither awareness of disability nor tolerance of non-payment, is that communicative rather than physical means should have been used to bring about compliance. Unfortunately, we do not know at this point whether and to what extent the officers tried to reason with Ethan, but one can assume they did not do it for very long or (judging by the escalation to violence) very effectively.

Those who complain about the use of force for not paying for a movie ticket are missing the point that force was used because Ethan did not comply with the order to vacate the theater (resisting a police officer could be a crime) and, apparently, for striking out at the officers after one of them put his hands on him (attacking a police officer is definitely a crime, although Ethan likely lacked the rational intent to have ever been charged). Grand jury proceedings are secret, but I would bet my house that the reason why none of the deputies was indicted or punished is that the jury as well as the department believed that the deputies were defending themselves against assaultive behavior by Ethan. He was a 300-pound man and one can assume he could do some damage if one of his punches or kicks connected. Still, whether or not one believes that the officers committed a crime, there is little doubt (at least in my mind) that the officers did not deal with the situation in a competent manner.

One way of defining foolishness is behavior that results in unwanted but foreseeable consequences. Surely, none of the officers wanted Ethan to die, none of them wanted to be sued for a lot of money, none of them wanted to bring their department into international disrepute, and none of them wanted to face a lifetime of scorn and (one would hope) remorse. Yet those four outcomes, which might have been foreseen when one of them put Ethan in a chokehold so strong that it fractured his larynx, had all taken place.

Whatever the tolerance level that police departments have for using potentially deadly force (and apparently the tolerance level was fairly high in the Frederick County Sherriff's department), one would like to think that are other departments and officers, including within the Frederick department, who would view the behavior of the three officers in this case as unprofessional. It was unprofessional because police officers, along with other professionals (such as therapists), are paid to accept a certain amount of abuse without responding in kind. They are also being paid to recognize when a subject is in an unstable state, and to practice responses intended to calm rather than inflame. Unfortunately, neither of those hallmarks of professionalism were demonstrated in this case.

The death of Ethan Saylor resulted from a "perfect storm" of collective foolish (risk-unaware) behavior by three parties: (a) the police officers and the theater manager (who I am certain later wished he had not called in the security guards/ police) who failed to appreciate the extent of Ethan's limitations, and responded too quickly with force; (b) Ethan himself, who lacked the social intelligence to understand that resisting police while striking out at them can be a very dangerous thing to do; and (c) the young caregiver who by leaving Ethan alone, inadvertently put him in harm's way and failed in her responsibility to serve as a buffer between a very brain-impaired young man and a complex social situation he lacked the ability to navigate on his own. Risk-awareness certainly contributed to the behavior of all three parties: in Ethan, by not understanding that saying "no" to a cop (and it is possible he did not even know the security guards were real cops) could get one arrested or killed; in the deputies (who, as mentioned, did not understand that by assaulting Ethan they were putting their careers, and even their freedom, at risk); and in the caregiver, who lacked the experience or wisdom (which one can define as advanced risk-awareness), to resist the terrible advice to leave Ethan alone while she went to get her car.

As in most cases of foolish behavior, *affect* entered into the picture, and when that happens, judgment/ *cognition* tends to suffer. For Ethan, judgment was impaired even in the absence of emotion, but here the emotion reflected his blind insistence on seeing the movie a second time and his knee-jerk angry response to being touched. For the caregiver, the emotion was frustration at being unable to get Ethan to leave and, presumably, a strong desire to resolve the stand-off. For the deputies, we do not know the role played by each of the three individuals, but most likely only someone in a very angry state would apply pressure sufficient to fracture a bone in a person's neck. Police officers tend, quite often, to impose their will physically on individuals who do not immediately follow their commands, and the level of coercion escalates substantially when someone strikes out at them. At this time, we do not know how angry or excited the individual deputies were, but it is safe to assume that through his words and deeds, Ethan activated an automatic coercive schema in one or more of the officers that involved a fair degree of annoyance. As mentioned above, truly professional officers would, in my judgment, have responded in a calmer and more clinical manner, especially once they recognized that they were dealing with a person with significant special needs.

It is not my desire to beat up on the then eighteen-year-old caregiver who, most likely, has suffered emotionally as a result of her involvement in this tragedy. But one wishes she (and also the deputies) had been coached in the communicative skills needed to influence someone with stubborn fixation issues. In my book Elements of Discipline (Greenspan 2012), I presented a scenario similar to the one posed by Ethan, in which a child stubbornly insisted that adults bend to his will, and started to throw a tantrum when they did not immediately comply. Trying to head off those adults who would use force (thus escalating the situation and teaching that might makes right) and those adults who would cave in (thus teaching the child that emotional blackmail works), I used what is termed "machine gun reflection" in which I rapidly asked a string of affective questions ("you really want to do this?" etc.) followed by a limit phrased as an "I-message" ("but the rule here is x because y"), followed by another reflective message about how the child felt about the imposed limit. Such an affectively-based method (which immediately deescalated the stand-off) might not have worked as well with Ethan, but if skillfully applied I am pretty sure it would have eventually defused the confrontation.

At one time, it was common for direct service workers in group homes, sheltered workshops, or other ID facilities to use coercive methods (including, believe it or not, cattle prods) to impose their will on clients, even for the most minor (and sometimes non-existent) of offenses. In his book Gentle Teaching , the late John McGee (1987) showed how positive methods—involving respect for the individual, negotiation, and most importantly a literal "turning of the other cheek" (tolerance) in the face of aggressive outbursts—could resolve most *situations* peacefully and help clients to become more competent. Today, fortunately, physically coercive methods are not as commonly used in the ID field as they were formerly, but I do not believe that *affective* communicative skills are any more likely to be taught to direct care workers than they are to police officers or other first responders. If there is any lesson to be learned from this tragic case, it is that the first instinct of the police, as well as direct care staff, when dealing with angry behavior exhibited by brain-impaired people like Ethan Saylor, should be tolerance combined with gentle insistence involving negotiation, both done in a spirit of love and an attempt to understand the individual and help them to regain self-control.

FOOLISH ACTS BY A MAN WITH BORDERLINE INTELLECTUAL FUNCTIONING

Our former cleaning lady "Shirley" used to bring her adolescent son "Matt" with her when she cleaned our house, as he had dropped out of high school and she was trying to teach him an employable skill. Matt has an IQ in the low 80s (I know that because Shirley once asked me to look at his special education records) and struggled with academics throughout his school years. Although labeled "Specific Learning Disabled" in school, Matt actually did equally poorly in all subjects, and more accurately could have been given the label "Borderline Intellectual Functioning" (BIF) or (the today less commonly used) "Slow Learner." These designations indicate that someone has a low IQ (in the high 70s or low 80s), putting him just over the 5th percentile of the population: low but not low enough to qualify for ID services (established at around the 2nd or 3rd percentile, along with deficits in "adaptive functioning."). Because people with BIF typically have life difficulties (adaptive deficits) similar to those who do qualify as having mild ID, it has been suggested (Greenspan 2017) that BIF be folded (actually refolded, as at one time it was a sub-category of ID) into the more serious ID category. After Shirley retired and moved to another state, Matt took over as our cleaning person and helped with lawn care and other chores. He was a genuinely nice person, but his life was filled with one poor decision after another. Here is one of them.

Matt was a very hard worker and subsisted by working multiple minimum wage jobs. Between overtime and a second (or third) job, it was not uncommon for him to work fifteen or eighteen hours in a twenty-four-hour period. One of his jobs was working the overnight shift as the only person staffing a gas station and convenience store late at night. It was understood by Matt that the owner was paying him off the books. One night around 2:00 A.M., Matt got a call from a man who said he was with the central office for the convenience chain store's national company. The man said he needed the serial numbers on a series of gift cards displayed by the cash register. Not having been given any instructions as to how to handle such a matter, Matt complied with the request. The owner informed him the next day that the business had been defrauded to the tune of $3,000. Matt was told he would have to pay the business back through deductions from his pay. This described arrangement (which under state law should have been agreed to by him in writing, if he had been legitimately placed on the payroll, and should still have allowed him to make minimum wage) was so extreme that Matt was basically expected to work for free for a period of several weeks. After this arrangement went on for a couple of pay periods, I told Matt he was being treated unfairly, and he should contact the state Labor Department and seek legal advice. When Matt mentioned something along those lines to the employer, he was immediately fired, a fate he likely would have suffered anyway after the owner recovered his $3,000. Lacking initiative, or skill in dealing with bureaucracies, Matt let the matter go and did not pursue any legal recourse for the money he had already been cheated out of.

I asked Matt the question that had been on my mind, namely "why did you go ahead and give the unknown man the gift card numbers he asked for?" His answer was "he was with the central office" (not "he *said* he was with the central office" but rather "he *was* with the central office"). This suggests to me that on some level he still thought the request was legitimate. As with low IQ people in general, Matt has coped (and covered up his limitations) by saying "yes" to any request from an authority figure, a tactic that has generally served him well. What he lacks are: (a) an ability to recognize when such a tactic could be risky, and (b) an ability to resist an inappropriate request, either by saying "no" or by coming up with a deflection tactic, such as "call back later when the boss is here."

I have learned that one of Matt's deficits is an inability to recognize when ambiguity requires him to seek clarification. Thus, I once walked him over to two wood piles, one on the right and the other on the left, and pointed to the logs on the right and asked him to cut them with a chop saw down to fireplace size. When he was done he went ahead and also cut the logs in a pile on the left (valuable pole logs I intended to use to construct a teepee) without thinking to ask if my saying "on the right" was meant to be taken as "cut all the logs, wherever they might be." Matt did not understand my reason for differentiating the two piles (my fault for not telling him) and therefore saw no reason to ask for clarification.

Following up on my inquiry about why Matt gave the unknown caller the card numbers, I asked him if he noticed any red flag that might have caused him to hesitate. Matt said "no," after which I asked whether he thought people at the main office were in the habit of working at 2:00 in the morning. Matt did not know what to make of that. I asked him if he could think of something he could have said (such as "I am not authorized to take such an action on my own") that could have enabled him to get out of complying and he again could not think of anything. Thus, one of his limitations is an absence of verbal heuristics for dealing with tricky situations. In fact, I suspect Matt did not experience the situation as tricky, and likely even felt proud of himself for dealing with the request on his own without bothering his boss.

If space allowed, I could write about many other stories (such as the time he bought a car under incredibly exploitative credit and purchase terms) that illustrate Matt's inability to reflect on or resist risky social pressure. Instead, using the four explanatory factors I shall attempt to briefly shed some light on why he was so prone to foolish action.

The main reason for someone with borderline intelligence to be so socially vulnerable is impaired *cognition*, specifically a failure to anticipate negative consequences of a particular course of action (such as the possibility that a man pretending to be from company headquarters could instead be a crook). Matt is a highly concrete thinker, who cannot and does not consider the possibility that someone could be other than he claims to be. The *situational* factor is that a faker with some persuasion skills knew that the night clerk at a convenience store might not be too bright and, furthermore, that a more knowledgeable supervisor was unlikely to be around. Matt's *personality* is one of compliance with requests from others, while his *state* was fear of doing the wrong thing, which ironically is exactly what he ended up doing.

TEN

Foolishness and Crime

The Greek tragedian Sophocles (441 BCE / 1986) wrote that "wickedness is, indeed, the sister of foolishness." Many criminal acts can be considered foolish: such as when the offender fails to take into account the long-term risk (for example, years in jail for himself, maiming or death for the victim) that far exceeds the short-term gain (for example, monetary gain or revenge satisfaction) of his action. Of course, enough people get away with crime to make it attractive, and the short-term benefits can be spectacular. That was certainly the experience of financial swindler Bernard Madoff, who lived the life of a successful and respected billionaire, before exposure of his fraudulent Ponzi scheme destroyed his family, created grave financial distress for thousands of his victims, and condemned him to spend the rest of his life in a prison cell.

To say that many criminal acts are foolish is not to deny that they may also be quite evil. Crimes vary according to their degree of both evil and foolishness, and examples can be found of crimes ranging from pure evil and minimal foolishness, to those with pure foolishness and little evil, to crimes where foolishness and evil are fairly evenly balanced. In this chapter, the contribution of risk-unawareness (foolishness) to assignment of blame will be explored in various crime stories, with (as in earlier chapters) an application of my four-factor model to analyze the foolishness aspects.

CULPABILITY OF FOOLISH ACTION

An interesting experiment, published in the top-tier journal *Intelligence*, was carried out in Hungary, by three academic psychologists (Aczel, Palfi, and Kekecs 2015). They wanted to find out the kinds of behaviors people considered to be foolish. They asked twenty-six university students to keep a journal for five days recording instances of people acting foolishly. A portion of the resulting stories were shown to 154 students, who were asked to rate the severity of the foolishness portrayed in the stories, and to indicate the psychological factors that they believed could be to blame.

The stories fell into three clusters: (a) confident ignorance, (b) lack of control (obsessiveness), and (c) absent-mindedness (clutziness). Culpability of the actors was judged greatest for the willful ignoramuses and lowest for the clutzes. Presumably, the culpability continuum reflected the extent to which an individual's foolishness was judged as something that could have been avoided (an ignorant person, unless brain-impaired, always has the ability to inform themself, and in the era of Google that is easy enough to do). *State* and *personality*, on the other hand, are harder to overcome.

In terms of the four-factor model, confident ignorance could be considered a combination of *cognition* (lack of knowledge) and *personality* (arrogance), lack of control could be considered an aspect of personality, while absent-mindedness reflects *state*. The role of situations was not apparently considered by the respondents, but there is much research indicating that coercion is a mitigating factor for culpability. Basically, this research suggests that foolishness born of ignorance, especially in someone with ability to become better informed, is the most deserving of blame.

FOOLISH RESPONSE TO FEELING MISTREATED

It is a little-known fact that most acts of violence are motivated not by a lack of morality in the offender but by an excess of (usually misplaced) morality. An example would be when a violent offender becomes convinced that a moral violation has been deliberately committed, one that needs to be severely punished. This insight is the major contribution to the criminal justice field made by sociologist Lonnie Atkins (Rhodes 2015), whose developmental model of violence I find generally convincing (even if I disagree somewhat with his formulation of an invariant stage sequence that violence-prone people supposedly go through over a period of years before they kill someone). In Atkins' opinion, most if not all extreme violence is motivated by a desire to punish the victim for some offense or defect which the perpetrator sees as inhering in the person's behavior or character. It is in the choice of punishment, however, that the offender crosses a line, often without understanding that an action seen by him as justified retaliation could be viewed by legal authorities as criminal conduct. Two examples of this (one involving violence, the other not) will be discussed, the first an obscure case of a man who once did odd jobs for me, and the other a famous case, involving former football great O. J. Simpson.

"Jeff" was a thirty-five-year-old handyman who had been in trouble with the law on numerous occasions, but they were mostly for "dumb" crimes that could have easily been avoided had he possessed better problem-solving skills and an understanding of the legal danger to which his behavior was exposing him. One example involved an automobile that he was interested in purchasing. Jeff was at a bar and someone he knew slightly asked if anyone wanted to buy a $500 car, which was described as being in good running condition. Jeff gave the seller a $50 down payment and started to drive the car home, promising to pay the balance in a week. On the way home, Jeff saw some smoke coming out of the engine compartment, and assumed that the car had a serious engine problem which the seller tried to cover up by loading it with oil additive. Instead of taking the car back, and asking the seller to explain himself, Jeff assumed the seller was trying to swindle him. He never notified the seller that he had changed his mind, or told him where the car had been left. After a week, the seller called the police and reported that the vehicle, which he falsely described as having a value in excess of $1,000 (which at that time was the threshold for a felony in that state), had been stolen. Jeff was arrested and eventually pled guilty to felony theft but avoided going to jail. He had two other equally ridiculous felonies on his record (one of them involved punching a fellow he believed had made a move on his girlfriend when he was eighteen years old), and thus put himself in danger of being labeled a habitual offender and spending the rest of his life in prison.

The *situational* pull here was the misrepresentation by the owner (as perceived by Jeff) of the condition of the automobile. Even assuming Jeff's perception of the situation was accurate, this is a minimal provocation, which one can expect to encounter on a frequent basis, especially when buying a vehicle from a private party in a bar. To Jeff, however, this was a serious affront, and one that required an equally serious response. Jeff actually thought that he showed admirable restraint, by not going to the man's home and beating him up.

In my view, Jeff is a man with borderline intelligence, and this showed in his *cognitive* inability to understand that by not returning the vehicle he was committing theft. He also lacked an ability to reflect on the many legally acceptable alternatives available to him, including giving the man a piece of his mind. Jeff's *personality* played an important role here as well, as he is a macho type, with a need to portray himself as tough and unwilling to take disrespect from anyone. Finally, *affect and state* played a huge role, as Jeff was motivated by strong anger and his already shaky judgment was likely further impaired by the ingestion of alcohol. Given these factors, and the ubiquity of similar situations likely to arise (especially in bars), it is not surprising that Jeff has spent a good portion of his life in jail, mostly for crimes that reflect poor judgment rather than truly malicious intent.

An even more bizarre (but less benign) example of foolish judgment resulting in criminal conviction involved Orenthal James ("O. J.") Simpson, a retired, professional football star (Toobin 2015). Simpson, a man likely more intelligent than Jeff, was very well-known not only for his athletic exploits but also for his post-football career as an actor, product spokesperson, and sportscaster. In 1995, when he was sixty-one years old, Simpson was tried by a jury for the double murder of his estranged wife Nicole Brown Simpson and her friend Ron Goldman. The trial, which received enormous publicity, resulted in an acquittal which most legal commentators felt was the wrong verdict. A subsequent civil wrongful death lawsuit was initiated by the families of the two victims, and resulted in a 1997 award of over $33 million. Simpson managed to avoid paying all but a token amount by successfully warding off efforts to garnish his sizeable pension, by moving to Florida (where his residence was protected from lawsuits), by allegedly hiding some of his income (for example from autograph signings), and by dispersing many of his valuable sports memorabilia assets.

In September 2007, Simpson was in Las Vegas to attend a wedding when he was tipped off by a friend, Thomas Riccio, that some of his possessions were being advertised for sale at a Las Vegas hotel. Outraged by what he saw as the theft of his possessions by one of the men who was helping him to hide them from the Goldman family, Simpson rounded up several large friends and headed over to the hotel room where the items were being displayed. Before heading over there, Simpson asked two acquaintances to each bring a gun in order to show the men selling the items that he meant business. Barging into the room while in a highly agitated state, accompanied by men flashing weapons, Simpson screamed (Norman, 2007) "Don't let nobody out of this room. Mother fucker, you think you can steal my shit and sell it?" After Simpson and his posse departed, one of the victims was taken to a hospital with a serious heart attack.

Simpson made off with a number of items, some of which turned out never to have belonged to him. He also took a cell phone, presumably to prevent the victims from calling the police. Although he later returned the items, Simpson was arrested and tried for a number of serious crimes, including armed robbery and kidnapping. Before the trial, Simpson made light of the matter, saying "I'm O.J. Simpson. How am I going to think that I'm going to rob somebody and get away with it? Besides, I thought what happens in Las Vegas stays in Las Vegas . . . [and] I just wanted to get my stuff back." (Glover, 2008). (As in earlier examples in this book, this is another case of inappropriate humor by a sports figure). Simpson was convicted after four of his five coconspirators agreed to testify against him in exchange for reduced sentences. The most critical piece of evidence was an audio recording that Thomas Riccio—the friend who had given him the original tip—had made on a surreptitious recording device while the incident was taking place. (Riccio later sold that recording to a gossip website for over $200,000). Simpson was sentenced to a maximum of thirty-three years (eligible for parole after nine) in a Nevada prison. He had been warned before the incident by several people, including his attorney, not to take the law into his own hands. That was good advice, which he foolishly chose to ignore. The attorney, Yale Galanter, admitted in his closing argument that Simpson's plan to recover his property forcefully was not a smart idea, and then added "but being stupid and being frustrated is not being a crook." The jury disagreed with that characterization, and the lengthy sentence was upheld by the courts, in spite of the surfacing of a hidden recording on which an investigating police officer was heard saying that convicting Simpson in Las Vegas would be proper payback for his having gotten away with murder in Los Angeles.

As with my handyman Jeff, the *situational* pull for Simpson's foolish conduct was fairly minimal, although there was also a gullibility component in that Thomas Riccio (who allegedly was setting Simpson up for a payday by making and selling the recording) told him about the sale of his property and encouraged him to retrieve it. It has been pointed out that there were legal options, such as going to the police, available to Simpson, but the obvious problem with that is that he wanted to keep Fred Goldman (the aggrieved father of the murdered Ron Goldman) from getting his hands on the items. *Cognition* enters in here as Simpson actually seems to have believed that the method he chose to recover what he considered his property was proper and legal. He also apparently did not understand that there were many people (including, probably, his codefendants) looking to exploit his notoriety, and others (the police) itching to put him in jail.

As if thinking his method of property recovery was legal was not a big enough mistake, Simpson's even bigger mistake—which greatly increased the sentence given him—was telling associates to bring guns and then forcing the victims to stay in the room (impeding someone's freedom of movement, even momentarily, technically qualifies as kidnapping). *Personality* and *affect/ state*, however, likely were the biggest explanatory factors, in that Simpson was in a very angry frame of mind, and he had a history of violence, ranging from road rage to (unpunished) homicide, when angered. A critical aspect of his personality is that he is a classic narcissist, whose vanity, conceit, selfishness, and sense of entitlement know few bounds. Narcissists are also prone to what has been described as "narcissistic rage" (Kohut 1972), an irrational seeking of revenge when their will is thwarted or when they feel disrespected. Simpson's self-destructive behavior in the Las Vegas incident certainly is an illustration of that.

CRIMINAL HAZING IN A MARCHING BAND

As dangerous hazing is an activity typically performed by a group of young people, the following account could just as easily have been included in the chapter on youth foolishness or in the chapter on collective foolishness. Hazing is an initiation practice in which members of a group—such as a fraternity, military unit, or sports teams—force newcomers to do unpleasant, humiliating, or dangerous activities as a prerequisite to becoming a full-fledged member of the group. Although hazing is generally applied equally to every initiate, it can merge into bullying, in which special abuse is directed at certain individuals.

At one time, hazing was seen as harmless fun and was at least tacitly tolerated by adults—such as college presidents, military officers, or team coaches—who possessed the power to end, or severely limit, the practice. Tolerance of hazing has declined, however, as a result of publicity and lawsuits (civil and criminal) resulting from incidents in which individuals were killed or maimed, such as through beating or coerced alcohol consumption. In spite of the fact that hazing is now banned in many institutions, and violent hazing is now a felony in many jurisdictions, notorious instances of abusive hazing still do occur.

Two tragic cases both became public towards the end of 2011: (a) the beating death of a marching band member, Robert Champion, at Florida A&M University, as the result of a hazing ritual (Inabinett 2016), and (b) the suicide in a US Army base in Afghanistan of Private Danny Chen, apparently just after he had been severely humiliated by racist hazing from members of his unit. The death of the nineteen-year-old Chen has been memorialized in the opera "An American Soldier," by the composer David Henry Hwang (Cooper 2018). In both of these cases, as in most other severe hazing episodes, the action can be seen as foolish, in that the perpetrators seemed unaware of the dangers their activity posed, both to the victims (who were grievously harmed or killed) and to themselves (some of whom came to face serious jail time). As a little more is known about the Robert Champion case, and also because Danny Chen's case appears to be more a matter of group punishment (he was allegedly targeted for some performance lapses and also for personal characteristics, including his ethnicity) rather than a rite of passage ritual, my analytic comments will be reserved mainly for the college marching band case.

Florida A&M University (FAMU) is what is referred to as a "historically black college and university," or HBCU, and, like several other HBCUs has a celebrated marching band that performs at half-time of the school's football games and on other occasions. FAMUs band, referred to as "The Marching 100" (it actually had over 300 members), is probably the most famous of these bands, as reflected in the fact that it was invited to France in 1989 to represent the United States in the festivities marking the centennial of the French Revolution. The Marching 100 is the model for many other such bands, and one of the things that they modeled was a culture of violent hazing. As reported in a 2010 piece by journalist Frank Deford (2017) in *Sports Illustrated*, "new band members—called 'crabs'—had to face choreographed assaults, with two-by-fours, belts, baseball bats, beer bottles, suffering literally hundreds of blows from their older compatriots." Usually, hazing does not result in serious injury or death, but predictably it sometimes does.

At first glance, the Champion hazing tragedy seems a little atypical, as he was an older student in his mid-twenties (he had earlier dropped out of school for financial reasons) and thus was not a new band member. However, there is an initiation rite aspect to the story, in that Champion had applied to ride on Bus C, the percussion vehicle that held the highest status among band members. As part of the process for being accepted on Bus C, a student had to run the gauntlet from the front to the rear of the bus, being beaten along the way by the occupants. This apparently is what happened to Champion, during which he suffered internal bleeding that caused him to collapse and go into fatal shock. Less than a month before Robert Champion was killed, a female freshman FAMU band member named Bria Hunter suffered a broken femur and blood clots after being beaten by three band members. Morevoer, such extreme cases are not a new thing at FAMU. For example, in 2001, a FAMU band member named Marcus Parker suffered severe kidney damage after being beaten hundreds of times with a paddle.

As a result of the Champion and Hunter beatings, the Marching 100 was suspended and there were serious calls for it to be disbanded. The state of Georgia (where Champion and Hunter were from) suspended marching bands at over twenty high schools, because of fear that a culture of violent hazing was developing within those organizations. Renewed attention is being paid nationally to the problem of violent hazing in college marching bands, a problem that seems to be localized mainly in HBCUs, the vast majority of which are located in Southern states. Scholars, most of them African American, have made efforts to understand why this culture of violent hazing arose and persists. One interesting theory espoused by Walter M. Kimbrough, president of Philander Smith College in Arkansas, is that it is an offshoot of a 1990 collective decision by college presidents to end pledging (which always involved hazing) at HBCU fraternities. Because opportunities for hazing in HBCUs suddenly became limited, they resurfaced in marching bands, which have many of the features of fraternities but which to some extent are freer from supervision and discipline by adults such as leaders of national organizations (which will suspend or terminate fraternity chapters where abusive hazing is tolerated).

In terms of the four-factor theory of foolish behavior, the most powerful explanation for what happened to Robert Champion is *situation*. Two situational aspects, in particular, seem especially relevant: (a) that members, including the victims, enter into the group knowing that hazing will occur and accepting it as a legitimate price to pay, and (b) that the practice occurs in secret, free from scrutiny by the outside world of adults except, of course, when something goes seriously wrong. There is a process of groupthink occurring here, in which an otherwise deviant act (assaulting someone with fists or objects) is defined by the collectivity as non-deviant and even valued. In such a case, individual conscience and judgment tends to fly out the window, and members of the group allow the behavior of others to guide their own actions. It takes a certain degree of courage to withstand such pressure, and few people possess that courage, especially given that the likely price of taking a stand is ostracism or expulsion.

Here it is necessary to make a somewhat sensitive point having to do with the partial complicity which victims of hazing play in their own victimization. It is difficult to imagine that anyone who joined the FAMU marching band was unaware that they would be hazed, both because such hazing was well-known on campus, and also because many of the members came from high school marching bands that emulated the practices of the famous HBCU bands. Certainly, Robert Champion must have known beforehand that he would have to run the gauntlet of Bus C before being allowed to ride on that high-status vehicle. He did not seem to feel oppressed by such practices (according to his parents, he was very happy with the band experience) or to consider saying "no, do not assault me, unless you are prepared to spend a year or more in jail." The willingness of most members to be assaulted (although, obviously, not to end up near death) made it, of course, much easier to carry out these heinous practices. Thus, a major engine that drove the whole sick process was the strong motivation of members to participate in the band, a topic covered more fully under *affect/ state* below.

Cognition enters into foolish hazing, as in most foolish behaviors, in that the perpetrators of the hazing did not seem to understand the real risks involved, both to the physical well-being (death, injury) of the victims and to the social well-being (freedom, money, and future) of themselves. One reason they did not understand these risks is because of what might be termed the "base-rate" phenomenon. Simply put, when a practice can go on for years without anything catastrophic occurring, there is a tendency to underestimate risks and assume that nothing bad can happen, especially to the perpetrators. The only thing that might have countered this false belief is if the college administrators (both President and band director, working closely with law enforcement) had worked hard at getting commitments from band members to avoid hazing and to report (and then prosecute) offenders, but this apparently never happened in any meaningful way. A major contributor to the *cognition* factor is the young age of most of the band members. Presumably, older age brings enhanced wisdom to understand the dangerous (not to mention morally abhorrent) nature of violent, or any, hazing. Unfortunately, band members still in, or barely out of, their teens, mostly lack that experience and wisdom.

The third explanatory factor, *personality*, is difficult to apply to a collectivity such as a band, given that in an organization of 300 members, one will likely find some who opposed hazing and resisted participating, a majority who went along with it half-heartedly, and a large minority who embraced it totally. This more enthusiastic sub-group, whom I shall dub the "brutes," likely play a leadership role in organizing and carrying out the hazing assaults, and also tend to do it with greater force and viciousness. Thus, if Robert Champion was struck by say twenty band members on the bus, I would guess that five barely touched him, ten used some force but were careful not to hurt him too badly, while the five remaining members struck him as hard and as often as they could. It is likely that the fatal injuries were caused by these more violent individuals. I suspect that one or more of the brutes has a history of violence, including involvement with the mental health and criminal justice systems. (In a 2016 book, Curtis Inabinett Jr., revealed that youth gang members, with their even more severe culture of initiation and exiting violence, had infiltrated the band).

One of the distressing things about hazing is that a few disturbed individuals are using the cover of a collective activity to express their need to abuse others and to do it with relative impunity. Thus, the most maladapted members of the group are using a bogus rationale (that hazing builds group coherence) to give vent to their sadistic tendencies. That seems to have been true in the coerced suicide of Army Private Danny Chen, as one of the ringleaders of his brutal assault is a man who had spent time in prison for domestic violence .

The fourth factor in the explanatory model, *affect/state*, is an important contributor to violent hazing, less in the excitement that perpetrators feel when they are hurting others, as in the fear that victims feel when they consider the consequences of refusing to participate. Becoming a member of the Marching 100, and of comparable other HBCU ensembles, is a tremendously prestigious accomplishment and one which some members (such as, apparently, Robert Champion) dream about from childhood on. The strong motivational drive to participate in these bands is the engine that drives acceptance of hazing, given that hazing is seen as a necessary prelude to becoming a member. I suspect that hazing will stop once it becomes clear that: (a) hazing is no longer necessary to achieve band membership, and (b) hazing in fact will prevent one from achieving that end. For both of these things to happen, it is necessary for mature adults to step in and end this "Lord of the Flies" drama, in which unchecked adolescents brutalize each other without reason or compassion.

A FOOLISH HIT-AND- RUN

In October 2001, a twenty-five-year-old Fort Worth woman named Chante Jawan Mallard was driving home from a night out drinking and doing drugs with her friends when her car hit a thirty-seven-year-old homeless man named Gregory Biggs (Rothe 2008, 154-55). The impact was so great that Biggs became lodged in the windshield, with his head stuck inside the vehicle. Not stopping to call for help, Mallard—a former nurse's aide—continued to drive home, parking the car in her garage. She was quite upset by what had happened, and she periodically tearfully apologized to the still-alive man, both during the drive home and after she parked the car in her garage. It is alleged that Mallard had sex with her boyfriend during the time when Biggs was still lodged in the windshield. Sometime over a period of several hours, Biggs died of his injuries; doctors testified that he would have survived if Mallard had sought medical help. Mallard's boyfriend and a male cousin helped her to cover up the crime by moving the body to a park and by destroying the automotive evidence.

Mallard might have gotten away with the crime, but she brought suspicion on herself when she joked at a party that she "hit this white man" with her car. After a widely publicized trial, Mallard was sentenced to fifty years for murder and ten years for evidence tampering, with the sentences to run concurrently. This incident has been the inspiration for several TV episodes and films. This event can be considered a variant on a hit-and-run accident, with the extra twist that the perpetrator brought the victim home with her. As with any hit-and-run accident, the main motive was that Mallard feared that she would get into trouble, in this case because she had been driving while impaired. So instead of a much milder penalty, Mallard wound up having to spend most of her life in prison.

The four-factor model helps to explain how Mallard could have made such a foolish trade-off. The *situational* component here is that having a man lodged in your windshield is a very rare and unique circumstance, which could not have been anticipated by Mallard or anyone else. Once she made the unfortunate split-second decision to keep on driving (helped by the fact that it was late at night and there were no other cars or pedestrians around), the *cognitive* and *affective* challenges of the situation became even greater. That is because the fear of punishment from having an accident while impaired was now compounded by the fear of punishment stemming from driving off. Thus, *affect* (in this case, fear) was a big part of the equation. *State* also played a role, as Mallard was intoxicated at the time of the accident and alcohol and drugs cause judgment to become seriously impaired.

Once Gregory Biggs died, of course, the prospect of turning herself in became even more challenging. Mallard also had the misfortune of turning for help to a boyfriend who provided the bad advice to cover up the deed rather than come clean. (Even at that late date, the punishment would likely have been much less had she gone to the authorities.) Mallard struck me as having a weak and dependent personality. Her behavior following the tragic accident, combined with a lack of perspective-taking in blabbing about it at a party, showed a level of naiveté and immaturity one might find in a young adolescent. For that reason, I feel that a fifty-year prison sentence in this case was grossly excessive, even by Texas standards. (I participated in a Texas court case where a young man with an IQ in the 40s received a ninety-nine-year sentence for allegedly exposing himself to a child, so I know something about the cruel nature of sentencing practices in that state).

WHY CHILD ABUSERS ARE FOOLISH

Child abuse is a form of violence, in which an adult uses excessive force to punish a child (Pardeck 1989). Violence can be defined broadly, to include such things as verbal aggression, suicide, and warfare. However, I am defining it more narrowly to mean the intentional use of physical force by one person against one or more other people and which has a high likelihood of inflicting harm. Thus, in this paper, I am mainly interested in physically aggressive acts committed by a single individual, even when the act is triggered or coerced by one or more other people.

Violent acts (Alvarez and Bachman 2008) can be placed along a "hot-cold" continuum, with hot violence occurring on the spur of the moment with little or no planning or forethought, while cold violence is planned and nurtured by the actor, over a period of time that could range from minutes to days or months. Violence can also be placed on a force continuum, ranging from minor force that leaves no visible signs of damage to major force the effects of which can involve permanent damage that can be visible for days, weeks or even years.

Violence can be: (a) instrumental, in the service of an end (for example, robbing a store or person, coercing sexual compliance, controlling the behavior of a child), or (b) it can be symbolic (expressing hatred or contempt, restoring damaged self-esteem, or righting what was perceived as a wrong), or (c) it can be both. Violent acts can be one-time events, in a person who is generally non-violent, or it can be part of a (sometimes escalating) pattern in a person who is habitually violent. Most violent acts can be prosecuted, with punishment depending on: (a) degree of conscious intent, (b) the actor's violence history, (c) the motive underlying the act, (d) the severity of the resulting harm, (e) the circumstances that led up to the act, and (f) evolving social mores (for example, disciplining a child with a belt or strap has gone from condoned to condemned in one generation). Although the harm implied in the above definition is mainly physical (ranging from slight pain to serious injury or death), emotional damage to the victim is also a common outcome of violence.

Often a violent act can be viewed as an attempt to achieve some goal, whether or not the actor is fully conscious of that goal. Using child abuse as an example, the use of physical punishment has the implicit goal of bringing about some desired change in the child's behavior (for example, ceasing crying or bedwetting, influencing the child to be better behaved, etc.), but it often has the opposite effect (for example, continuing and even heightening crying or bedwetting, producing very maladaptive child behavior patterns, etc.). Most reputable childrearing experts, for example, emphasize that punishment should be a relatively small part of effective caregiving (which should mainly rely on a skillful combining of praise and ignoring), and physical (that is, violent) correction is virtually never called for. If the social competence outcome of parenting is to be successful in influencing the short- and long-term behavior of children, then parents who are abusive are, almost without exception, miserable failures.

In addition to failing to achieve implicit childrearing goals, violence directed against a child can also bring very undesired consequences for the actor, ranging from loss of employment and assets (for an example see the football player Adrian Peterson who was suspended for a year and lost multimillion dollar product endorsement contracts, after pleading guilty to beating his child with a tree branch), to being universally scorned, to ending up in jail. Almost all human beings would prefer to be employed, well-off, respected, and free from incarceration. To the extent that violence against children jeopardizes one or all of those implicit goals, then the behavior can be considered both foolish and incompetent.

An additional form of incompetence, for which Adrian Peterson again provides an example, is the leaving of very visible signs of the abuse. Whenever committing any crime (and I fully agree that child abuse is a crime) a smart perpetrator takes pains to cover up, and not advertise, their illegal activity. Given that physical punishment of children is commonplace, and widely accepted in the United States (unlike Sweden, where even spanking was outlawed in 1979), if Adrian Peterson had been more restrained and careful in his use of corporal punishment he likely would not have suffered any negative consequences.

Evidence that Peterson did not show restraint can be found in police photos (posted on several websites) of the four-year-old child's wounds. To anyone who might think that this was just a case of corporal punishment but not really abuse, the truly shocking photos will hopefully change his or her mind. Peterson has asserted that he did not intend to cause any injuries, and that using a switch was a mistake. However, the making of visible cuts and scratches on the child's body indicates not only a lack of self-control, but ignorance of child abuse laws and a lack of understanding that such visible signs would possibly draw the attention of police, courts and the NFL.

If there is one truism about violence, it is that violent acts can rarely be attributed to a single cause. Every actor behaves violently for a unique combination of reasons, and even within the same individual, a violent incident can be explained by more than one factor, and violence on one occasion can be explained differently than violence on another occasion. Here are the four explanatory factors in my model; again, I use child abuse—particularly the Adrian Peterson case—as an illustration.

The first explanatory factor, *situation*, reflects the fact that almost every violent act is in response to some situation, although sometimes the situational trigger (such as a victim wearing a shirt in the wrong gang or sports team color) is extremely minimal. In the case of physical child abuse, the situational trigger is typically a child saying or doing something which the abuser finds unacceptable. In the case of Adrian Peterson the incident that triggered his violent reaction was when his son pushed another child off of a video game. Peterson, not understanding that this is very typical four-year-old behavior, saw this as a serious form of misbehavior, and he set out to teach the child "right from wrong." Furthermore, while most of us would agree that it is appropriate to teach a child the importance of taking turns, the majority can think of non-violent ways of getting that point across, even if (as is possible, but unknown to me) this was not the first time the child had exhibited that behavior.

Another *situational* factor that was not present in the Peterson case, but which is found in many other abuse cases, occurs when the perpetrator is pressured or encouraged by another person, such as a spouse. That was the case in a notorious murder trial in which I was peripherally involved as an expert, where a child was fatally abused by his father who acted in part because his wife (the child's stepmother) told him that he needed to act like a man and not allow his daughter's habitual bedwetting to go unpunished.

The second factor, *cognition*, enters in when a foolish actor lacks the knowledge, skills, or understanding of alternative (and legal) methods for solving a childrearing problem. Obviously, Adrian Peterson has a very limited childrearing repertoire, as his default position for dealing with what he sees as defiance from a child appears to be coercive and violent. *Cognition* enters in here also, in his inability to discern risk (a) to the child (it is hard to believe that he could be so unaware that repeated use of a stick by a physically powerful man such as himself could cause serious injuries to a four-year-old), and (b) to his own reputation and career (as the reader knows well by now, risk-unawareness is the core defining feature of what I term "foolish action"). Such behavior can only be termed "stupid," although I am not implying anything about Peterson's general intelligence (smart people often behave stupidly, as so many stories in this book illustrate). However, there is a recent study which shows that less intelligent people are more likely to behave violently, which makes some sense although there are many likely confounds, such as social class.

The third explanatory factor, *personality*, refers to individual differences in temperament, self-regulation, motivation, emotional reactivity, interpersonal style, worldview, and behavior tendencies (all of which can be broken into sub-factors). In terms of child abuse, the most obvious personality contributions are: (a) a tendency to misattribute intentional defiance to child behaviors, (b) a low tolerance of perceived child misbehavior, (c) a preference for physical control techniques, and (d) a pattern of similar acts in the past. In fact, there was at least one earlier credible allegation of physical abuse directed by Peterson involving another of his several children.

The fourth factor—*affect / state*—refers to an imbalance in self-regulation, which impels someone to behave violently or which reduces his or her ability to behave non-violently. Alcohol consumption reduces the ability to resist behaving violently, and it is commonly found that violent acts occur when someone was under the influence of drugs or alcohol. I have seen no evidence that Peterson had been drinking when he assaulted his child with a stick, but it would not surprise me if he had been. An affective factor that is almost always operating in cases of child abuse is anger. Clearly, this was operating with Peterson, as it is inconceivable that he would have assaulted his son so repeatedly and harshly unless he was very angry at him. The most shocking thing about Peterson is that after experiencing so many financial, reputational, and legal hits as a result of the abusive behavior towards his son, he recently admitted to a journalist that he still disciplines his son with a belt (New York Post Staff 2018). It appears, thusly, that he has learned little or nothing about what constitutes child abuse and the risk such behavior opens up to both his child and himself (the NFL announced that they may impose a new suspension as a result of this admission). For Peterson I will relax my usual avoidance of name-calling and assert that he certainly seems to be a fool.

IV

From Foolishness to Wisdom

In *The Count of Monte Cristo*, Alexandre Dumas père (1845–1846) wrote "if it is one's lot to be cast among fools, one must learn about foolishness." In previous sections, I defined foolishness as unwise (that is, risk-oblivious) behavior, and pointed to the widespread use of the term in everyday life but its relative ignoring by scholars. I proposed and explained a four-factor explanatory model (figure 3.1), and demonstrated the utility of the model by analyzing stories of incompetent behavior in three domains (practical, social-noninduced, social-induced) and some applied problem areas. In this concluding section, I use the explanatory framework to address the question "how can foolishness be avoided (and wisdom thus attained?)" preceded by one question of great current interest: "What makes US president Donald Trump a Fool?"

ELEVEN

What Makes Donald Trump a Fool?

> As democracy is perfected, the office of the president represents, more and more closely, the inner soul of the people. On some great and glorious day, the plain folks of the land will reach their heart's desire at last, and the White House will be occupied by a downright fool and complete narcissistic moron.
> —H. L. Mencken, *Baltimore Evening Sun*, July 26, 1920.

As someone who studied history and political science before deciding on psychology, I am struck by how many contemporary political commentators, of all political persuasions (and from many countries), use the terms "fool" and "foolish" to describe the 45th president of the United States and his policies. One, North Korea's President Kim Jong Un, called him a "dotard," a term meaning senile (Ramzy, 2017). If there has been a previous US president called a fool as frequently as Trump, I am not aware of who he might be. Here is a typical example, in an article by historian Walter G. Moss (2016) titled "The Main Problem with Donald Trump: He's a Fool." Moss begins his article as follows: "By calling Donald Trump a fool, I do not wish to engage in mindless name-calling. Borrowing from the Oxford Dictionary, which defines a fool as 'a person who acts unwisely or imprudently,' I merely wish to say that Mr. Trump often demonstrates unwise behavior."

As is typically the case in the scholarly foolishness literature, Moss did not mention relative degree of risk-unawareness (to me the central factor) as the essence of Trump's foolishness. Instead, he focused on Trump's character defects, such as his narcissism and unkindness. In the following sections of this chapter, I elaborate on Trump's foolishness and make the case that it his lack of risk-awareness, rather than (or in combination with) mental illness and deviant personality (especially his fundamental lack of decency), which mainly puts him, the country, and the world at risk.

TRUMP'S EXTREME GULLIBILITY

One of the factors that contributes to success or failure in life and in work is the ability to see through and resist false information or manipulative influence (Greenspan 2009a). Trump seems very lacking in that ability, as pointed out by journalist Jennifer Rubin (2017) when she wrote (in a column titled "Russia's Mark: A Dangerous Fool for a President" that Trump's "gullibility threatens our national security." This gullibility partly explains his becoming a mouthpiece for Russian propaganda, but also some of his many stupid statements, his flip-flopping on positions, and his very many questionable and likely doomed actions. In this section, I explore various aspects of his gullibility and the related concept of credulity. In a later section, I explore those aspects of Trump's personality and cognition that explain, or at least make more understandable, his gullibility and foolish behavior.

CREDULITY TOWARDS MYTHS

Donald Trump is commonly accused of telling untruths. In fact, he is a pathological liar. Those who keep track of his falsehoods in speeches and twitter posts have counted an average of around eight per day. In a survey by Daniel Dale (2018) covering an eighteenth-month period ending in mid-2018, Trump made almost 2,000 misstatements, and the trend indicated that his lying was getting worse. Many claim that he is by far the least truthful president in United States' history. While many of these lies arise wholly out of Trump's imagination, the majority of them are "factoids" (untruths posing as truths) that he finds on alt-right websites or that are brought to his attention by irresponsible journalists, staffers, or acquaintances. A question that remains to be answered is whether Trump then promotes these factoids because he believes them to be true (which makes him gullible), or because he knows them to be untrue but uses them anyway (which makes him deplorable). Probably the truth is somewhere in between, and varies according to the nature, source, and usefulness of the specific falsehood.

Here is one of Trump's many outrageous claims, made when he was running for the 2016 Republican presidential nomination. The story told by Trump during a news interview was that Rafael Cruz, the father of Trump's main primary opponent Ted Cruz, was connected to the 1963 assassination of President John F. Kennedy. Trump asserted (McCaskill 2016) that Rafael Cruz "was with Lee Harvey Oswald prior to Oswald's being—you know, shot ... what is this, right prior to his being shot, and nobody even brings it up. They don't even talk about that. That was reported, and nobody talks about it."

By "reported" Trump meant that it was written up in the supermarket tabloid *National Enquirer* and on the conspiracy website *infowars.com*. It should be noted that both have well-known reputations for making facts up out of whole cloth. The "evidence" cited was a 1963 photo showing a man who looked vaguely like Rafael Cruz standing next to Lee Harvey Oswald, with both of them distributing "Hands Off of Cuba" pamphlets on a street corner in New Orleans. After Trump repeated this claim, various news organizations checked it out and found zero support for any connection between Ted Cruz's father and Oswald. It was labelled a false rumor by *snopes.com*, a website that investigates internet misinformation. A short while later, in an interview on "Meet the Press," Trump was asked about another rumor he obtained from the internet that also turned out to be false. Trump's reply was "all I know is what's on the internet" (Savransky, 2016).

In other words, Trump's position is that anything posted on the internet that he finds interesting is fair game for incorporating into his speeches or tweets, regardless of the dubiousness of the source or the obviousness of red flags. Furthermore, he does not make a distinction between an allegation (whether credible or not) and a fact (as in his asserting categorically that Cruz "was with" Oswald). That Trump relied on *infowars.com* is especially troubling, as that website is owned by the conspiracy theorist Alex Jones, who is reviled for his cruel claims that national tragedies such as the Sandy Hook slaughter of young children (no one was killed according to Jones, and the children shown in photos were actors) either never happened and/or were "false flag ops," that is, inside jobs carried out by government agencies to increase their allegedly despotic power.

One of the more dangerous of Jones' claims, generally known as "pizzagate," involved a conspiracy theory (subsequently also thoroughly debunked) to the effect that the emails of the Democratic National Committee hacked and distributed by WikiLeaks (wikileaks.org) contained coded messages referring to sex trafficking of children. Jones claimed that this criminal scheme operated out of various pizza restaurants around the country, including a DC establishment called Comet Ping Pong (Kang 2016). Numerous death threats were received by its owner and staff, and one highly gullible man showed up shooting off a rifle and demanding to see the basement where *infowars.com* claimed the children were being held. In an earlier interview on a radio station owned by *infowars.com*, Trump started off by telling Jones that "your reputation is amazing. I will not let you down" (Stableford, 2016). A question one could legitimately ask Trump is "reputation for what?"

SUSCEPTIBILITY TO INFLUENCE

One of Trump's biggest problems as president is an inability to take a position and stick to it. Because he has few deep convictions, does not read or understand policy documents, and lacks relevant knowledge and analytic skills, he can take a position one day and then take an opposite position the next day, without seeing or explaining contradictions. The main contributor to these switches is who last happens to get his ear, either in person, through a phone conversation, or from a TV news show. This is one of the main reasons why the former White House Chief of Staff John Kelly attempted to limit casual drop-in access to the Oval Office, as Trump would quickly take an extreme action (such as the aerial bombing of Syria, despite criticism by him of such actions in the past) after his daughter told him about innocent children being gassed by Syrian military planes.

Once a position is taken impulsively and with little planning, deliberation, or inter-agency collaboration, it is often implemented poorly and having little of the intended effect. As example, the initial Muslim immigration ban, overturned quickly by the courts, reflected the then outsized influence of Steve Bannon, and is but one example of Donald Trump's extreme and highly unstable susceptibility to social influence. (An example of how pervasive Trump's gullible acceptance of nonsense continues to be, I am writing this passage just two days after he ordered the U.S. Secretary of State to protest and investigate the killing of white farmers by South African blacks, a long-discredited myth propagated by White Supremacists, but which the President tweeted about just minutes after hearing it mentioned on Fox News).

FAILURE TO UNDERSTAND CONSEQUENCES

What defines a foolish act, and what most marks many of Donald Trump's actions as foolish, is an inability to anticipate or understand the negative social or other consequences of those acts. If one commits the same foolish act over and over again, even after the consequences become clear (and especially if one is warned repeatedly of those consequences by a knowledgeable adviser such as an attorney) then it is safe to conclude that the person is a "fool" in both the vernacular and clinical uses of the term.

There are many examples of Trump's lack of foresight for undesirable consequences. An example that I shall use for deconstruction purposes is his repeated actions that put him and his associates at risk for a charge of obstructing justice by attempting to block the work of the special prosecutor Robert Mueller and his predecessor former FBI Director James Comey. Here I shall use my four-factor explanatory model of foolish action, as these factors (*situation*, *cognition*, *personality*, *state*) working in combination, may shed additional light on Trump's penchant for foolishness. I shall use it now to analyze one of Trump's most foolish acts: his firing of former FBI Director James Comey (the unintended, indirect consequence of which was the appointment of Special Counsel Robert Mueller, who became a vastly greater threat), and then quickly abandoning the ridiculous invented cover story (that Comey was being punished for hijacking Hillary Clinton's campaign). He admitted this in a subsequent TV interview, when he stated that his real motive was to derail the investigation into alleged Russian collusion with Trump's presidential campaign.

Situation: The precipitating event was Comey's refusal to give Trump the loyalty pledge he asked for. To Trump, this was both sinful (according to his Tony Soprano-like moral code) and threatening. He was also egged on by his son-in-law Jared Kushner, who naively thought firing Comey would eliminate his own legal jeopardy. (Kushner's father ended up in a federal prison, a fate he himself greatly wished to avoid). Trump was warned by more mature and sophisticated advisers, but he arrogantly went ahead anyway, and clearly become almost unhinged by the inevitable but unanticipated (by him) consequences.

Cognition: Trump is profoundly ignorant of the law, and thus failed to understand that eliminating someone investigating oneself could itself constitute a crime (later, he took the Justice Department to task on political grounds for prosecuting two Republican Congressmen; a stupider public stance is difficult to imagine). He also lacks any understanding of professional ethics, particularly the core concept of conflict of interest. This explains his puzzlement over why Attorney General Jeff Sessions, had no choice but to recuse himself from any oversight of the Special Counsel or the investigation of Russian collusion, as he himself was a potential witness or target for such an investigation. Trump's lack of social foresight also contributed to admitting to a TV journalist his real motive for firing Comey, namely to kill the Russia collusion inquiry. Trump continued openly for well over a year to fume over Sessions' recusal, repeatedly berating his Attorney General in a most disrespectful manner. As detailed in *Fear*, by Bob Woodward (2018), Trump allegedly called Sessions "mentally retarded" and mocked his southern accent. In this, and many other acts, Trump demonstrated what could only be characterized as supreme failure to demonstrate social appropriateness or recognition of legal risk.

In response to the many who have publicly questioned both Trump's intelligence and his sanity, Donald Trump has referred to himself as a "stable genius" (Gstalter 2018). Hardly anyone today takes seriously Trump's claim of being a genius; to the contrary, the question that many have been asking is "just how severe is Trump's level of cognitive impairment?" The contrary claim by the former White House physician Ronny Jackson that Trump received a perfect score on the Montreal Cognitive

Assessment (MoCA) should be given little weight as it is an unreliable and intentionally easy brief screening test. Furthermore, Jackson—an emergency physician and thus untrained in administering cognitive instruments—was seeking a big promotion (head of the US Department of Veterans Affairs) and certainly knew what Trump's reaction would be if his doctor failed to describe him as brilliant.

An aspect of Trump's *cognition* that is even more disabling than his striking degree of ignorance and possibly defective intelligence, is his obvious deficiency in "executive functioning" (a double entendre in this case). The term refers to processes that have to do with managing oneself and one's resources in seeking to attain complicated goals. It includes a number of neurologically-based (particularly frontal lobe-based) skills, such as self-regulation, planning, attention, prioritizing, short-term memory, cause-effect reasoning, juggling of multiple tasks, filtering of distractions. and self-monitoring of behavior. In looking at this list, it should be evident to most readers that whatever the 45th president's IQ might be, he is unlikely to do well on measures of these neuropsychological processes. Problems in executive functioning are suggestive of a wide range of brain-based disorders, including ADHD (a label likely to be ascribed today to any child who slugged his second-grade music teacher, as Trump admits to having done) and Neurocognitive Disorder (an adult-onset diagnosis which I argue later may be appropriate for Donald Trump).

State: As for Trump's claim of having a stable temperament, that is an even bigger joke, as on almost any day Trump reacts in a wildly emotional manner, that could be characterized somewhere between "emotionally disturbed" and "crazy." Trump's default emotional state is anger, and he expresses anger (usually accompanied by disparaging comments to or about the target of his anger) several times a day. Barbara Res, a high-up executive in Trump's business for eighteen years, up until 1998, has described him as a very angry man (Res 2018) who would get red in the face and scream and shout at employees on a regular basis. In an interview with the *Daily Beast* (Nuzzi 2016), Res stated "as far as the anger is concerned, that's real for sure. He's not faking it." Res told a TV interviewer that Trump seems to be an even angrier person today than when she worked with him in the 1980s and 1990s. Typically, people mellow somewhat as they age, and are able to take more things in stride or express their disappointment more moderately. In the case of Donald Trump, there seems to have been little or no emotional maturation, and his penchant for anger appears to have worsened. That is certainly in line with a diagnosis of a brain-based disorder as emotional lability is a very common symptom of various forms of brain damage (Kim 2016).

Personality: While *state* refers to fluctuating internal forces (affect, exhaustion, lust, etc.) which could influence behavior in a specific situation, *personality* refers to relatively stable individual patterns of thinking, feeling, and behaving. Anger is a *state* domain (in that it can spur someone to do a risky thing such as assault someone) but it also could be a *personality* domain if such a feeling surfaced routinely and with different targets. In such a sense, we could thus conclude that Donald Trump is an angry person as opposed to someone whose anger caused him to engage in a specific foolish act (such as insult Goldstar parents). Several classification systems have been developed to describe and to differentiate the personality of individuals; the two that I shall use to describe Trump's personality are the Five Factor Model (Digman 1990), often referred to as the "Big Five," and the 16 Basic Desires Theory of Steven Reiss (2000), also referred to as the "Reiss Profile." A difference is that the Big Five is a trait model based on broad personal tendencies, while the Reiss Profile (which I prefer, as it is more context sensitive and thus can more easily explain behavior) is a needs model, based on specific personal motivators. Both models have been well validated empirically, but Reiss (a late colleague of mine in the developmental disabilities field) also drew inspiration from 2,500-year-old ideas of Aristotle (whose name in ancient Greek meant "best purpose").

The Big Five *personality* traits are: Openness to Experience, Conscientiousness, Extraversion, Agreeableness, and Neuroticism, represented by the acronym OCEAN. Each of these traits contains variable numbers of sub-factors, which can be a problem in terms of using the model diagnostically, as someone can be positive on some sub-factors and negative on others within the same broad factor. Nevertheless, here is an attempt to use the Big Five to describe Donald Trump.

- *Openness to Experience* refers to appreciation for art, unusual ideas, creativity, novelty, etc. Trump seems pretty low on this domain. For example, while other billionaires are collectors of fine art who generously give money and valuable paintings or sculptures to museums, Trump has not done such things, and his taste in art (gilded Louis quatorze furniture, etc.) is gaudy and conventional. Trump's main form of creativity was understanding how to use Reality TV tactics to be elected and to govern.
- *Conscientiousness* refers to a tendency to be self-disciplined, dependable, reliable, driven, organized, etc. Trump seems to be a mixed bag on this domain, as he has little sense of personal loyalty and is anything but organized (his bedroom, which he resists having cleaned, is reportedly a pigsty) or disciplined, but he obviously has strong drive, which one needs to survive a presidential campaign.
- *Extraversion* refers to a tendency towards talkativeness, attention-seeking, high emotional reactivity, assertiveness, sociability, being often in the company of others, being perceived as domineering, and having high energy. Extraverts are not seen as aloof, reserved, or reflective. Politicians often are described as extraverted, and

Donald Trump is clearly someone who fits that description, as reflected in the fact that when he has free time in the evening, he fills it by calling people to talk.

- *Agreeableness* refers to a tendency to be kind, compassionate, helpful, polite, trusting, respectful, non-competitive, and generally nice. While Donald Trump is able to feign agreeableness, such as when golfing with others, he is a highly disagreeable person, as reflected in his rejection of politeness norms, his lack of empathy (as when he cruelly mocked the speech and movements of a reporter with a disability), and a relative absence of long-term close friendships.

- *Neuroticism* refers to a lack of emotional stability, and a tendency to excitability as reflected in a high frequency of experiencing unpleasant emotions such as anger, anxiety, and depression. Trump is very high on neuroticism, as a lack of emotional stability is one of his chief defining qualities. As an extravert, however, his emotionality is directed outward, through anger and verbal assaults, and he does not appear to have internalizing or self-directed issues such as depression. But he clearly is an overly sensitive, nervous, and insecure person, as reflected in an inability to take criticism in stride without going on the attack.

A recent attempted improvement of the Big Five was developed in the Netherlands, and is termed the HEXACO Model (Lee and Ashton 2004), for the addition of a sixth factor. It also takes a more systematic approach to the problem of sub-factors, including four within each major factor, for a total of twenty-four domains. Keeping four of the OCEAN domains, the HEXACO model has dropped Neuroticism, and added two new traits: Honesty (fairness, humility, greed avoidance) and Emotionality (fearfulness, anxiety, dependence, sentimentality) which emphasizes the internalizing aspects of Neuroticism. In addition, the HEXACO model has an "interstitial factor" termed "altruism," which cuts across several other factors. Trump is clearly very low on Honesty (uttering dozens of lies per week and acting very greedy) and also seems to lack Altruism (as reflected in an almost complete absence of charitable giving). But, as mentioned, he seems to lack internalizing (depression, anxiety) psychopathology, and thus is low on Emotionality as defined in this model, unless one takes a Freudian approach and sees Trump's externalizing behavior as a defense against feelings of anxiety, unworthiness, and low self-esteem.

The Basic Desires theory ("Reiss Profile") consists of a list of sixteen needs on which all adult humans can be differentiated according to how strongly they desire gratification of each need. Here is the list (not necessarily in the usual order), with a brief description and comment on Donald Trump next to each need.

- *Power,* the need to control and dominate others—this is clearly a need that Trump has in spades.

- *Curiosity*, the need to gain knowledge—not important to someone who disputes established science, who gullibly believes anything, and makes decisions based solely on gut feelings
- *Independence*, the need to be autonomous—very important, as Trump routinely ignores advice from lawyers and other advisers.
- *Status* (need to feel significant)—very important throughout his life, as when he was planting stories about himself in New York gossip columns.
- *Social Contact* (need for relationships)—important for Trump, as he constantly works the phones and seems to have a high need to talk to people.
- *Vengeance* (punishment of others perceived as enemies)—this appears to be one of Trump's defining needs and explains the viciousness of his personal attacks on people.
- *Honor* (traditional rule-following)—Trump is not an honorable person. There are many examples of this, two of them being an inability to tell the truth and a history of cheating on his wives.
- *Idealism,* the need for social justice—a less idealistic person would be hard to find. Nor does Trump have any appreciation of social justice.
- *Physical Exercise*—not important to someone whose only exercise is golf, without even the benefit of walking between holes.
- *Romance* (sex)—obviously a high priority for the thrice-married serial philanderer and accused sexual harasser.
- *Family*, the need to take care of one's offspring—a mixed bag for Trump. He employs adult children from his first marriage in his real estate enterprise and in the in the White House, but he never embraced the idea of nurturing young children and does not appear to be close to his extended family.
- *Order,* the need for sameness and inflexible routines—a clear need for someone who flew home almost every night during the 2016 campaign to sleep (and eat cheeseburgers) in his own bed.
- *Eating*, the need for food—important to the borderline obese Trump, but he is far from sophisticated or health-conscious about what he eats.
- *Acceptance*, a need to feel appreciated—Trump has a strong need to tell people (or be told) how wonderful and special he is.
- *Tranquility*, the need to feel secure—not important to someone who creates chaos on a daily basis.
- *Savings*, the need to accumulate possessions—very important to the acquisitive, boastful and greedy chief executive.

PUTTING THE ELEMENTS OF TRUMP'S PERSONALITY TOGETHER

Most people, when being analyzed with the Big Five or the Reiss Profile, fall in the middle on many of the domains, or present a mixed picture, being high on some good qualities and high on some bad qualities. One thing that is striking about Donald Trump is how strongly he is defined by being extremely high on most bad qualities and extremely low on most good qualities. In short, Donald Trump is a cartoon-like caricature of a villain, or to use technical terminology, sociopath. Whether talking about Trump's behavioral traits, or his personal needs, he is extremely consistent in his (usually nasty) responses to things, and as a result his behavior is fairly easy to predict. Thus, when Trump's severe critic John McCain died, many people assumed that Trump would do the usual thing and pretend to be sorry over his passing. I was pretty certain he would be unable to give up his disdain (for McCain criticizing him and defying him on Obamacare repeal), and I was proved correct when he said nothing and (after someone else lowered the flag) ordered the White House flag to be quickly raised again, thus making it the only building in Washington with flags fully raised. He relented later by lowering the flag again and giving a weak statement that started, as usual, with a mention of himself. This occurred only after enormous backlash from veterans groups and his own military staff. This is yet another example of Trump's lack of perspective-taking or risk recognition (not to mention decency). Trump's personality, and other personal qualities detailed above, paint a picture of someone with apparent mental illness. But I argue below that there is more to the story than that.

TRUMP'S FOOLISHNESS IS NOT DUE SOLELY TO MENTAL ILLNESS

On April 20, 2017, exactly three months after the inauguration of Donald Trump as president, a meeting chaired by Yale University psychiatry professor Bandy X. Lee was held in New Haven, Connecticut. Termed the "duty to warn conference" it was later turned into a book titled *The Dangerous Case of Donald Trump: 27 Psychiatrists and Mental Health Experts Assess a President* (B. X. Lee 2017). The focus of the book was on the widespread belief among the contributors (mostly psychiatrists and psychologists along with a few others) that Donald Trump has serious mental health problems and that his serving as president constituted a danger to the country.

The conference was widely perceived as a challenge to the American Psychiatric Association's so-called Goldwater Rule (preventing members of that organization from publicly diagnosing political candidates with whose politics they disagree). It was enacted after many psychiatrists engaged in that heavily criticized practice during the 1964 Presidential election. In fact, although the universal sentiment among the contributors to the Yale conference was that Trump was unfit to be president, only a few authors suggested a specific category of psychopathology that likely applied to him, and they all stopped short of diagnosing Trump and, thus, directly challenging the Goldwater Rule. In fact, a number of the chapters dealt only with the responsibility of mental health professionals to raise an alarm when a president poses a severe danger, and several addressed the legal mechanisms and difficulties of removing a US president under both the impeachment and the 25th Amendment (unfitness) provisions of the Constitution.

The most common diagnosis discussed in the book was Narcissistic Personality Disorder (NPD). As noted by Zimbardo and Sword (2017) NPD involves more than the trait of narcissism (extreme self-centeredness) as one can be narcissistic and still be an effective leader. For example, Steve Jobs was often pointed to as a highly narcissistic person, but he was still capable of operating in a healthy (that is, reality-based) manner. Trump's narcissism, on the other hand, could be characterized as "pathological" (Malkin 2017) in that it drives him to distort and misrepresent reality and to "lie, cheat, steal, betray, and even hurt those closest" to him in order to meet his ever-present need to feel special.

People with NPD, according to Malkin (2017) have three characteristics: (a) a sense of entitlement, requiring others to always bend to one's will, (b) exploitation of others, no matter what the emotional or even physical cost to the others might be, and (c) a lack of empathy or concern for the needs or feelings of others. This absence of empathy explains why the most vicious and disrespectful of utterances are routinely hurled by Trump at those who criticize or oppose him in any way. An example would be his description of Congresswoman Maxine Waters as a "low IQ individual." "Honestly, she's somewhere in the mid-60s, I believe" (Schwartz, 2018). Such a characterization violates norms of decent discourse, but also reveals Trump's pervasive racism, as Ms. Walters is a prominent, African-American politician, and racists often justify their prejudice against minority individuals by disparaging their intelligence.

Unlike Steve Jobs, whose narcissism, as mentioned, did not interfere with his ability to make smart decisions, Trump's more severe narcissism, according to several contributors to the Lee book, has led him to often make very unwise decisions. However, while NPD offered a useful hook for describing and to some extent explaining Trump's dramatic psychopathology, it does not in itself provide a basis for declaring him unfit or for that matter dangerous. That is because NPD qualifies as a character disorder and while Trump's character defects are substantial, few psychiatrists see NPD or for that matter any other character disorder as grounds for automatically characterizing someone as legally incompetent. Nor did more than one or two of the attendees at the Yale conference see Trump as psychotic, that is, possessing an almost total inability to deal with reality (although he sometimes comes close). NPD, or any other character-based mental illness can obviously contribute to a foolish act, within the framework of the four-factor explanatory model (under either "personality" or "state"). But in my opinion, any attempt to argue that a disordered personality (a characterization that can be applied to many politicians or others who generally function adequately) is both dangerous and inappropriate.

TRUMP'S FOOLISHNESS MAY REFLECT
A NEUROCOGNITIVE DISORDER

While there is support for diagnosing Donald Trump with a character disorder (specifically NPD), such a diagnosis by itself is not sufficient, for reasons stated above, to meet the legal or constitutional standard of unfitness. There is, however, one disability category within the *Diagnostic and Statistical manual of Mental Disorders, Version 5* (DSM-5) (American Psychiatric Association 2013) that can co-exist with NPD, and which could justify the determination that Trump is too foolish (that is, lacking in risk-aware judgment) to function safely in the role of President. Amazingly, only one of the contributors to the Lee book (Reiss 2017) mentioned it as a possibility, although others commented on the president's likely cognitive limitations.

Before DSM-5, adult-onset cognitive impairment was termed dementia, but in 2013 it was renamed "neurocognitive disorder" or NCD. In DSM-5, the core symptom of NCD is loss of thinking ability below what was present in childhood or adolescence (where cognition was reputedly normal) and thus has onset in adulthood and represents a decline from earlier levels of functioning. Many people who have known Trump for years, including both Oprah Winfery and Omarosa Manigault Newman, have commented on how dramatically less intelligent and verbally skilled — much more of a diminution than one would expect from normal aging — he appears compared to how he was during his heyday.

In DSM-IV and DSM-IVTR, the emphasis had been on dementia first manifesting during old age (as in Alzheimer's Disease, only one of many possible causes of NCD), while in DSM-5, it is noted that NCD can occur at any point in adulthood. There are many potential causes of NCD, including genetic disorders, traumatic brain injury (TBI), hydrocephalus, strokes, substance abuse, Alzheimer's Disease, prion disease, infections (for example, tertiary syphilis — which one prominent physician has suggested can explain many of Trump's symptoms, including his unusual pattern of hair loss), and other or unknown causes. NCD can take mild or major forms, depending on the number of impairments and the degree to which everyday functioning and independence are affected. In DSM-IV the emphasis was on major forms, while today there is more of a spectrum emphasis (for Major NCD's such as Alzheimer's, cognitive and independent functioning below the 3rd percentile or below IQ of 70-75, for Mild NCD's below the 15th percentile, or IQ of 85–90 or less).

Another difference is that previously the *cognitive* domain receiving the most emphasis was memory loss. While memory loss remains a common indicator of NCD, it is far from the only cognitive sign, and is not an essential one. For mild NCD, one or more areas need to have shown decline (which must be noted not only from test results, but also from observations by relatives or other acquaintances): Memory and Learning, Executive Functioning, Attention, Language, Perception, and Social Cognition (a new area of emphasis, as impaired understanding of people and social consequences is now found especially useful in diagnosing milder forms of NCD such as most TBIs). DSM-5 notes that the cognitive deficits in NCD should not be explainable by another mental disorder, such as schizophrenia (where cognition, including social cognition, is typically impaired, but unlike NCD is not the core feature). Social cognition (also termed social intelligence) has been my main area of research emphasis since the 1970s, and it is notable how impaired Trump seems to be in this domain.

COGNITION EMPHASIZED AS THE CORE IMPAIRMENT IN RISK-BASED UNFITNESS

Within the legal framework of the US Constitution, two involuntary removal options exist: (a) impeachment, generally believed to require commission of a crime, such as obstruction of justice, and (b) being found unfit under Section 4 of the Constitution's 25th amendment (Feerick 1992). A problem with implementing Section 4 is the absence of any clear statement or definition of "fitness" or of the criteria to use in determining if a Presidential unfitness threshold is met. Implicit, however, in Section 4 and in its legislative history (inspired by the coma-state JFK was temporarily in after he was fatally shot in the head), is that a president has been rendered unconscious or seriously diminished in cognitive ability. (For example, George H. W. Bush caused it to be activated when he was scheduled for a colonoscopy when he was to be temporarily rendered unconscious by anesthesia). An easy case for invoking Section 4 would have been the severe stroke suffered by Woodrow Wilson in October 1919, following which his wife secretly governed in his name for the remaining seventeen months of his presidency (Hazelgrove 2016). Donald Trump poses a more subtle case, however, as mental illness (which has been the main candidate for applying Section 4 to him) is an ambiguous and often unreliable concept, especially when (as argued earlier) it is based on a character disorder such as NPD.

In my opinion, the key to understanding Donald Trump's unfitness to serve as president is not solely to be found in his *personality* (cruelty, hypersensitivity to criticism, grandiosity, dishonesty, impulsivity, etc.), deviant and disturbing as it is, but in his largely *cognitive* characteristic of irrationality. By irrationality, I am referring to a failure to base one's actions or beliefs on objective facts or on logical thought processes. In the case of Trump, such irrationality (but one example of which is continuing to insist that his inauguration crowd was bigger than Obama's, despite clear evidence to the contrary) likely reflects brain impairment. In the case of people with brain impairment, irrationality is less dramatic and all-encompassing than would be the case if one were blatantly psychotic (which Trump probably is not), where the detachment from reality or reason is total and immediately obvious to all.

For someone with a broken brain, irrationality is more subtle than in a psychotic state, in that one can be semi-rational about some things but not others. There is, thus, an interaction between Trump's probable NPD (and related *personality* characteristics) and his broken brain (which I argue he also may have), in that deteriorating brain function likely has made his NPD worse. Cambridge University psychology professor Simon Baron-Cohen (2011) has argued that NPD and other "empathy deficit disorders" reflect to some extent abnormal brain pathways), and his NPD likely sheds light on the kinds of *situations* when Trump as President is most likely to go off the deep end. An example is when being called names by a dangerous opponent, such as the sociopathic, nuke-wielding leader of North Korea (sociopathy is another variant of an empathy deficit disorder). Thus, the unfitness of Donald Trump is not just a function of his mental illness, but possibly of brain impairments interacting with his overly sensitive and highly confrontational *personality*. However, even when someone's irrationality is not all-pervasive, a brain-based partial diminution of rationality, in combination with an unstable temperament, is a formula for eventual disaster.

TRUMP'S PAST SUCCESS IS NOT AN ARGUMENT AGAINST LATER FOOLISHNESS

One of the arguments used by supporters to dispute Trump's unfitness is that he must be quite intelligent and otherwise competent to have assembled significant wealth, achieved notoriety and fame as a reality TV star, and attained the most esteemed and powerful elected position in the United States and, arguably, the world. In this view, Trump's foolish behavior is an intentional charade, whose purpose is to activate and retain the support of his political "base" (evangelical Christians naïve enough to believe Trump's dubious claim to have been born again, and poorly educated and unworldly working-class whites, many of them racist or with limited critical thinking skills almost all of them receiving their political information from Fox News and alt-right websites).

There are several points that can be raised to dispute this claim that Trump's accomplishents disprove the possibility that he has impaired intelligence:

a. dementia (time-based diminution of competence reflecting underlying brain changes) may have eroded Trump's competence in recent years;
b. existence of supports from others created a false aura of competence (in every phase of Trump's career, much of what he took credit for was actually done or directed by others, including real estate—where his current wealth mainly accrues from licensing fees arranged by underlings for use of his brand—and in TV shows where his words were largely scripted by writers and producers);
c. non-transferability of competence from one domain to another (there are untold examples of people successful in business or the arts who proved incompetent in public life) is a common phenomenon;
d. evidence that his wealth (which benefited from much early help from his father) is wildly inflated;
e. his graduation from an Ivy League school (with the help of his brother's friend in Penn's admissions office who arranged a transfer from Fordham University into the University of Pennsylvania's non-challenging real estate degree program, where he never achieved distinction) is hardly evidence of brilliance; and
f. he drove several business ventures into bankruptcy through unwise and impulsive investments, surviving afterwards in business mainly through forgiveness by banks and alternate funding by corrupt oligarchs.

Even the great accomplishment of being elected president is diminished by several factors: (a) Hillary Clinton's campaign was incompetently run (as was the case eight years earlier when she blew a big lead to Barack Obama); (b) Bill Clinton's clumsy attempt to influence Attorney General Lynch forced her to turn responsibility for a prosecution decision on Hillary's dangerous email practices over to James Comey, whose improper interference in the last stage of the election was greatly harmful; and (c) massive Russian interference in the election by its hacking and voter-targeting activities, facilitated by cheaters associated with the Trump campaign, all contributed to his unlikely electoral victory.

The argument (once advanced by a friend of mine) that Trump's seemingly foolish behavior is actually a sign of canniness and wisdom is contradicted by the many serious legal and other consequences, outcomes that hardly advanced his interests. All that said, there is no doubt that Trump has showed some skill (and doggedness) in playing to his rabid and unsophisticated base, which is a form of competence more suitable to a professional wrestling ring (where Trump once actually performed a clownish cameo role) than to his subsequent role as leader of the free world.

WHEN DID TRUMP BECOME A FOOL?

Trump's childhood and adolescence, including his college years, are a closely guarded secret. (Trump's former attorney sent a letter to his high school, colleges, and the College Board, threatening legal action if his grades or SAT scores were made public). So, it is difficult to know exactly when and how he became the extreme fool he is today. But there are hints that he was already on the foolishness spectrum as a child and adolescent. According to schoolmates, he was a very disturbing child in elementary school, frequently disrupting class and acting out. In his *Trump: The Art of the Deal*, he stated that he was almost expelled from a private elementary school after he punched his second-grade music teacher (Trump, with Schwartz 1987). When the teacher, Charles Walker, was on his deathbed, he reportedly said this about Trump: "even back then he was a little shit" (Schneider, 2017). His parents exiled him to a military school during high school, and that is often done by affluent families to "straighten out" a young man seemingly on track for delinquency. He speaks of the school to this day fondly and became the captain of cadets, although his authority over other students was removed, as he apparently misused that power. Despite his expressed fondness for the place, he turned down a request for a big donation a few years ago, when the school was in imminent danger of going under.

One cannot blame parents when children turn out badly (an interesting thing to say about someone who became president), but he apparently idolized his father and adopted many of his habits, such as his choice of real estate as a career, his racial prejudices, and a tendency to dominate and control others. Trump's mother was apparently a sweet person, but it is interesting that the president placed a picture only of his father on his Oval Office desk until someone pointed out the strangeness of such an omission. His siblings apparently turned out very differently from him: an older brother who disliked business, became an airline pilot and died young from alcoholism (Trump says he has never tasted alcohol), an older sister who became a federal judge and who (according to a Newark court reporter I met when I testified there) is much revered, and a younger brother and older sister, both apparently normal.

He must not have been much of a student or test taker, as he enrolled in a medium rank college (Fordham) until a family member pulled some strings and got him transferred into Penn. He claimed to graduate at the top of his class, but there is no record that he received any honors, and other students remember him as an undistinguished classmate. He started his work career at his father's successful firm (owning and operating middle-class rental properties in Brooklyn and Queens) until he decided to enter the big time, and struck out on his own in Manhattan real estate (bankrolling a quickly-closed Broadway show on the way). His mentor (whom he met when dealing with a federal lawsuit over racial discrimination in his family's rental properties) was the infamous lawyer Roy Cohen, who encouraged Trump to always be as nasty and combative as possible when defending himself against lawsuits or criticism. I grew up and spent much of my life in the New York area and followed Trump's career from his earliest days, when his local media coverage was a harbinger of what it is nationally today. (If Trump has a spark of genius it is in his talent for self-promotion).

Donald Trump was a fool then, but today he seems an even bigger fool. I would attribute that to two factors: (a) possibly, he has brain impairment (Neurocognitive Disorder), which has reduced his judgment and self-control, while exaggerating his already existing *affective, personality,* and attentional problems, and (b) he has become something of a slave to his base, and the buffoon role they expect and encourage him to play. Unfortunately, the dangers of having a fool in charge of the United States of America are substantial and scary to contemplate.

TWELVE

Some Advice for Surmounting Foolishness

No one can completely avoid behaving foolishly from time to time, but the key to surviving and doing well in the world is to avoid making (and repeating) big mistakes, especially when they are fairly obvious and predictable. This does not require one to avoid all risk, as that would be a formula for boredom and non-accomplishment. Furthermore, there are times when one is justified in taking a risk when a matter of principle or conscience is involved. I did that once when publicly taking on my university Dean, a man who had a pattern of unethical conduct. I did not get fired (being a tenured professor has some advantages) but things were unpleasant for a couple of years, until he was pushed out, and I ended up receiving some belated thanks from less courageous (or less foolish) colleagues.

In this chapter, my intent is to impart some lessons for how foolish risk can be surmounted or avoided. Some of these lessons are taken from news stories, with a few from other sources. These kinds of stories can be accumulated rather quickly, as every day brings at least one news article about a bad outcome stemming from a foolish act. After a summary of each story, I present a brief analysis pointing out some lesson for competence improvement. I also present a few examples of wise (risk-aware) incidents, but these are harder to find in the news, as catastrophic outcomes are the ones that get the most attention.

LESSON #1: LEARN TO KEEP YOUR MOUTH SHUT,
UNLIKE LYNNE STEWART

Knowing I have a big mouth, a mentor of mine, A. J. Pappanikou (one of the people to whom this book is dedicated), often used to share with me this World War II slogan: "loose lips sink ships." There are untold numbers of people who have been done in (or did other people in) inadvertently due to their inability to follow this advice.

Lynne Stewart was a prominent left-wing attorney who took on controversial clients, such as the New York-residing, radical Muslim leader Omar Abdel-Rahman (the so-called Blind Sheikh). Her husband, also an attorney, warned her not to take on that case, figuring that in the aftermath of 9/11 beefed-up government surveillance would require more caution than his headstrong wife possessed. Abdel-Rahman was accused of conspiring to overthrow the government of Egypt, of plotting to assassinate various political leaders and of planning to blow up various New York tunnels and bridges. One of the conditions that Stewart accepted when she became Abdel-Rahman's attorney was that she would not use her attorney immunity from search to convey messages to his supporters. Stewart, who naively saw her client as a progressive hope for Egypt rather than a depraved terrorist (whose group took credit for killing sixty-two people, mostly tourists, in the 1997 Luxor Massacre), violated this condition both by publicly reading a letter from him and by smuggling a message to his supporters (Chadha 2006).

In addition to being disbarred, Stewart was given a relatively modest sentence of twenty-eight months. When heading off to prison, Stewart made a dismissive public statement along the lines of "I can serve two years while standing on my head" (Preston, 2006). The judge responded by saying in that case he would increase the sentence to ten years, figuring such a sentence might be taken more seriously. That tactic worked, as Stewart admitted her foolishness and humbly begged for earlier release. That was granted four years later, but on compassionate grounds, as she then had terminal breast cancer. Stewart, like some of the excellent lawyers I know and work with, had a great deal of passion and feistiness, but learned that it is not a good idea to tick off a Federal judge who (given his great discretion in sentencing) has the power to put one away for the remainder of one's life.

LESSON #2: LEARN THAT YOU MIGHT BE MISINFORMED,
UNLIKE AYN RAND

It is astounding to me that smart people can often be led by their emotions into holding obviously untrue beliefs, without considering for a moment the possibility that those beliefs could be mistaken. One notable example of this came from a speech I attended around 1961 by the famous writer Ayn Rand. Ms. Rand, born in Russia in 1905 as Alisa Rosenbaum, emigrated to the United States in 1925, where she achieved success, and eventual fame, as a Hollywood screenwriter, author of two blockbuster novels (*The Fountainhead*, 1943, and *Atlas Shrugged*, 1957) and inventor of a philosophical system that she named Objectivism. Rand's writings glorified the role of the free and creative individual, in contrast to the collective state and its tendencies towards controlling and conforming totalitarianism. Obviously motivated by her suffering under Soviet Communism (which confiscated her father's successful business and expelled her from film school as a bourgeois), Ms. Rand glorified unfettered capitalism, as reflected in the final scene in *Atlas Shrugged*, in which the book's protagonist, John Galt, traced a dollar sign in the earth. Ms. Rand's portrayal of rich and successful people as an oppressed minority, and unfettered Capitalism as the path to greatest happiness, had obvious resonance to libertarians, such as then Congressman (later House Speaker) Paul Ryan, who used to hand out copies of *Atlas Shrugged* as Christmas presents.

A source of disappointment to Ayn Rand was the fact that her books and ideas were not taken seriously, either as literature or as philosophy, by university-based scholars. It was, therefore, pleasing to her when my good friend Lyman Heine (now deceased) and I invited her to speak at a meeting of a public affairs club that we cochaired at Johns Hopkins University. I was later told by a biographer of Ms. Rand that this event was important to her as a first indication of academic respectability, although in reality, it was not the university that invited her, but just two undergraduates, one of whom (me) barely even knew who she was. The large auditorium in which Ms. Rand spoke was packed (this was at the height of her fame as a novelist) but she received a generally negative response, as reflected in the derisive tone of most of the questions directed at her from the audience. She came across to me (I spent time with her and her entourage both before and after the talk) as a paranoid nut-case, a view supported in an excellent biographical profile by Johann Hari (2009). After the event was over, I asked one very distinguished-looking gentleman how he enjoyed the (free-of-charge) talk and he replied that it was "worth the price of admission."

The thing that most sticks out in my mind about the talk was Rand's insistence that Sputnik (the satellite which in 1957 enabled the Soviet Union to beat the United States in putting such an object [carrying a dog] into a space orbit) was a lie fabricated by the Russians to create the illusion that they actually possessed technological and industrial competence. When asked what evidence she possessed for this extreme claim, her answer was "I know the Russians, and they are incapable of pulling off such a feat." What Ms. Rand apparently did not know is that the Russian space program, as was the United States program, was headed by captured German scientists, as reflected in Soviet leader Nikita Khrushchev's famous boast to John F. Kennedy that "our Nazis and better than your Nazis" (Little, 2018).

While it is clear how a philosophy marked by a rejection of collective responsibility for others (what Rand dismissed as "ethical altruism") would appeal to someone with Paul Ryan's anti-government leanings, there is another, more fundamental similarity between the two individuals. That has to do with a tendency to believe the truth of an assertion without requiring empirical proof or, for that matter, even in the face of considerable evidence contradicting the assertion. In the case of Ayn Rand, there is the example of her unshakable belief that the Soviets were lying about Sputnik, in spite of the ease with which she could have solicited reliable information from trustworthy experts who would have informed her that her belief was false. In the case of Congressman Ryan, there was his belief that cutting income taxes, especially for the rich, is the path to balancing the Federal budget, in spite of the fact that on the several occasions when that policy has been followed, it has had exactly the opposite effect.

However smart one is (and Rand obviously had a high IQ, as clearly also is true of Ryan), a failure to acknowledge obvious reality is a form of stupidity. The driving force here obviously is *affect*, namely the holding of emotionally charged beliefs that are articles of quasi-religious faith and that are so strong that they cannot be questioned. In the case of Ayn Rand, the emotionally-charged belief that could not be questioned was that the Russians were lying incompetents, while in the case of Congressman Ryan, the emotionally charged belief that cannot be questioned was that taxes are bad and cutting them is always good. In the face of such rigidly held beliefs, even the smartest among us will stubbornly hold onto positions that can only be described as foolish.

Years after the lecture (see Mayhew 2005), Ms. Rand finally came to accept the truth that Sputnik had in fact orbited the earth. However, in line with the theory of cognitive dissonance (which describes the maneuvers we use to make an inconvenient fact jibe with a deeply held belief), she explained that while a totalitarian state cannot do good science, it is capable of stealing good science from scientists in free countries. Not admitting that the science behind the Russian space program was developed by captured Germans (because Nazi Germany was also a totalitarian state), Rand made the (to my knowledge untrue) assertion that the Russian space program was stolen from the United States. The lesson from this story is that truth is truth regardless of how it makes one feel, and that twisting the facts to make them fit with one's values is not a smart thing to do.

LESSON #3: LEARN TO LET ANTIPATHY GO, LIKE WALT WHITMAN

One of the hallmarks of a mature and mentally healthy person is an ability to decide when and where they will respond to provocation or disappointment. Here is a century-old description of an eminently mature person by the Canadian psychiatrist William Bucke (1901) in his book *Cosmic Consciousness.* This description was cited just a year later by William James (1902) in a chapter on the "the religion of healthy-mindedness" in his *The Varieties of Religious Experience.* The person who Bucke and James so honored was the great US poet and humanist Walt Whitman (1819-1892). Here is how Whitman was described by Bucke, as quoted by James:

> Perhaps no man who ever lived liked so many things and disliked so few as Walt Whitman. All natural objects seemed to have a charm for him. All sights and sounds seemed to please him. He appeared to like (and I believe he did like) all the men, women and children he saw . . . [and] each who knew him felt that he liked him or her, and that he liked others also. I never knew him to argue or dispute, and he never spoke about money. He always justified . . . those who spoke harshly of himself or his writings, and I even thought he took pleasure in the opposition of enemies. When I first knew him I used to think that he watched himself, and would not allow his tongue to give expression to fretfulness, antipathy, complaint and remonstrance. It did not occur to me to be possible that these mental states could be absent in him. After long observation, however, I satisfied myself that such absence or unconsciousness was entirely real. He never spoke deprecatingly of any nationality or class of men, or time in the world's history, or against any trades or occupations—not even against any animals, insects or inanimate things, nor any of the laws of nature, nor any of the results of those laws, such as illness, deformity and death. He never complained or grumbled either at the weather, pain, illness or anything else. He never swore. He could not very well, since he never spoke in anger and apparently never was angry. He never exhibited fear, and I do not believe he ever felt it (Bucke 1901, as quoted in James, 1902, 82).

Anger is a feeling that most people assume is caused by an event (being victimized or treated unfairly, experiencing a bitter disappointment, etc.), but truly evolved people do not experience much if any anger, or any other strong negative feeling (such as depression) for that matter. It is not a matter of suppression (as Bucke once suspected) but rather of having a philosophical view of the world which does not assume that one's needs are always to be met, that other people must behave as we would like them to, or that someone who opposes us is evil. Such insights can occur while in a mystical *state* (as Bucke, a hero of the psychedelic crowd, suspected happened to Whitman) but it can be trained through immersion in Skeptical philosophy or its offshoots, such as Rational-Emotive

Therapy (RET) and Cognitive-Behavioral Therapy (CBT). Before I attended some lectures by Albert Ellis—founder of RET—I was a walking basket case, while today there is little that can upset me. Undoubtedly, some of my emotional evolution is due to normal aging, but I think mostly it reflects the *affect* reframing techniques taught by Ellis.

Much foolishness is driven by strong emotion that overrides judgment, with anger probably at the head of the list. One reason so many describe Donald Trump as both immature and mentally ill is that he is always angry about something and this anger often pushes him to say and do foolish things. Social effectiveness requires us to pick and choose when and how we react to other people. Learning to ignore some things is an absolute requirement, if one is not to be an emotional prisoner of events or of other people.

LESSON #4: LEARN FROM EXPERIENCE, LIKE KING LEAR

As stated in the first chapter, foolishness has been a frequent topic for writers of fiction. William Shakespeare frequently explored the comic or tragic consequences accruing from foolish decisions, and nowhere was this theme explored more fully than in *King Lear*, first performed in 1606. The following highly simplified treatment of foolishness in Shakespeare's great tragedy owes much to the paper "'Reason in Madness': The Wisdom in Folly in the New Testament and *King Lear*," by Kim Paffenroth (2004).

The basic story goes as follows. Lear was a medieval king of Britain who felt he was getting too old to continue ruling and decided to retire by dividing his kingdom up among his three daughters. Two of them, Goneril and Regan, were evil and duplicitous, while the third and youngest, Cordelia, was good and lacking in guile. Before dividing up his kingdom, Lear held an event where he asked his daughters to first show that they deserved his generosity by proclaiming their love for him publicly. Goneril and Regan disguised their true feelings by directing one flattering lie after another to their gullible and narcissistic dad. This exercise reminds me of the event on June 12, 2017, when Donald Trump prompted his Cabinet secretaries to declare their regard for him, and with one exception (Defense Secretary James Mattis) they all responded by telling the narcissistic president just how wonderful he was.

When it was the turn of Lear's youngest and truly loving daughter, she basically replied that her father should know how she felt about him and she refused to play this game. This was naïve on Cordelia's part (assuming she wanted her inheritance) and triggered a foolish reaction from the King, as he angrily announced that he was cutting her out of her inheritance, and would split her share up among her two sisters. The rest of the play is a dawning realization by Lear, helped by feedback from a few others (especially the king's "wise fool"), who tell him how stupidly and unjustly he had handled that situation. Eventually, Lear achieved wisdom on his own (helped by duplicitous action by Goneril and Regan, when they cut off promised support and lodging) and he tried to make it up to the grievously wronged Cordelia, who ended up betrothed to the King of France, who greatly admired her for her honesty and character.

While Shakespeare's play is often seen as uniformly grim, it also has a hopeful message, as Lear did change and learn from his foolishness. On a practical level, Lear learned the related lessons that betrayal is an ever-present possibility and that one should always take care to protect one-self from that possibility. On a transformational level, the king acquired insight into his neurotic need for flattery, the role emotion played in driving him to act foolishly, and the superficiality of being so dependent on the blandishments of power. Lear also acquired an understanding of his own selfishness, and developed the beginnings of empathy for others who suffer indignities and privations such as those he caused or experienced.

The lesson of this story for wisdom acquisition is that experiencing the consequences of a foolish act, especially with interpretive guidance from one or more friends, can help someone to acquire greater insight and wisdom. Positive *personality* transformation usually occurs incrementally (as in older people becoming more accepting of their offspring's divergent lifestyle choices) but sometimes one can achieve profound insights, such as from a mystical experience, and change fundamentally as a result.

LESSON #5: LEARN TO REJECT BAD ADVICE, LIKE EISENHOWER

When I was an undergraduate at Johns Hopkins University in the late 1950s, the university's president was Milton Eisenhower, whose older brother Dwight was then president of the United States. Influenced by the media, I considered "Ike" to have ordinary intelligence, because his performances at press conferences were inelegant and characterized by tortured syntax. Milton defended his brother, by saying that while he was not an intellectual in the academic sense, he possessed more "common sense" than any man he had ever known.

At the time, I considered Milton Eisenhower's characterization of his brother a strange form of praise, as I valued book learning and verbal facility above all else. Today, on the other hand, I consider such a statement to be a high form of praise, especially when it causes a leader to avoid the kinds of catastrophic mistakes that were committed by several of Eisenhower's more verbally facile successors: Kennedy in the Bay of Pigs and the escalation in Vietnam; Johnson and Nixon in getting us even more deeply mired in Vietnam. In contrast, Eisenhower made an explicit decision not to get seriously involved in Vietnam, as when he turned down a desperate plea from the French to help with their losing cause (Ambrose 1990). He reasoned that it would be folly for the United States to become directly involved in a ground war in Asia, especially after he extricated the country from the Korea quagmire he inherited from Harry Truman.

In short, Eisenhower's common sense (which in my taxonomy is better described as wisdom) translated into his ability, flowing from deep experience in matters military, logistical, and organizational, to make correct decisions under conditions of uncertainty, emotion, social pressure and danger. In short, Eisenhower's wisdom contributed to his understanding of risk and when to avoid it, and this quality is what causes him today to be viewed as one of the wisest and most effective leaders that the United States produced in the twentieth century.

The history of the United States and other countries, and of countless business CEOs, has been replete, however, with examples of leaders (George W. Bush in invading Iraq, Gerald Levin in merging Time-Warner with AOL) who graduated from prestigious colleges (Bush from Yale and Harvard; Levin from Haverford and Penn) but who lacked the sense to know when to say "no" to what turned out to be a very bad idea.

I would describe a wise leader as someone who can perceive hidden and subtle risk for the organization (or country) that is not obvious to many if not most leaders. In contrast, I would describe a foolish leader as someone who demonstrates a failure to give obvious risk the weight it deserves. Leaders of organizations, including nations, are paid to be "deciders" (to use George W. Bush's term) but their best decisions often involve having the sense to stand pat. The survival of an organization, as well as of a person, often rests on the ability to recognize and avoid both obvious and non-obvious risk. This is an aspect of leadership that typically receives little attention, but it may be that one of best things a leader could say about their tenure is "I recognized risks that could have jeopardized the organization's survival and I avoided them."

LESSON #6: LEARN TO BE RATIONAL, UNLIKE NIXON AND CLINTON

A foolish act can often be described as irrational, in that the risks are both obvious and serious, and the potential benefit to the actor pales in comparison to what they stand to lose if and when the foolish act backfires. An example can be found in the Watergate incident which imperiled (and ultimately ended) the presidency of Richard Nixon. He was widely considered a shoe-in for re-election in 1972, an assessment borne out by the fact that his subsequent victory was the biggest landslide in US political history. He jeapordized that, however, when a few months before the election, burglars tied to his re-election committee (one of them on its payroll) were arrested while engaged in a failed attempt to wiretap the Democratic National Committee's headquarters in the Watergate office complex. As if that was not dumb enough, Nixon subsequently led an illegal effort to obstruct justice (captured on a taping system that he himself had installed) by ordering hush money payments from campaign funds to the captured burglars, and by his attempt to get the FBI to abandon its investigation of the Watergate break-in. When the whole scheme unraveled, several of Nixon's top associates (including Attorney General John Mitchell) went to prison, and only Nixon's resignation (to head off impeachment) followed by a presidential pardon from his successor, kept Nixon from being prosecuted. So one can ask why Nixon (a man widely considered one of the brightest people ever to serve as president) engaged in such blatantly stupid acts? He was probably driven by deep-seated paranoia and by a lifetime of successful cheating, especially in electoral matters, that was a core part of his *personality* (Weiner 2015).

As mentioned, the term "irrationality" is often used to describe behavior that makes little or no sense. The link between irrationality, intelligence, and foolishness was explored in a September 16, 2016 essay in the *New York Times*. The authors of that essay, David Z. Hambrick and Alexander P. Burgoyne, made an interesting distinction between intelligence and rationality. Drawing mainly on the work of noted cognitive psychologist Keith Stanovich (Hambrick and Burgoyne 2016), they referred to "dysrationalia" (a term coined decades earlier by Stanovich 1994; 1999) as the failure of people with average or above-average intelligence (as measured by IQ) to apply their intelligence adequately in addressing real-world problems.

An example (termed the "Linda Problem") used by Hambrick and Burgoyne (2016) was drawn from work in behavioral economics, and involved the following scenario "Linda is 31 years old, single, outspoken and very bright. She majored in philosophy. As a student, she was deeply concerned with issues of discrimination and social justice, and also participated in antinuclear demonstrations." Then the researchers asked the subjects which was more probable: (a) Linda is a bank teller or (b) Linda is a bank teller and is active in the feminist movement.

The correct answer is (a), because feminist bank tellers are included in the larger total class of tellers and it is possible that some non-feminist tellers will also be concerned about discrimination and social justice. But a very large percentage of respondents, including students at elite colleges, fell for the logical illusion created by the conjunction of feminism and social justice, and answered (b). Hambrick and Burgoyne (2016) used this finding to make the point that having a high IQ does not ensure that one has a high "rationality quotient," as reflected in the fact that even smart people demonstrate *cognitive* biases that undermine their ability to make rational real-world decisions.

The fact that smart people sometimes behave stupidly is, of course, not exactly news (in fact, it is the main topic of this book). In his edited book *Why Smart People Can Be So Stupid*, Robert Sternberg (2002a) (like Stanovich, also a noted cognitive psychologist) used the example of Bill Clinton's disastrous Oval Office dalliance with college intern Monica Lewinsky to illustrate the phenomenon of irrational conduct (although Sternberg preferred the term "foolishness" to the term irrationality) (2002b). Sternberg and other contributors to his book, operated—like the authors cited earlier—within a largely cognitive (but even if beyond IQ) framework, by attributing to smart-stupid people an absence of what Sternberg termed "tacit knowledge." That term reflects the fact that in most social settings there are certain keys to success that are not explicitly taught, but which when not followed are likely to lead to failure. An example often used by Sternberg is about an assistant professor at a research university who was denied tenure for failure to publish sufficiently, but then complained that "nobody told me that publishing a lot is so important for obtaining tenure here" (2002b). She was not given that information by the institution, because research universities want to protect an important secret, namely that teaching excellence in the very top schools is a low priority, and because it is assumed that anyone smart enough to land a job at an elite university should be smart enough to figure out what is required to stay there.

However, applying the tacit knowledge explanation to Clinton-Lewinsky was problematic for Sternberg and his colleague Richard Wagner, for the simple reason that a worldly and very savvy person like Bill Clinton would surely possess the tacit knowledge that an office affair with an intern was a very politically risky activity. So, they came up with a supplementary *personality* explanation for Clinton's foolishness, namely profound arrogance and a sense of immunity, stemming from past success in getting away with sexual misconduct. By thus bringing a *personality* factor into their explanation of foolishness/irrationality, Sternberg and Wagner acknowledged that a purely *cognitive* approach to foolish irrational behavior is not always sufficient. However, they can be faulted for omitting two other important causal elements: *situation* (Monica flirtatiously snapping her thong at Bill) and biological *state* disequilibrium (Clinton's likely horniness, coupled with chronic sleep-deprivation) (see Sternberg, Wagner, and Okagaki 1993).

The basic problem with equating irrationality with failure to solve logic illusions is that in most settings (including economics, where the term seems most widely used) rationality has to do less with inefficient thought and more to do with behavior in line with or contrary to self-interest. It is understandable that economists, who for the most part study decisions of relatively trivial importance (such as buying house A as opposed to house B), would over-value the contribution of logical efficiency to rationality, as a smart home, or any other large purchase clearly would benefit substantially from financial acumen. However, even there, *affect* should be factored in, as falling in love with a house is more important than cost or investment potential for many home buyers (such as myself). In fact, the main contribution that behavioral economics (essentially the merging of economics and psychology) has made to economic theory, is the correction of the classical economic assumption that individuals always make financial decisions based on reasoned self-interest.

When rationality is applied in non-economic contexts, however, the limitations of equating irrationality with deficient thought processes becomes even more obvious. Here an example from Stanovich's (1994; 1999) early writings about dysrationalia can be illustrative. He wrote about two Holocaust-denying school teachers in Illinois who defied the state's curricular mandate to teach about the Shoah, when they sent out 6,000 letters (presumably one for each 1,000 mythical murdered Jews) telling parents in their school district why they felt unable to teach about an event they firmly believed had never happened. As a consequence, the teachers were fired from their jobs, a highly predictable outcome but one which the two clueless individuals apparently never anticipated.

The teachers' behavior was irrational, not so much because it showed a lack of formal logic (which may have contributed to their mistaken reading of history) but because it showed a lack of social risk-awareness (the risk of being insubordinate to their employers, and the risk of offending taxpayers in a state with many Holocaust victims and their relatives). The irrationality of their behavior was, in that case, driven mainly by emotion (deeply-held political beliefs), which derailed their (likely limited) ability to reflect on social reality. In his original writings about dysrationalia, Stanovich described the condition as an "intuition pump," a term earlier coined by Daniel Dennett (2013), by which he meant that the inability to use one's intelligence in the real-world is affected by the presence of strongly interfering *personality* or *state* factors such as emotion and impulsivity. In a very limited sense, logical illusions such as the Linda problem can be considered analogous (in that they trigger heuristic associations that substitute for thinking) to emotion-driven impulsivity, but non-economic irrationality (such as in the Illinois example) usually reflects much stronger non-cognitive influences.

Rationality is one of those constructs that is widely used in everyday parlance, and in various professional contexts besides economics (for example, philosophy, psychology, legal theory), but which has never really been adequately defined. In most contexts (including, for the most part, economics), rationality refers to smart action (and irrationality to stupid action) rather than efficient or inefficient thinking processes. The latter may, obviously, contribute to smart/stupid behavior, but it is a mistake, in my opinion, to conflate the two and imply (as Hambrick and Burgoyne

[2016] appeared to do) that rationality is nothing more than non-IQ aspects of *cognition*.

In criminal law (where I have been functioning as a psychological consultant for years), irrationality refers to criminal behavior where the actor fails to reflect on the likely physical or social consequences of his or her behavior. In fact, on June 20, 2002, in the US Supreme Court decision in *Atkins vs. Virginia* which abolished execution of people with Intellectual Disability (ID), Justice John Paul Stevens wrote that the impaired rationality of people with ID causes them to partially lack *mens rea* (criminal intent). The definition of a crime, in British and US jurisprudence, is based on conscious intent coupled with understanding of likely consequences. The essence of legal irrationality, therefore, is found in action which at least partially reflects a lack of risk awareness (in this case, risk to the interests of the victim). As noted repeatedly in this book, I define foolishness as action which reveals a relative absence of risk-awareness. Within the criminal justice field, therefore, irrationality is another word for foolishness.

The basic mistake made by Hambrick and Burgoyne (2016) was in confusing rationality with reasoning. Poor reasoning involves faulty thinking while irrationality involves clueless behavior. How many of the Princeton or Stanford students who flunked the Linda problem would be likely to do anything as stupid as sending out a signed letter denying the Holocaust, even if they held such a factually incorrect belief? Zero, or close to it, in my opinion. Dumb behavior by smart people is a topic deserving of attention, but defining dumb behavior as poor performance on tricky tests of formal logic is not likely to add much to the understanding of that phenomenon.

LESSON #7: LEARN ONE'S LIMITATIONS, UNLIKE DISTRESSED HIKERS

I am writing these words in early September 2018 in New York's Adirondack Mountains, while at a summer compound that has been in my wife Helen's family for over a century. One day, she returned from a moderately strenuous hike with Susan (her visiting climbing buddy from Colorado) up Gothic Mountain and told a story of running into a couple of fifty-ish women who were having a seriously hard time. One of them had a gimpy knee and was barely able to walk. They had started their (non-technical but steep and scrambly) climb too late the day before and got to the peak when dusk was setting in. Wisely deciding against heading down in the dark, they ended up spending the night on the top, without sleeping bags or minimal essentials for overnight camping.

Fortunately, the weather was relatively mild, but it was a little chilly and they suffered considerably. When Helen and her friend ran into them, they were all beaten up from having taken a wrong turn and bush-whacked for quite a distance through rough and brambly downhill terrain (more experienced hikers would have quickly recognized their mistake and turned around rather than kept on going). They had run out of food and water and were hungry and thirsty. They had what normally would have been an hour (at their rate, more like three or four hours) more downhill to go, and then about a two or three mile walk on a dirt road to get to their car. Giving them water and snacks, and taking one of the packs, Helen and Susan headed down and when able used a phone to arrange for a ride when they reached the road. The story ended up having a happy (or at least non-tragic) ending, but it could have been worse had the women not been fortunate enough to run into compassionate and knowledgeable strangers.

In the Adirondacks, death when hiking in warm months is infrequent, but people sometimes end up coming close. The same day that this event happened, I read a web story about two solo hikers who became separately lost on Longs Peak, a very popular but potentially dangerous 14,259 foot mountain in the Colorado Rockies (where Helen and Susan typically hike). One of the hikers, sixty-year-old Jens "Jay" Lambert, had become lost and was eventually found dead after a few nights on the mountain (where evenings can become quite cold that time of year), while the other, a woman, was found injured from a fall (while searchers were looking for Lambert) and had to be airlifted to a hospital (Lotus 2018). Amazingly, Mr. Lambert, an Illinois resident who loved coming to Colorado, had become lost when hiking in the same general area in 2014. At that time, he was found by searchers who traced his cell signal after he called his family to say he was okay but had gotten lost in a fog. When found, Mr. Lambert was surprised to find out he was on Longs, as he thought he was on neighboring Mount Meeker.

It is understandable and laudable that people seek exercise and adventure in the mountains, but it is not smart from a survival standpoint (or an ethical standpoint, as searches put others at risk) to do so in a slapdash manner that lacks adequate preparation, maps, nourishment, equipment, risk-awareness, and backup plans, such as giving others precise information about routes and timetables (shades of Chris McCandless). Hiking alone, as in the two Colorado incidents, is especially foolhardy (the more damaged of the two distressed Adirondack hikers would have been in much greater jeopardy if she had attempted such a thing). Most critically, it is important to be honest with yourself about your capabilities and the possibility that one could be taking on too big a challenge. It is not coincidental that all of the people described above were at an age (forties and fifties) where stamina, flexibility, and strength start to decline, but where one is still young enough that this reality may not yet have fully sunk in. When one suffers a near-catastrophic experience in the wilderness, most people acquire the wisdom to be more cautious in the future. Repeating the same mistake, this time with a tragic consequence, has to be counted not just as the product of bad luck, but of defective *cognition*, combined with an obstinate *personality*.

Parenthetically, the story of incompetent hikers who overestimated their ability to cope in the wild can be considered a variant of the "Dunning Kruger effect." This phenomenon has achieved some currency due to its use by Vicky Ward (2019) in her book "Kushner, Inc." to explain how a young man with zero background in foreign affairs became convinced of his ability to single-handedly solve the intractable Arab-Israeli conflict. The effect, proposed by two social psychologists—David Dunning and Justin Kruger--is based on the simple idea that if you are too dumb to know how to solve a problem, you are also likely too dumb to recognize how incompetent you really are. For a chuckle, listen to the "Dunning Kruger song," an aria in the spoof "Incompetence Opera" (https://www.youtube.com/watch?v=BdnH19KsVVc) presented to honor Dunning and Kruger for winning the "Ig Nobel Prize" for improbable research.

LESSON #8: LEARN TO KEEP IT IN YOUR PANTS, UNLIKE WEINSTEIN AND C.K.

Foolish acts take many forms, but the most common form may be a scenario in which a strong desire conflicts with a reason to be cautious, and the desire wins out, facilitated by an over-confident determination that the reason to be cautious (the risk, in this book's terminology) is not something worth worrying about. Often this dismissive determination reflects the fact that the person has run such a risk numerous times in the past and nothing bad happened.

Certainly, such a scenario seems to describe the dynamic in the previous story (distressed hikers), when the two women (who probably had muddled through other poorly prepared hikes in the past) had plenty of reason to abort their hike early on when impending darkness and their obvious lack of fitness or preparation should have been evident. But their strong reluctance to alter their plan (or even turn around when they lost the trail) created a challenging situation they were ill-equipped to deal with.

This may seem a strange lead-in to men who behave badly, but the same dynamic applies in that a strong desire (in this case, sexual gratification) motivates a behavior with both legal (in the case of sexual coercion) or career (in the case of sexual harassment) risks that could be very serious, but that are dismissed at the time, likely because the offender has gotten away with similar behavior many (or at least a few) times in the past. Two famous men who exemplified this pattern are the movie executive Harvey Weinstein (Kantor and Twohey 2017) and the comedian

Louis C.K. (Jones 2017), the former for harassing women (including by exposing himself) and allegedly committing rape, the latter for pressuring women to watch him masturbate. At the time of this writing Weinstein is disputing the claims (some of them criminal), while Louis C.K. quickly admitted to the allegations (none of them criminal). Both men have suffered enormous career consequences, in the case of Weinstein probably permanently, in the case of C.K. possibly temporarily. In either case, the accused behavior turned out to have serious unwanted consequences, and can in hindsight be termed profoundly foolish.

Sex, either of the old-fashioned ("Hollywood casting couch") or sick (Weinstein and C.K. exhibitionist) variety, has always been a big motivator of bad behavior, especially among higher-status men. However, the "#MeToo Movement," which came to fullest fruition in 2017, has encouraged sexual harassment victims (mostly, but not exclusively, females) to speak out against harassment, and this changed environment has made things much more dangerous for serial harassers such as Weinstein, C.K. (stands for Szkeley but sounds like sick and also shmeckele) and others. The other environmental change, of course, is that in the age of texting, Facebook, Twitter, Instagram, and Snapchat, any accusation against a famous person, even from a relatively unknown accuser, can become big news literally overnight. Obviously, this has potential for abuse (behaving in a sexually boorish manner does not automatically make one the moral equivalent of Harvey Weinstein) but in an age when private behavior has the potential of easily becoming public, it seems advisable when in doubt to keep one's private parts private.

LESSON #9: ACQUIRE SOME SOCIAL FORESIGHT, UNLIKE JAMES WATSON

James Watson is an American molecular biologist and geneticist who in 1962 was the cowinner of the Nobel Prize in Physiology and Medicine along with Francis Crick and Maurice Wilkins for discovering the double helix structure of DNA when Watson was a twenty-five-year-old postdoctoral researcher at the University of Cambridge's Cavendish laboratory in England. Several prestigious positions followed, including a professorship at Harvard University, directorship (later chancellorship) of the acclaimed Cold Spring Harbor National Laboratory, and chairmanship of the path-breaking Human Genome Project at the National Institutes of Health, plus many honors. All of this was put in jeopardy in 2007 after Watson made highly controversial public comments in a magazine interview about what he believed to be the genetic inferiority of blacks (Belluz 2019).

Even though Watson (a person with otherwise progressive political views) made what seemed a sincere apology, he was forced to resign his position as Chancellor of the Cold Springs Harbor Lab (although he kept the title Chancellor Emeritus and was allowed to keep an office) and was fired from a number of lucrative corporate board memberships. Complaining about the consequences, both financial and social (shunning by former friends), that flowed from his offensive statements, Watson, always interested in money, even resorted to auctioning off his Nobel Prize medal for $4 million, to make up for lost revenue.

Given the disastrous consequences that followed Watson's 2007 racist remarks, one would have thought that he would come to exercise greater prudence and discretion if the topic of race ever came up again. But when he was interviewed four times in 2018 for a PBS documentary "Decoding Watson" (which aired in January 2019), Watson repeated his claims, even more forcefully, about the genetic inferiority of Black people. This time the consequences were even greater. For example, the Cold Spring Lab, which had just a few months earlier celebrated Watson's ninetieth birthday, removed his honorary title of Chancellor Emeritus and cut off any further ties with him, and Ireland's University College Cork, which had honored him as recently as 2016 by naming a medical building after him (his maternal grandmother emigrated from Ireland) ordered his name taken down from the building.

This tragic story of Watson's fall from almost mythic status to shunned outcast likely has several explanations including his advanced age and the possibility (which I doubt) that he basically did not care what happened. Watson has always been a bit of a loose cannon who says what he thinks (for example, highly offensive generalizations about women, the Irish, colleagues, etc.) often in a very indiscreet fashion. There is a naïve, almost Aspergerish, quality to these utterances, showing a lack of sophisticated thinking, accompanied by a certain arrogance in thinking he is completely correct in his opinions. But I have to think that this tendency is exacerbated by an absence of tacit knowledge about how offensive such comments are likely to be experienced, especially given changes in societal norms about race, gender, and other matters now affected by political correctness strictures.

Watson's *cognitive* failings go beyond a failure to anticipate social condemnation and also includes the holding of very unsophisticated beliefs about race and other matters in the first place. The assumption is that he is a genius but he would be the first to admit that his intellect was never first tier (and nowhere near that of Crick), and that his main skill was his single-minded focus and willingness to accept help from others who he knew to be smarter. But even if he were a genius in the narrow field of molecular biology, that does not mean that he knows what he is talking about when he ventures into other fields or subjects.

As with most examples of foolishness, *affect* played an important role here, and that had to do with Watson's obsessive need to believe that genes explain not only human biology but also human psychology. But he appears to know little or nothing about human psychology, including intelligence, the focus of his claims about Black inferiority. An important fact that came out in the 2019 documentary is that Watson and his wife have an adult son with schizophrenia, and Watson would obviously prefer to think that is due to nature rather than nurture. But there are many biological factors, other than genes, that contribute to schizophrenia, including prenatal infections (for example, cytomegalovirus) and postnatal brain injuries (my brother was dropped on his head only two days after birth, which according to some research could explain why a few years later he was given the label "childhood schizophrenia," a category which subsequently morphed into autism).

The *affective* obsession that Watson has with regard to the importance of genes clouded his judgment not only about human development, but also about how his comments would be received. Had he been able to exercise some self-control and shown greater social foresight, it is likely James Watson would still be considered a great citizen of the United States and he also would have a more substantial bank balance.

LESSON #10: LEARN TO BE SKEPTICAL, UNLIKE GEORGE SCHULTZ

George Schultz is a ninety-eight-year-old economist who was a great public servant, serving his country in four different cabinet positions (including Treasury and State) under two different presidents (Nixon and Reagan). He is also credited with playing a central role in bringing about detente between the United States and the then Soviet Union. Upon retiring from government service (and a stint as chairman of the giant Bechtel Corporation), Schultz became a Fellow of Stanford University's Hoover Institution, and served on a number of corporate boards. One of those boards was the Theranos Corporation, founded in 2003 by a nineteen-year-old named Elizabeth Holmes who dropped out of Stanford University during her Freshman year to pursue an entrepreneurial dream. That dream involved developing a small machine that could do reliable blood screening with immediate results using only a drop or two (1,000th the usual amount) of blood from a finger stick, and at a fraction of the usual cost.

Acting as the CEO, and with the help of her older COO boyfriend Ramesh "Sunny" Balwani, Ms. Holmes in ten years raised over $700 million in venture capital funds, signed a valuable contract with Walgreen's to have her machines in its stores, and achieved a corporate valuation of over $9 billion and a personal paper wealth of over $4 billion. George Schultz, who took a grandfatherly interest in Ms. Holmes, played an important role in the company's success, by serving on its board and by recruiting from the Hoover Institution a Who's Who of the US rich and powerful, including Henry Kissinger, Larry Ellison, and General

James Mattis, who also made their own sizeable investments in the company. A curious thing about this board is that not a single one of its members had any background in science or medicine.

The first public doubts about the company were raised by John Ioannidis (2015), a Stanford University medical school professor, famed for being a gadfly about over-valued Silicon Valley biomedical firms. Ioannidis was especially incredulous that not a single article had been published in a scientific journal describing Theranos' methodology or validating its claims about the effectiveness of its product. Amazingly, the whistle blower who played the most crucial role in exposing what turns out to have been one of the biggest investment frauds in US history was Tyler Schultz, George's grandson. As an undergraduate at Stanford, Schultz was so inspired by the promise of Theranos' technology that he switched his major to biology and went to work for the company shortly after graduating. Unlike other talented Theranos employees who came to understand the gross inaccuracy of the test screenings, but either kept their doubts to themselves or quietly left for other jobs, Tyler was appalled enough (driven by ethical concerns about sick patients being damaged by the scam) to do something about it.

Tyler sought to warn his grandfather by telling him the story, but the old man (whose deep knowledge of foreign affairs was matched only by his deeper ignorance of science) continued to believe in Ms. Holmes and the Theranos fantasy. Tyler also brought his concerns to Ms. Holmes, but when that failed to produce anything but threats (from Sunny Balwani), he sent a memo (under a pseudonym) to a government regulatory agency detailing how the company corruptly manipulated quality control data. He then got in touch with a *Wall Street Journal* reporter John Carreyrou (2018), whose articles (detailed in his recent book, *Bad Blood: Secrets and Lies in a Silicon Valley Startup*) utilizing Tyler's information brought the whole house of cards crashing down. Holmes and Balwani received strong penalties and likely will end up in prison.

When Tyler Schultz emerged as a threat to Theranos, fellow Board member David Boies (the prominent lawyer whose inept representation of Al Gore before the US Supreme Court likely brought the country eight years of George Bush) sent an associate to the Schultz house (when George tipped the lawyers off that his grandson would be there) to threaten the younger Schultz and tried to coerce him into retracting his claims. Tyler was saved by George's wife, who was bothered by how her grandson was being treated and who helped him escape the trap by hooking him up with high-powered legal representation. Tyler is now considered a great moral hero, while George continued being loyal to Elizabeth, even inviting her to his ninety-fifth birthday party at which Tyler was not present. The Theranos story, which seems straight out of Hans Christian Andersen's "Emperor's New Clothes" playbook, is a sad story of how so many accomplished people, including the great George

Schultz, could be led by a skilled con artist and by their own naiveté, into being so foolish. This is but one more piece of evidence for the importance of skepticism in the face of claims that seem to be too good to be true.

THIRTEEN
In Pursuit of Common Sense

Common sense refers to the use of good judgment in practical matters. As mentioned in chapter 2, common sense is usually thought of as intuitive or self-acquired, and not as something requiring formal instruction. While common sense typically refers to avoidance of bad (and obvious) physical outcomes it can refer to obvious social outcomes as well, as illustrated by a high school friend of mine who got suspended in the prudish 1950s by shockingly uttering the word "shit" in a public forum. (What is considered a punishable offense in one time can become almost routine in another). In this final chapter, I explore aspects of the common sense construct, which are used in many instances as a stand-in for non-foolishness. In this way, the themes explored throughout this book are revisited somewhat.

A FOOLISH ACT CAN REFLECT STAGGERING NAIVETÉ

Here is a recent, highly publicized example of someone who demonstrated a remarkable absence of social common sense. It involved a female kindergarten principal in China who proudly welcomed new students and their parents with a striptease pole dance (China News 2018). To her great surprise, she was fired as a result. Ironically, it is likely that the woman's prudishness (in a very prudish society) is what impelled her to engage in such a raunchy and foolish act, as I would bet that she thought (and probably had been told by a dance mentor) that a pole dance is a respectable athletic and artistic activity. Thus, she most likely lacked background knowledge of its sexual connotations. Her behavior smacks of naiveté, and the first listed definition of naiveté is "lack of experience." *Affect* undoubtedly also played a role, in this case the prideful wish the young woman likely possessed to bask in the approval she naively assumed would ensue.

Within the four-factor explanatory model (figure 3.1), ignorance is embedded within *cognition*, and cognition includes both information and processing of information. Obviously, as reflected in many of the stories in this book, the other three factors—*situation*, *personality*, and *affect/ state*—also contribute in important ways to foolish action, or its obverse—wise action (or commonly, wise non-action). But cognition, specifically the possession of information, plays a particularly important role. Experience in the world, and in different contexts and settings, helps one to understand what kinds of behaviors are safe or unsafe, both socially and physically. When we age, we acquire greater experience and it is because of this increased experience, rather than improved information processing (which usually declines somewhat) that we become "wiser."

CAN COMPUTERS ACQUIRE COMMON SENSE?

Marvin Minsky, one of many famous scholars who attended my high school (Bronx Science), was a pioneering computer theorist who cofounded MIT's computing laboratory and served as a leading Artificial Intelligence (AI) philosopher and futurologist. One of his preoccupations, expressed in several books and papers, was the inability of computers to demonstrate common sense (Roush 2006). It continues to be a challenge, as reflected in the fact that before he died in 2018, Microsoft cofounder and tech entrepreneur Paul Allen identified it as the main goal of the Allen Institute, the centerpiece of which is project Mosaic (mosaic.allenai. org) described as having the purpose of teaching machines to exhibit common sense.

Minsky noted in the 1980s that while computers could solve math problems at an advanced level, they could not demonstrate common sense at the level of an average preschooler. For example, if you showed a preschooler a picture of someone with a party hat blowing out the candles on a cake, the preschooler would say "Birthday Party" while a computer shown the same picture would be dumbfounded. The solution chosen by Minsky and others was to expend considerable resources to get a computer to recognize a birthday party, but that same computer would then fail to correctly attribute meaning to some other simple recognition task also within the behavioral repertoire of a preschooler. This is a technically solvable problem (by inputting information about hundreds or thousands of routine situations) but situation labeling hardly captures the quality of independent thinking, particularly understanding of hidden risk.

Getting computers to demonstrate common sense has become one of the two Holy Grails of AI. The other is autonomous cars, which involves a variant of common sense, namely recognizing and adapting to various driving situations (many of which involve significant risk). The reason for seeking to establish common sense in computers is because it is considered an essential aspect of being human, and of human thought. The great computing pioneer Alan Turing (1950) established a challenge now known as the "Turing Test," which stated that a computer would demonstrate human intelligence when it could carry on a conversation with a person and the person would not know she was conversing with a computer.

There are problems with using such a criterion, however, one being that many humans are credulous, and the other being that it would be fairly easy to program a computer to produce some conversational blather that could fool an average recipient. A more meaningful test of a computer's common sense, it seems to me, would be to reverse the task, and see if a computer could detect some problem (not necessarily the humanness of the computer) on the receiving end. If one framed the problem to be identified as some kind of risk, then one would be approaching a definition of common sense (relative non-foolishness) close to the one I have been proposing throughout this book, as opposed to Minsky's somewhat simplistic view of common sense as general situation labeling.

Just as human non-foolishness exists on a continuum (figures 2.2 and 2.3) from common sense (awareness of obvious risk) to wisdom (awareness of subtle risk), then one would have to grade the relative humanness of computers on such a continuum as well. Ability to recognize risk is generally not something shown by young children, except for wired-in wariness around unprotected heights, so such a reversed humanness challenge would require a computer to show adolescent or adult social judgment.

There have been a few large projects that attempt to program a computer to demonstrate common sense, but they have all gone down the path of teaching it the truth or falseness of hundreds of thousands if not millions of everyday statements, and tell which are true or nonsensical. Forgive me for being a spoil sport, but I do not see how this will help a computer to acquire the judgment to avoid entering a dark alley, let alone not doing a pole dance for the parents of kindergarten students.

SELF-DRIVING CARS LACK COMMON SENSE

Of all the problems in artificial intelligence, the one that has attracted the most attention, and certainly the most money, has been the development of self-driving motor vehicles. Many different enterprises, including car companies (Tesla, General Motors), software companies (Google, Argus), and ride-share companies (Uber) have poured many billions into a competition that likely will go on for another decade or more. It has been approached as a great technology challenge, with two components: hardware (development of sensors capable of fully and adequately mapping the driving environment) and software (developing and programming car-mounted computers capable of processing that environment and making correct driving decisions). Significant progress has been made but the ultimate goal (cars without steering wheels or operators, capable of driving safely at all speeds and in all conditions, and reliable enough to acquire the trust of human potential passengers) seems far in the future (The Week Staff 2018).

The reason why such a task may be unattainable is that so far techies (who themselves often lack social intelligence) have failed to recognize that to make a computer-operated car show driving common sense it will be necessary for it to demonstrate social information-processing in real time and with some degree of sophistication. This is because driving is as much a social as a physical task (predicting and reacting to the behavior of other drivers is an exercise in social cognition) and that is an aspect of human competence that AI researchers have failed to master or even address.

COMMON SENSE AS A KEY TO SURVIVAL

The word that best describes the basic purpose of common sense, and conversely the thing most at risk from foolish (non-commonsensical) behavior, is "survival." It can take many forms, but in its most literal form survival involves staying alive. The scholar who has devoted the most attention to common sense explanations for surviving or not surviving deadly situations is Laurence Gonzales, a Fellow of the systems theory-oriented Santa Fe Institute. His two best-known books in this vein are *Deep Survival: Who Lives, Who Dies, and Why* (2005) and *Everyday Survival: Why Smart People Do Stupid Things* (2008). While Gonzales recognizes that survival is in part a matter of luck and is obviously affected by the objective size of the danger, his stories of people who succumbed to relatively small dangers and others who overcame huge dangers, provide a systems theory of survival that has some similarities to the multi-factorial model that forms the basis for my own book.

As in my analyses of foolish episodes, Gonzales believes that the biggest threat to exercising survival common sense is emotion, especially fear. While some level of fear when facing possible demise is rational (that is, it keeps one in touch with reality), too much fear causes one to narrow one's attentional focus and to forget the survival rules one might otherwise remember to follow. An example is falling out of a raft when traveling down a whitewater river. An experienced rafter knows to float on their back with feet and toes facing downstream and, most importantly, elevated out of the water. Inexperienced or panicked rafters will attempt to stand up with their arms outstretched over their heads. This causes them to drop down into the water with an increased likelihood that one or both feet will become wedged between rocks. Once that happens, the process of extracting someone from a river becomes very difficult, even after they have drowned.

Situation contributes to absence of survival common sense in two related ways: (a) group pressure to cut corners, and (b) the fact that situations labeled easy or safe may in fact be anything but. An example Gonzalez used which illustrated both of these phenomena involved four rock climbers who were tackling what they and others deemed an easy rock face. On the descent they were in a hurry to get down quickly (*affect* likely contributed to this decision), and they made the fundamental mistake of not using fixed belay ropes but instead used ice axes to break a possible fall. When the top-most climber slipped and fell, it became almost inevitable that the other three would also fall, taking two climbers below them along for the ride. This multi-fatality accident could have been avoided if the climbers had followed the simple rule of never disengaging from a secured rope.

Cognition obviously plays a critical role in lapses of survival common sense, with the most frequent example being ignorance. Gonzales gave an example of the time he visited a beach on the Hawaiian island of Kauai. He was about to go into the ocean for a swim but luckily stopped to ask a lifeguard (who turned out to be a very experienced surfer) for advice. The lifeguard explained that the surf in the seemingly calm area where Gonzales planned to swim was in fact extremely dangerous, and there was a strong possibility that the uninformed visitor would have been swept out to sea. Gonzales gave an example of the opposite side of the coin, involving basic knowledge of tsunami signs. As example, a ten-year-old British girl named Tilly Smith learned about tsunamis in her geography class. She was vacationing with her family on the beach in Phuket, Thailand on Boxing Day 2004 when she felt a slight tremor and saw water trickling out to sea and bubbling. She warned her parents, and they sounded the alarm and saved one hundred people on the beach and at their nearby hotel (where everyone below the fourth floor, and thousands in the vicinity, drowned). For her precocious risk-awareness, Tilly was named "child of the year" by the French newspaper *Mon Quotidien*.

Personality contributes to common sense survival and non-survival in various ways. One of them is a willingness to alter plans when circumstances—such as weather conditions—change. Non-survivors tend to stick to a behavioral script even when basic assumptions (such as about the weather staying mild) turn out to no longer be applicable. Survivors, in contrast, tend to be more flexible, if not during the lead-in to a catastrophe, then during its critical aftermath. Perhaps the three most important *personality* qualities that Gonzales sees in extreme survivors (as reflected for example in accounts by people stranded for days or weeks in lifeboats) are: (a) an acceptance of the situation (rather than bitching about it), (b) a creative ability to see the experience as an interesting puzzle to solve, and (c) a firm conviction that they would survive, even as others around them were dying.

As mentioned, *affect/state*, particularly fear, plays a central role in explaining failure to use survival common sense. The underlying skill, according to Gonzales, is self-regulatory ability, an aspect of executive functioning. While regulation of fear (keeping it from crossing over into full-blown panic, for example) is an important part of executive functioning, it also involves maintaining attentional focus, without becoming so focused that one gets tunnel vision, and staying reflective and calm. (A common mistake of people who are lost in the wilderness is to immediately plow ahead which both uses up energy and is likely to make finding the correct way out more difficult.)

Gonzales ends "Deep Survival" with a lengthy list of survival principles. Here are just some of them:

a. stop and think before acting;
b. be aware of changing circumstances;
c. have back-up plans to adopt when things go awry;
d. avoid behaving impulsively;
e. know the forces you are dealing with (for example, multiple climbers tethered only to themselves create far more momentum when one [especially at the top] falls than they can arrest with their axes);
f. seek information about danger zones (where and how people have died);
g. be humble (arrogant Rambo types are often the first to die);
h. when in doubt bail out (difficult advice to follow, as many people are reluctant to give up a goal they are invested in emotionally or financially); and
i. believe in your ability to prevail (adopt what psychologists term "self efficacy").

ENGINEERING AS A COMMON SENSE SCIENCE

It is interesting that one of the most thoughtful discussions I have seen on the relationship between common sense and wisdom is to be found not in the psychology literature but in an engineering publication. In an online newsletter titled *TheEngineeringDaily.net*, one finds the following assertion by Sajid Kahn (2009): "common sense is very clear while wisdom is fuzzy. Perhaps when some particular common action is proven wise then it graduates to becoming common sense. All proven human behavior that results in a wise result is common sense." This view of common sense as more basic and established than wisdom is close to my formulation, but differs from it mainly in the degree to which it can be accessed intuitively (my view) as opposed to verified empirically.

For engineers, inadequate practice implicated in bad outcomes (for example, a bridge collapsing) poses serious financial and existential threats to a practitioner and the profession itself. For this reason, engineering can be considered the applied study of risk and its management in construction, operation and maintenance of structures, machines, and other physical entities or processes. As a result of careful development of, and adherence to, science-based engineering practices, training, and building codes, major fiascos are relatively rare in conventional engineering-based projects in the United States and other advanced countries. That is not so much the case in less technically or ethically developed societies, where failure of conventional structures occur on a routine basis.

However, when dealing with novel engineering situations or methods, established common sense engineering principles can be inadequate even in highly regulated countries, and can lead to foolishly dangerous results (Levy and Salvadori 1987). An example can be found in a 1978 case often used in courses in engineering ethics. It involved New York's Citibank building, at that time the seventh tallest structure in the world. The major challenge to that project was that the seller of the building site, a Lutheran church, insisted that its demolished structure be replaced, and that the tower be built over the new church. Thus, the bottom nine of the building's fifty-nine stories were stilts, and these are inherently less sturdy than bedrock.

To make this project possible, the building was made unusually light for a skyscraper, using a novel chevron bracing structure. An eminent structural engineer named William LeMessurier did the required calculations and determined that the design was safe. To keep the lighter than usual tower from swaying too much in the wind, LeMessurier added a unique tuned mass damper, a 400-ton electrically operated device. As required by building codes, the wind force calculations by LeMessurier examined only the effect of perpendicular wind gusts, which were considered the most dangerous.

For her undergraduate thesis project, an architecture student named Diane Lee Hartley asked LeMessurier's firm whether quartering (diagonal) wind gusts had been looked at. The answer was no, and when LeMessurier did new calculations and wind tunnel tests, it turned out for this type of unique structure quartering winds were far more dangerous than perpendicular winds, and that he had also failed to take into account the possibility that the balancing device would be disabled if a storm caused a city-wide power outage. Furthermore, LeMessurier discovered (something that as the supervising engineer he should have known) that to save money the contractor had weakened the building by using screwed bolts, rather than much stronger welded rivets, on the supporting structure. As a result, LeMessurier determined that the Citibank building was likely to collapse in a fifty-year storm, and in a sixteen-year storm if the balancing device was disabled.

In terms of the ethics aspect of the case, LeMessurier is generally considered (McGinn 2018) a hero, for quickly confessing (rather than covering up) his mistake to the client, and notifying the appropriate government agencies. A successful, but very expensive, retro-fix was implemented, which involved adding a generator staffed around the clock for the damper, and doing nocturnal repairs to the rivet problem. An additional ethical complication focused on the fact that the public, including workers in the tower and surrounding buildings, were never informed of the risks they faced. (Authorities were prepared to issue an evacuation order when a hurricane came up the East coast while the work was still going on, but scrapped the order when the storm took a turn out to sea.)

LeMessurier justified this use of deception (the problem was not disclosed for well over a decade), including not informing other architects and engineers who might have learned from it, on the ground that going public with the story would have caused mass panic and great harm to Citibank (which generously spared the famous engineer from bearing any financial consequences for his sloppy work). Nobody seems to have raised a more fundamental ethical concern, which is that LeMessurier maybe should have refused to proceed on the project in the first place, telling the architect and client that it would be foolhardy to go ahead with building a fifty-nine-story building on stilts using untested construction methods and novel wind-mitigating technology. An update: Citibank eventually sold the building and moved to another office tower built with more conventional methods. To this non-engineer, that seems like a wise move.

PHILOSOPHY OF COMMON SENSE

Common sense (as an intuitive path to direct knowledge and not necessarily as awareness of risk) has been an important and recurring topic for philosophers, ever since it was first mentioned in 350 BCE by Aristotle, in *De Anima* (a Latin translation of the original Greek title). According to Pavel Gregovic's 2007 *Aristotle on Common Sense*, common sense (*koine aisthesis*) was viewed by Aristotle as a cognitive process midway between simple sense perceptions and abstract reasoning. It enabled organisms (humans as well as higher animals) to "regularly and effortlessly perform a number of complex perceptual operations that cannot be explained in terms of the five senses taken individually" (Gregovic 2007). It is an important skill enabling those possessing it (for example, a monkey knowing that what looks like a stick is actually a snake) to survive challenges posed by environmental dangers. However, I do not believe that the survival (danger-recognizing) implications of common sense were extensively addressed in Aristotle's few and somewhat inconsistent references to this concept.

Roman philosophical writings, much influenced by Aristotle, also made reference to common sense (*sensus commuas*), although it took on a somewhat different and higher-level dimension, referring to inborn meanings that humans (but not animals) share in common. This view of common sense has more of an ethical and political emphasis, which can be viewed positively (a shared commitment to human virtues) or negatively (in the ignorant notion held by many right-wing politicians that an occasional snow storm or cold snap disproves the reality of global warming).

In early modern philosophy, the concept of common sense was most fully realized in "Scottish common sense realism," also known as the "Scottish school of common sense." This is a philosophical framework that originated in Scotland in the mid-to- late eighteenth century, through the writings of Thomas Reid and others. Reid's treatise *An Inquiry into the Human Mind on the Principles of Common Sense* (1869; originally published, 1764) was rightly seen as a criticism of the influential skeptical school of epistemology best embodied in the writings of another Scotsman, David Hume (1711–1776). Reid (basically an early psychologist) believed that the primary objects of perception are actual objects, not (as Hume believed) mental associations. Reid's ideas, and the common sense school generally, was extremely influential in France and the Americas, as reflected in the publication of Thomas Paine's (1776) small book titled *Common Sense*. It was a polemical pamphlet (the most widely read book title relative to population in American history), which played a crucial role in changing the American Revolution from an attack on an unpopular taxation policy to a more fundamental attack on monarchy and a call for complete independence from England.

This emphasis was directly related to another aspect of Reid's common sense project, namely his theory of action (Yaffe 2004), which extolled human freedom and autonomy as core values. There is much empirical support today for this idea, as reflected in work on intrinsic motivation by Edward L. Deci (1975) and others and in work on the psychology of parenting, such as my own book *Elements of Discipline* (Greenspan 2012). In the eighteenth century, when obeisance to deity, monarchy and hierarchy was so ingrained, the idea that it was commonsensical to seek autonomy from conventional beliefs or external controls (Paine was an atheist and Reid a free thinker) was truly revolutionary.

Common sense has continued to be an important philosophical topic in modern times, particularly in the writings of G. E. Moore (who founded the school of "common sense realism") and Moore's Cambridge University colleague and mentee Ludwig Wittgenstein. The latter made famous what he named "Moore's Paradox," a state of absurdity captured by the example "it is raining but I [or you] don't believe that it is raining" and other variations of "It is P but I [or someone else] believe it is not P." Many tomes have been written about this paradox (for example, Green and Williams 2007), but I know of a real-life example that makes it seem less absurd than it is generally believed to be. My buddy Harvey (a well-known cognitive psychologist) and I were in a hotel room at a conference and I looked out the fifth story window and said "boy it's really raining." Harvey went over to the window and said "no it isn't." When asked why, Harvey replied "see that guy walking by? He is not wearing a hat or carrying an umbrella, plus the weather forecast did not call for rain." To which I replied "look at that puddle and see the raindrops falling in it. Also, when you stick your hand out the window you will feel raindrops hitting your hand." To me (not knowing or caring much about philosophy at that time), the thing most interesting about this exchange is that it illustrated a basic problem in psychology, which is a preference for indirect indices of cognitive incompetence (such as IQ) over real world indices (such as adaptive functioning). To me, the most commonsensical way of construing reality is to look at direct (sticking your hand out) rather than indirect (a weather forecast) forms of evidence, especially when at a distance (looking out a fifth story window) and when the phenomenon (in this case, rain) is not in an extreme form.

POLITICS OF COMMON SENSE

Another arena in which the term common sense refers to intuitive knowledge without necessarily including risk (except in pointing out dangers of people or groups perceived as dangerous enemies) is "political common sense." According to Sophia Rosenfeld (2011), as spelled out in her book *Common Sense: A Political History,* "common sense has always been an awareness cornerstone of American politics." As mentioned in the previous section, the American Revolution was decisively influenced by Thomas Paine's 1776 pamphlet of that title, which created a near consensus among colonists to the effect that continued loyalty to England violated common sense. In light of that example, it became widely believed that political common sense (shared wisdom about governing so obvious as to not require debate) is always on the side of reason and good action, but that turned out to be a naive belief. For example, in the antebellum South (and North too, for that matter), and continuing to almost the present day, it seemed commonsensical (such as to a college-educated relative of mine) that the presumed inferiority of black people justified denying them equal rights.

The basic idea behind political common sense is that one does not need policy studies or elaborate analyses to know what is the right course of action in addressing a particular issue. Rather, it is sufficient to merely check what your gut tells you. There are two problems with this, of course: (a) many matters (such as climate change) are too complex to be addressed by simple solutions grounded in ignorance of the underlying phenomenon, and (b) what seems commonsensical to one person because it fits with their worldview (for example, a paranoid-style suspicion of foreigners) may be abhorrent to someone with a different (more welcoming and tolerant) worldview.

Appeals to common sense can be found across the political spectrum, but they seem most prevalent among conservative politicians, such as Ronald Reagan, who, frequently appealed to common sense by telling folksy stories from his youth. The 2012 presidential candidate Herman Caine, a leader of the Tea Party (extreme anti-tax) wing of the Republican party, referred to himself as "president of the university of common sense." The most ominous examples of appeal to political common sense are found in xenophobic propaganda, such as the fear-mongering used by Donald Trump in his rants against Mexican immigrants. In an article titled "The Only Thing More Dangerous Than Trump's Appeal to Common Sense Is His Dismissal of It," Sophia Rosenfeld (2017) points out that a big part of Trump's justification for his border wall is in making common sense analogies to what home owners do to protect their property from criminals. As is his wont however, Trump took it to another level when he told his supporters to ignore what their senses tell them (such as the fact that his inaugural crowd was demonstrably smaller than Obama's) as part of his assault on anything conveyed by mainstream "fake news."

Common sense is based on the notion that many questions we encounter in everyday life are fairly easy to answer (for example, is it thundering out or isn't it?). However, in the realm of politics, where truth and reality are harder to pin down, we have to rely on others (or Wikipedia, which is the same thing) to answer most questions about what is happening on a simple factual level (for example, how many criminals and terrorists are actually attempting to cross over from Mexico?) let alone on a more complex level (for example, has a physical wall really been an effective way of keeping drugs or people from illegally crossing into the country?). The heart of populism (which has had both positive and negative manifestations) is distrust of elites and a turn for leadership to people claiming to be just like oneself.

Having studied economics, history, and public policy (and being a regular consumer of responsible journalism), I consider myself more informed than the average person on such questions, but I still rely on candidates who seem trustworthy to help me understand complex policy matters. Pity the high school-educated voter whose evidence of reality comes from fear-mongering conspiracy theorists who lack any need to be truthful and who use non-factual appeals to emotion to manipulate gullible voters. In the political realm the main challenge to common sense of citizens is the ever-present need to see through lies and half truths. This ultimately is an exercise in risk-awareness, as the danger flowing from an absence of such common sense in the face of Orwellian manipulation of the truth is the undermining of a civil and democratic society.

SERIOUS MENTAL ILLNESS AS A LACK OF COMMON SENSE

Mental Illness takes various forms, and most of these bring an increased likelihood of behaving foolishly, that is, exhibiting reduced (mainly social) risk awareness. Here I shall address the role of common sense in "major" mental illness, particularly schizophrenia or related conditions (such as mania) on or close to being on the "psychosis" spectrum. I shall not address character disorders (which often impel people to do foolish acts of commission), "neurotic" conditions such as anxiety disorders (for which foolishness typically involves acts of omission) or neurocognitive (such as dementia) and neurodevelopmental (such as autism) disorders, in all of which lack of common sense is a very central symptom.

The scholar who has done the most to address the possibility that severe mental illness can be a "common sense deficit disorder" is an Italian psychiatrist named Giovanni Stanghellini (2000), whose paper "At Issue: Vulnerability to Schizophrenia and Lack of Common Sense," provides a very in-depth treatment of the subject. Because of the comprehensiveness of that paper, my comments in this section shall not stray much beyond the confines of Stanghellini's excellent analysis.

It is an understatement that people with serious mental illness do not act wisely. For example, there is "Gail," a very unstable older woman I know slightly who, despite her meager income (a result of many foolish financial decisions over the years), had purchased on credit a very expensive automobile which she could not afford and had very little opportunity or need to drive. Gail also has alienated her adult children and most of her friends, with very hurtful verbal attacks or other cruel actions. In my opinion, Gail likely has Borderline Personality Disorder (BPD) a condition whose name indicates that someone is on the schizophrenia spectrum but not quite psychotic (that is, so detached from reality that she is unable to function independently). The basic disabling condition in BPD is an inability to regulate emotion, such that a triggering event (which could be quite trivial) sets off a wildly disproportionate reaction that persists for a long time (Elsevier 2013). Needless to say, people with BPD (who can be quite charming and seductive) are unable to maintain romantic or other close relationships, and go through life sowing chaos and hurt feelings without anticipating the serious consequences that flow from their emotion-driven actions.

Stanghellini (2000) agrees with those who see impairments in social functioning as central to schizophrenia, but in contrast to those who see such impairments as one outcome feature (among several) of the disorder, Stanghellini sees it as central to understanding "vulnerability" (increased likelihood) for acquiring schizophrenia. He agrees with Blankenburg (1971) that schizophrenia is a "crisis of common sense." By common sense he means understanding people and social rules, and explicitly points to deficient "social cognition" (perspective-taking; a topic which I first explored in the 1970s) as the defining element in common sense. Unfortunately, Stanghellini did not specifically link common sense to risk-awareness, although in several case examples he mentions the disastrous unwanted social and practical consequences that flow from poor common sense. So, without using the f-word or bringing risk avoidance into the equation, Stanghellini described schizophrenia as a foolishness (that is, common sense deficit) disorder that exposes an individual to serious social risk. Stanghellini did not explore implications of common sense deficiency for treating serious mental illness (which today are treated mainly pharmacologically) but it should be noted that in the burgeoning "moral treatment" movement (Peloquin 1989) that impelled the building of humane psychiatric asylums in the late eighteenth and early nineteenth centuries, the emphasis was on gently providing (mainly in pastoral settings) an opportunity for people who had lost their common sense a chance to recover what Stanghellini termed an "attunement" with the social world.

As with most of the other examples in this book, all of the four explanatory factors can play a role in explaining episodes of schizophrenic foolishness, even if *cognition* (social non-attunement) is implicated in virtually all such episodes. Stanghellini discussed three forms of schizophrenic psychopathology: (a) sensory level disorders (disordered perception of self and the world), (b) conceptualization-level disorders (lack or loss of social knowledge, such as making sense of others' behavior), and (c) attitudinal level disorders (eccentric values and distrust of conventional knowledge). The last of the three (attitudinal) is the only one where lack of social attunement (sense-making) is not of primary importance, even if bizarre rejection of common beliefs result in behaviors that are profoundly risky. Stanghellini noted that Bipolar-Affective disorder also leads to social incompetence, but here the issue can be described as "hyper" as opposed to the "hypo" psychopathology seen in most cases of schizophrenia. What this means, I believe, is that schizophrenics withdraw from social interactions because of fear that they have not cracked the human behavior code (that is, they have inadequate social attunement) while Bipolar people, especially in their manic phase, are so convinced of the superiority of their social attunement that they are impelled (as in the example of Gail provided earlier) to do profoundly foolish things.

CONCLUSION

By ending this book with a chapter on common sense, and by emphasizing that it is a reflection of knowledge (largely innate and intuitive, but still knowledge), I mean to imply that the problem of foolishness (which can be thought of as an absence of common sense) is at heart a *cognitive* phenomenon. Obviously, as most of the stories in this book illustrate, *situational, personality,* and *affective-state* factors also play an important contributing role. But by describing foolishness as risk-unawareness, I mean to indicate that an absence of knowledge (in the case of foolishness, knowledge that something is potentially dangerous) is ultimately what we are talking about when we describe an action or a person as foolish.

A challenge in sending this book off to the printer is that every day brings one or more dramatic new examples of foolish behavior. There is, thus, a strong temptation to keep adding new stories and insights about foolishness and how one might avoid it. My basic point has been made, however, which is that many if not most unwanted social or practical outcomes could have been avoided if the person had stopped and thought about possible undesired consequences (see figure 3.3 in particular).

In most cases of foolish action there is some combination of two or more of the four explanatory factors operating. As a rule, every person on the planet has the potential to behave foolishly on any given day. However, people with significant affective issues (as in mental illness) or self-regulation issues (as in attention deficit or obsessive-compulsive disorder) or cognitive issues (as in Intellectual Disability) have an increased likelihood of behaving foolishly, sometimes with extreme (for example, bankruptcy, jail, death) consequences, or to other cognitive factors (as when one lacks an understanding of cause and effect).

Some people will always behave foolishly, especially when strong social or affective forces are present. Hopefully, readers of this book will take to heart some of its lessons, and will stop themselves from doing something seriously foolish in the future. As captured in the first line of a song cowritten by Aretha Franklin (1968), who passed away a few months before I finished this book: "You better think." To be more specific, you better think about the ways in which what seems like a good course of action could end up being very foolish.

References

Aczel, B., B. Palfi, and Z. Kekecs. 2015. What Is Stupid?: People's Conception of Unintelligent Behavior. *Intelligence* 53: 51–58.

Alvarez, A., and R. D. Bachman. 2008. *Violence: The Enduring Problem.* Los Angeles: Sage.

Ambrose, S. E. 1990. *Eisenhower: Soldier and President.* 2 vols. in one. New York: Simon & Schuster.

American Psychiatric Association. 2013. *Diagnostic and Statistical Manual of Mental Disorders.* 5th edition (DSM-5). Washington, DC: APA.

Anderson, T. 2007. *Buddhist Tales for Young and Old: Stories of the Enlightened Being.* 5 vols. N.p.: Buddhist Literature Society.

Armin, R. (1605). *Fool upon Fool, or Six Sorts of Sots: A Fat Fool and a Flat Fool, a Lean Fool and a Clean Fool, a Merry Fool and a very Fool, Showing Their Lives, Humors and Behaviors, with Their Want of Wit in Their Show of Wisdom. Not so Strange as True.* London: William Ferbrand.

Asch, S. E. 1956. Studies of Independence and Conformity: I. A Minority of One against a Unanimous Majority. *Psychological Monographs: General and Applied* 70 (9): 1–70.

Associated Press. 1995. Harassed Moose Stomps Man to Death. *Spokane Spokesman-Review,* January 11, 1995.

Ayduk, O., and W. Mischel. 2002. When Smart People Behave Stupidly: Reconciling Inconsistencies in Social-Emotional Intelligence. In *Why Smart People Can Be So Stupid,* edited by R. J. Sternberg, 86–105. New Haven, CT: Yale University Press.

Bandura, A. 1977. Self-Efficacy: Toward a Unifying Theory of Behavioral Change. *Psychological Review* 84 (2): 191–215.

Baron-Cohen, S. 2011. *The Science of Evil: On Empathy and the Origins of Cruelty.* New York: Basic Books.

Baumeister, R. F. 2001. Ego Depletion, the Executive Function, and Self-Control: An Energy Model of the Self in Personality. In *Personality Psychology in the Workplace,* edited by B. W. Roberts and R. Hogan, 299–316. Washington, DC: American Psychological Association.

Baumeister, R. F., and J. Tierney, J. 2011. *Willpower: Rediscovering the Greatest Human Strength.* New York: Penguin Press.

Beatty, J. 2005. Bush's Folly. *Atlantic,* January 20. Online July 2005.

Belluz, J. 2019. DNA Scientist James Watson Has a Remarkably Long History of Sexist, Racist Public Comments. *Vox,* January 15, 2019.

Berecz, J. M. 1992. *Understanding Tourette Syndrome, Obsessive Compulsive Disorder, and Related Problems: A Developmental and Catastrophe Theory Perspective.* New York: Springer.

Bergler, E. 1998. *The Talent for Stupidity: The Psychology of the Bungler, the Incompetent, and the Ineffectual.* Madison, CT: International Universities Press.

Berkshire, M. 2013. *Anthony Weiner, the Scandalous Sexter: 100 Questions & Answers About the Scandal.* N.p.: KAW Publisher.

Berrior, G. E., and M. Gili. 1995. Will and Its Disorders: A Conceptual History. *History of Psychiatry* 6.21: 87–104.

Birner, L. 1984. The Schlemiel and the Shlep: A Psychoanalytic Note on Two Masochistic Styles. *Modern Psychoanalysis* 9(2): 179–89.

Blagrove, M. 1996. Effects of Length of Sleep Deprivation on Interrogative Suggestibility. *Journal of Experimental Psychology: Applied*. 2: 1, 48–59.

Blankenburg, W. 1971. *Der verlust der natrlichen selbstvertaendlichkeit: Ein beitrag zur psychopathologie symptomarmer schizophrenein*. Stuttgart: Enke.

Boccaccio, G. 1353/2003. *The Decameron*. Translated by G. H. McWilliam. New York: Penguin Classics.

Branch, J. 2012. Snow Fall: The Avalanche at Tunnel Creek. *New York Times*. December 20, 2012. http://www.nytimes.com/projects/2012/snow-fall/index.html#/?part=tunnel-creek.

Brant, S. 1494/1944. *The Ship of Fools*. Translated by E. H. Zeydel: New York: Columbia University Press.

Bricusse, L., and A. Newley. 1962. *What Kind of Fool Am I - and Other Show-Stoppers*. Burbank, CA: Reprise Records

Bucke, R. M. 1901. *Cosmic Consciousness: A Study in the Evolution of the Human Mind*. New York: E.P. Dutton and Company.

Burrough, B. 2009. Marc Dreier's Crime of Destiny. *Vanity Fair*, November 2009.

Burton, R. 1621. *The Anatomy of Melancholy, What it is: With all the Kinds, Causes, Symptomes, Prognostickes, and Several Cures of it. In Three Maine Partitions with their several Sections, Members, and Subsections. Philosophically, Historically, Opened and Cut up*. London: William Veazie.

Caputi, S. 2015. *I Should Have Stayed in Morocco: My Misadventures with Billionaire Ponzi-Schemer Scott Rothstein*. Kingsport, TN: Twilight Times Books.

Carreyrou, J. 2018. *Bad Blood: Secrets and Lies in a Silicon Valley Startup*. New York: Alfred A. Knopf.

Carver, C. S., and M. F. Scheier. 1998. On the Structure of Behavioral Self-Regulation. In *Handbook of Self-Regulation*, edited by M. Boekaerts, P. R. Pintrich, and M. Zeidner, 41–84. San Diego, CA: Academic Press.

Chadha, 2006. Lynne Stewart, Jihadi Lawyer, *Middle East Quarterly*, 13:1, 59–65.

Chandler, M. J., and S. Greenspan. 1972. Ersatz Egocentirsm: A Rejoinder. *Developmental Psychology* 7.2: 107–9.

Chayefsky, P. 2000. *The Collected Works of Paddy Chayefsky: The Screenplays*. 2 vols. New York: Applause Books.

China News. 2018. Scantily-Clad Pole Dancers Greet Chinese Kindergarten Pupils on Return to Classroom. *China News*, September 3, 2018.

Cialdini, R. B. 1984. *Influence: The Psychology of Persuasion*. New York: William Morrow.

Clair, S. 1998. A Cusp Catastrophe Model for Adolescent Alcohol Use: An Empirical Test. *Nonlinear Dynamics Psychology, and Life Sciences* 2.3: 217–41.

CNN. 2010. Teen Arrested in Wal-Mart Racial Announcement Incident. *CNN*. March 20, 2010. http://www.cnn.com/2010/CRIME/03/20/walmart.racial.remark/index.html.

Commonwealth of Massachusetts v. Alexander Pring-Wilson. 2007. 448 Mass. 718, January 2, 2007–April 10, 2007. Middlesex County.

Connery, D. S. 1977. *Guilty Until Proven Innocent*. New York: G. P. Putnam.

Cooper, M. 2018. A Soldier Died After Racist Hazing. Now His Story Is an Opera. *New York Times*, June 1, 2018. https://www.nytimes.com/2018/06/01/arts/music/american-soldier-opera-danny-chen.html.

Crean, R. D., S. F. Tapert, A. Minassian, K. MacDonald, N. A. Crane, and B. J. Mason. 2011. Effects of Chronic, Heavy Cannabis Use on Executive Functions. *Journal of Addiction Medicine* 5.1: 9–15

Dale, D. 2018. Trump Has Said 1,340,330 Words as President. They're Getting More Dishonest, a Star Study Shows. *Toronto Star*, July 14, 2018.

Dayen, D. 2018. How Sears Was Gutted by Its Own CEO. *American Prospect*, October 17, 2018. https://prospect.org/article/how-sears-was-gutted-its-own-ceo.

Deci, E. L. 1975. *Intrinsic Motivation*. New York: Plenum Press.

Deford, F. 2017. The Best of Frank Deford. *Sports Illustrated*, May 29, 2017. https://www.si.com/2017/05/29/best-frank-deford-stories.

Denburg N. L., C. A. Cole, M. Hernandez, T. H. Yamada, D. Tranel, A. Bechara, and R. B. Wallace. 2007. The Orbitofrontal Cortex, Real-World Decision Making, and Normal Aging. *Annals of the New York Academy of Science* 1121 (December): 480–98.

Dennett, D. C. 2013. *Intuition Pumps and Other Tools for Thinking*. New York: W. W. Norton.

Deutsch, C. H. 2000. The Fading Copier King: Xerox Has Failed to Capitalize on Its Own Innovations. *New York Times*, October 19, 2000.

Digman, J. M. 1990. Personality Structure: Emergence of the Five-Factor Model. *Annual Review of Psychology* 41: 417–40.

Dostoevsky, F. 1869/1998. *The Idiot*. Translated by R. Pevear and L. Volokhonsky. New York: Oxford University Press.

Dumas, A. (1845-1956). *Le Comte de Monte-Cristo*. Bruxelles: Societe Belge de Librairie.

Dunning, John (1998). *On the Air: The Encyclopedia of Old-Time Radio*. Oxford, UK: Oxford University Press.

Dweck, C. S. 2002. Beliefs That Make Smart People Dumb. In *Why Smart People Can Be So Stupid*, edited by R. J. Sternberg, 24–41. New Haven, CT: Yale University Press.

Edgerton, R. (1993). *The Cloak of Competence*. Berkeley, CA: University of California Press.

Elrod, A. L. 2014. *Visualizing Child-Witch Narratives in Seventeenth-Century Cologne*. Durham, NC: Duke University Press.

Elsevier. 2013. Borderline Personality Disorder: The "Perfect storm" of Emotion Dysregulation. *ScienceDaily*, January 15, 2013.

Erasmus, D. 1509. *The Praise of Folly*. Originally published in Latin. Rotterdam.

Feerick, J. 1992. *The Twenty-Fifth Amendment: Its Complete History and Applications*. New York: Fordham University Press.

Ferris, T. 1997. De-Programming Heaven's Gate: The Wrong Stuff. *New Yorker*, April 14, 1997.

Feuer, A., and C. Haughney. 2008. Standing Accused: A Pillar of Finance and Charity. *New York Times*, December 12, 2008.

Flay, B. 1978. Catastrophe Theory in Social Psychology: Some Applications to Attitudes and Social Behavior. *Behavioral Science* 23.4: 335–50.

Ford, M. E. 1992. *Motivating Humans: Goals, Emotions, and Personal Agency Beliefs*. Newbury Park, CA: Sage.

Forrester, L., and H. Oguni. 1970. *Tora! Tora! Tora!* Ashiya, Japan: Twentieth Century Fox.

Fowler, J. 2005. *An Introduction to the Philosophy and Religion of Taoism: Pathways to Immortality*. Eastbourne, East Sussex: Sussex Academic Press.

freedictionary.com. 2018. s.v. "arrogance." http://www.freedictionary.com/arrogance.

Freud, S. 1901/1990a. *The Psychopathology of Everyday Life*. New York: W. W. Norton.

———. 1923/1990b. *The Ego and the Id*. New York: W. W. Norton.

Fulford, R. 2008. Ponzi Would Have Been Proud. *National Post*. December 27, 2008. http://www.robertfulford.com/2008-12-27-ponzi.html.

Galland, N. 2005/2009. *The Fool's Tale: A Novel*. New York: William Morrow/HarperCollins.

Gardner, H. 1983. *Frames of Mind: The Theory of Multiple Intelligences*. New York: Basic.

Gaylin, W. 2003. *Hatred: The Psychological Descent Into Violence*. New York: Public Affairs Press.

Glover, S. (2007, Sept. 16). O. J. on Las Vegas Hotel Incident: "I've Done Nothing Wrong." Los Angeles Times.

Goldman, D. P., and J. P. Smith. 2002. Can Patient Self-Management Help explain the SES Health Gradient? *Proceedings of the National Academy of Sciences* 99.6: 10929–34.

Goldstein, J. 2017. *101 Amazing Unusual Deaths*. Luton, Bedfordshire: Andrews UK.

Gollwitzer, P. M. 1990. Action Phases and Mind-Sets. In *Handbook of Motivation and Cognition: Foundations of Social Behavior*, edited by E. T. Higgins and R. M. Sorrentino, vol. 2, 53–92. New York: Guilford Press.

———. 1996. The Volitional Benefits of Planning. In *The Psychology of Action: Linking Cognition and Motivation in Behavior*, edited by P. M. Gollwitzer and J. A. Bargh, 287–312. New York: Guilford Press.

Gonzales, L. 2005. *Deep Survival: Who Lives, Who Dies, and Why*. New York: W. W. Norton.

———. 2008. *Everyday Survival: Why Smart People Do Stupid Things*. New York: W. W. Norton.

Goodgame, D. 1990. Read My Hips: Bush's Flip-Flops Add New Confusion to the Budget Battle and Raise Doubts About His Domestic Leadership. *Time*, October 22, 1990, 26–28.

Green, M., and J. N. Williams, eds. 2007. *Moore's Paradox: New Essays on Belief, Rationality, and the First Person*. Oxford: Oxford University Press.

Greenspan, S. 2008. Fooled by Ponzi (and Madoff): How Bernard Madoff Made Off with My Money. *eSkeptic*. December 23, 2008. https://www.skeptic.com/eskeptic/08-12-23/#feature (accessed January 20, 2019).

———. 2009a. *Annals of Gullibility: Why We Get Duped and How to Avoid It* . Westport, CT: Praeger.

———. 2009b. Foolish Action in Adults with Intellectual Disabilities: The Forgotten Problem of Risk-Unawareness. In *International Review of Research in Mental Retardation*, edited by L. M. Glidden, vol. 36, 147-94. Amsterdam and Boston: Academic Press.

———. 2009c. Foolish sex: Three Perspectives on Eliot Spitzer. Paper presented at the International Psychoanalysis Symposium, February 21, 2009.

———. 2009d. Why We Keep Falling for Financial Scams. *Wall Street Journal.* January 3, 2009. https://www.wsj.com/articles/SB123093987596650197.

———. 2012. *Elements of Discipline: Nine Principles for Teachers and Parents*. Philadelphia: Temple University Press.

———. 2017. Borderline Intellectual Functioning: An Update. *Current Opinion in Psychiatry* 30.2: 113–22.

Greenspan, S., G. Loughlin, and R. S. Black. 2001. Credulity and Gullibility in Persons with Mental Disorders: A Framework for Future Research. In *International Review of Research in Mental Retardation*, edited by L. M. Glidden, vol. 24, 101–35. San Diego: Academic Press.

Greenspan S., H. N. Switzky, and G. W. Woods. 2011. Intelligence Involves Risk-Awareness and Intellectual Disability Involves Risk-Unawareness: Implications of a Theory of Common Sense. *Journal of Intellectual and Developmental Disabilities* 36.4: 242–53.

Greenspan, S., and G. Woods. 2016. Personal and Situational Contributors to Fraud Victimization: Implications of a Four-Factor Model of Gullible Investing. *Financial Crimes: Psychological, Technological, and Ethics Issues*, edited by M. Dion, D. Weisstub, and J.-L. Richet, 141–66. Amsterdam: Springer.

Gregovic, P. 2007. *Aristotle on the Common Sense*. Oxford: Oxford University Press.

Groce, N. (1992). The "Town Fool": An Oral History of a Mentally Retarded Individual in Small Town Society. In *Interpreting Disability: A Qualitative Reader*, edited by P. M. Ferguson, D. L. Ferguson, and S. J. Taylor, 175–96. New York: Teachers College Press.

Gstalter, M. 2018. Trump Again Labels Himself a "Very Stable Genius." *Hill*, July 12, 2018. https://thehill.com/homenews/administration/396628-trump-calls-himself-a-stable-genius.

Gudjonsson, G. H. 2018. *The Psychology of False Confessions: Forty Years of Science and Practice*. Chichester, UK: John Wiley and Sons.

Halpern, D. F. 2002. Sex, Lies, and Audiotapes: The Clinton-Lewinsky Scandal. In *Why Smart People Can Be So Stupid*, edited by R. J. Sternberg, 106-23. New Haven, CT: Yale University Press.

Hambrick, D. Z., and A. P. Burgoyne. 2016. The Difference Between Rationality and Intelligence. *New York Times*, September 16, 2016.

Handwerk, B. 2013. 5 Tips for Staying Safe in Avalanche Country. *National Geographic News*, April 22, 2013. https://news.nationalgeographic.com/news/2013/13/130422-avalanche-safety-tips/.

Hardcastle, G.K. (2006). *Monty Python and Philosophy: Nudge Nudge, Think Think!* Peru, IL: Carus Publishing Company.

Hari, J. 2009. How Ayn Rand Became an American Icon: The Perverse Allure of a Damaged Woman. *Slate*, November 2, 2009. https://slate.com/culture/2009/11/two-biographies-of-ayn-rand.html.

Hazelgrove, W. 2016. *Madam President: The Secret Presidency of Edith Wilson*. Washington, DC: Regnery History.

Hedlund, J., J. Antonakis, and R. J. Sternberg. 2002. Tacit Knowledge and Practical Intelligence: Understanding the Lessons of Experience. *ARI Research Note 2003-04*. Alexandria, VA: United States Army Research Institute for the Behavioral and Social Sciences.

Hester, E. N. 1999. Bad Passenger, Bad! *Salon*. April 13, 1999. https://www.salon.com/1999/04/13/passenger/.

Heywood, J. 1963. *A Dialogue of Proverbs*. Berkeley: University of California Press.

Hill, A., and A. Michaels. 2002. Paw Taste Condemns Kozlowski: Report Says Tyco Bought $15,000 Dog Umbrella Stand for Chief's Apartment. *Financial Times*, September 18, 2002.

Huffington, A. (2017, Jan.28). A Modest Proposal: Mr. President, Get Some Sleep. *The Huffington Report*.

Hyman, R. 1989. *The Elusive Quarry: A Scientific Appraisal of Psychical Research*. Buffalo, NY: Prometheus Books.

Inabinett, C., Jr. 2016. *The Legendary Florida A&M University Marching Band: The History of "the Hundred."* New York: Page Publishing.

Ioannidis, J. P. A. 2015. Stealth Research: Is Biomedical Innovation Happening Outside the Peer-Reviewed Literature? *JAMA* 313.7: 663-64.

James, W. 1902. *The Varieties of Religious Experience: A Study in Human Nature*. New York: Longmans, Green.

Jones, N. 2017. A Timeline of Louis C.K. Masturbation Allegations. *Vulture New York*,

Joseph, A. 1995. *We Get Confessions*. Rochester, NY: Paladin Press.

Kahneman, D. 2013. *Thinking, Fast and Slow*. New York: Farrar, Strauss and Giroux.

Kang, C. 2016. Fake News Onslaught Targets Pizzeria as Nest of Child-Trafficking. *New York Times*, November 21, 2016. https://www.nytimes.com/2016/11/21/technology/fact-check-this-pizzeria-is-not-a-child-trafficking-site.html.

Kantor, J., and M. Twohey. 2017. Harvey Weinstein Paid Off Sexual Harassment Accusers for Decades. *New York Times*, October 5, 2017.

Kaplan, D. A. (2015, March 1). Tyco's "Piggy," Out of Prison and Living Small. *New York Times*.

Kavet, G., and A. Robin. 1995. The Jimmy. Directed by Andy Ackerman. *Seinfeld*. Los Angeles: CBS

Khan, S. 2009. The Science of Common Sense; Proven Wisdom is Common Sense? *EngineeringDaily*. (blog). April 1, 2009. http://www.engineeringdaily.net/the-science-of-common-sense-proven-wisdom-is-common-sense/.

Kim, J. S. 2016. Post-stroke Mood and Emotional Disturbances: Pharmacological Therapy Based on Mechanisms. *Journal of Stroke* 18.3: 244–55.

Koenigs, M., and J. Grafman. 2009. Posttraumatic Stress Disorder: The Role of Medial Prefrontal Cortex and Amygdala. *Neuroscientist* 15.5: 540–48.

Kohlberg, L. 1981. *The Philosophy of Moral Development: Moral Stages and the Idea of Justice*. New York: Harper & Row.

Kohut, H. 1972. Thoughts on Narcissism and Narcissistic Rage . In *The Search for the Self: Selected Writings of Heinz Kohut, 1950-1978* , edited by P. Ornstein, v ol. 2, 615–58. New York: International Universities Press.

Kotin, A. A. 2015. *The Narrative Imagination: Comic Tales by Phillippe de Vigneulles*. Lexington: University of Kentucky Press.

Krakauer, J. 1996. *Into the Wild*. New York: Villard Books.

LaBute, N. 2004/2014. *Fat Pig: A Play*. New York: Broadway Play Publishing.

Lee, B. X., ed. 2017. *The Dangerous Case of Donald Trump: 27 Psychiatrists and Mental Health Experts Assess a President*. New York: Thomas Dunne/St. Martin's Press.

Lee, K., and M. C. Ashton. 2004. Psychometric Properties of the HEXACO Personality Inventory. *Multivariate Behavioral Research* 39.2: 329–58.

Lee, N. 2014. *Facebook Nation: Total Information Awareness*. 2nd ed. New York: Springer.

Lehrer, J. 2009. Passions of the Brain. *NPR Fresh Air*. March 2, 2009. https://www.npr.org/templates/story/story.php?storyId=101334645.

Levy, M., and M. Salvadori. 1987. *Why Buildings Fall Down: How Structures Fail*. New York: W. W. Norton.

Lewis, M. K. 2015. *Understanding Ponzi Schemes: Can Better Financial Regulation Prevent Investors from Being Defrauded?* Northampton, MA: Edward Elgar Publishing.

Lipsitt, L. P., and L. L. Mitnick. 1991. *Self-Regulatory Behavior and Risk Taking: Causes and Consequences*. Norwood, NJ: Ablex Publishing.

Little, B. (2018, Aug. 26). JFK Was Completely Unprepared for his Summit with Khrushchev. *Inside History Newsletter* (www.history.com).

Loftus, E., and K. Ketcham. 1994. *The Myth of Repressed Memory: False Memories and Allegations of Sexual Abuse*. New York: St. Martins Griffin.

Lotus, J. 2018. Woman Rescued After Fall by Searchers Looking for Missing Hiker. *Patch*, August 31, 2018. https://patch.com/colorado/across-co/woman-rescued-after-fall-searchers-looking-missing-hiker.

Lovitt, B. 2011. Death by Selfie: 11 Disturbing Stories of Social Media Pics Gone Wrong. *Rolling Stone*, July 14, 2011.

Lynch, J. 2015. Little Rock Man is Guilty of Killing Girl, 15, After Prank. *Arkansas Online*, November 5, 2015. https://www.arkansasonline.com/news/2015/nov/05/lr-man-is-guilty-of-killing-girl-15-201/.

Malkin, C. 2017. Pathological Narcissism and Politics: A Lethal Mix. In *The Dangerous Case of Donald Trump: 27 Psychiatrists and Mental Health Experts Assess a President*, edited by B. X. Lee, 51–68 New York: Thomas Dunne/St. Martin's Press.

Malkus, C. 2013. *The Ultimate Ponzi: The Scott Rothstein Story*. Gretna, LA: Pelican Publishing.

Manegold, C. S. 1992. Judge and Heiress: The Rise and Fall of a Private Affair. *New York Times*, November 15, 1992. https://www.nytimes.com/1992/11/15/nyregion/judge-and-heiress-the-rise-and-fall-of-a-private-affair.html.

Martin, C. 2016. *Love and Lies: An Essay on Truthfulness, Deceit, and the Growth and Care of Erotic Love*. New York: Picador Press.

Mayhew, R., ed. 2005. *Ayn Rand Answers: The Best of Her Q & A*. New York: New American Library/Penguin.

Mazo, G., M. Trautschold, and K. Michaluk. 2010. *CrackBerry: True Tales of BlackBerry Use and Abuse*. New York: Apress Books.

McCandless, C. 2014. *The Wild Truth*. New York: HarperOne.

McCartin, J. A. 2011. *Collision Course: Ronald Reagan, the Air Traffic Controllers, and the Strike that Changed America*. New York: Oxford University Press.

McCartney, P. 1967. The Fool on the Hill. *Magical Mystery Tour*, by The Beatles. Capitol Records.

McCaskill, N. D. 2016. Trump Accuses Cruz's Father of Helping JFK's Assassin. *Politico*. May 3, 2016. https://www.politico.com/blogs/2016-gop-primary-live-updates-and-results/2016/05/trump-ted-cruz-father-222730.

McCormack, S. 2013. Robert Saylor's Death Ruled A Homicide: Man With Down Syndrome Died In Police Custody. *Huffington Post*, February 18, 2013. https://www.huffingtonpost.com/2013/02/18/robert-saylors-death-homicide-mentally-ill_n_2711629.html.

McGee, J. 1987. *Gentle Teaching: A Nonaversive Approach for Helping Persons with Mental Retardation*. New York: Human Sciences Press.

McGinn, R. 2018. *The Ethical Engineer: Contemporary Concepts and Cases.* Princeton, NJ: Princeton University Press.

Medina, J. 2011. Doctor Found Guilty in Michael Jackson's Death. *New York Times,* November 7, 2011. https://www.nytimes.com/2011/11/08/us/doctor-found-guilty-in-michael-jacksons-death.html.

Medred, C. 2007. Into the Wild: McCandless' Story Isn't Really Told in Book or Film. *Ledger-Enquirer, McClatchy Newspapers,* November 8, 2007. https://www.ledger-enquirer.com/living/article28974580.html.

Mehlman, P. 1994. The Wife. Directed by Tom Cherones. *Seinfeld.* Los Angeles: CBS.

Meserve, M. 2012. Meet Ivan Boesky, the Infamous Wall Streeter Who Inspired Gordon Gekko. *Business Insider,* July 26, 2012. https://www.businessinsider.com/meet-ivan-boesky-the-infamous-wall-streeter-who-inspired-gordon-gecko-2012-7.

Miller, A. 1987. *Timebends: A Life.* New York: Grove Press.

Moss, W. G. 2016. The Main Problem with Donald Trump: He's a Fool. *History News Network* (George Washington University), May 29, 2016.

Moushey, B., and R. Dvorchak. 2011. *Game Over: Jerry Sandusky, Penn State, and the Culture of Silence.* New York: William Morrow/Harper Collins.

Nath, C. 2013. Five Men Killed in Loveland Pass Avalanche Identified. *Summit Daily,* June 3, 2013. https://www.summitdaily.com/news/local/five-men-killed-in-loveland-pass-avalanche-identified/.

Newcomb, M. D., and L. McGee. 1989. Adolescent Alcohol Use and Other Delinquent Behaviors: One-Year Longitudinal Analysis Controlling for Sensation Seeking. *Criminal Justice and Behavior* 16.3: 345–369.

New York Post Staff. 2018. Adrian Peterson Shocker: "I still spank my child with a belt." *New York Post,* November 21, 2018. https://nypost.com/2018/11/21/adrian-peterson-shocker-i-still-spank-my-son-with-belt/.

Norman, T. (2007, Sept. 17). O.J. Simpson has done it again. *Pittsburgh Post-Gazette.*

Nossiter, A. 1994. A Daughter's Death, a Father's Guilt. *New York Times,* November 10, 1994. https://www.nytimes.com/1994/11/10/us/a-daughter-s-death-a-father-s-guilt.html.

Nuzzi, O. 2016. Former Donald Trump Executive: "He's a Supreme Sexist." *Daily Beast,* October 11, 2016. https://www.thedailybeast.com/former-donald-trump-executive-hes-a-supreme-sexist.

Ogrodniczuk, J. S. 2013. *Understanding and Treating Pathological Narcissism.* Washington, DC: American Psychological Association.

Osuagwu, N. G. 2009. *Facebook Addiction: The Life and Times of Social Networking Addiction.* Breinigsville, PA: Ice Cream Melts Publisher.

Paffenroth, K. (2004). "Reason in Madness": The Wisdom in Folly in the New Testament and *King Lear.* In *In Praise of Wisdom: Literary and Theological Reflections on Faith and Reason,* 53–83. New York: Continuum.

Paine, T. 1776. *Common Sense: Addressed to the Inhabitants of America.* New ed. Thomson. Philadelphia: W. and T. Bradford.

Pardeck, J. T., ed. 1989. *Child Abuse and Neglect: Theory, Research, and Practice.* London: Taylor & Francis.

Peloquin S. M. 1989. Moral Treatment: Contexts Considered. *American Journal of Occupational Therapy* 43.8: 537–44.

Peter, L. J. and R. Hull. 1969. *The Peter Principle.* New York: William Morrow & Co.

Perkins, D. N. 2002. The Engine of Folly. In *Why Smart People Can Be So Stupid,* edited by R. J. Sternberg, 64–85. New Haven, CT: Yale University Press.

Piaget, J., and B. Inhelder. 2011. *The Psychology of the Child.* New York: Basic Books.

Polanyi, M. 1966. *The Tacit Dimension.* London: Routledge & Kegan Paul; Chicago: University of Chicago Press.

Porter, K. A. 1962. *Ship of Fools.* Boston: Little, Brown.

Powers, D. (2008, Oct.6). Simpson "Stupid," but No Crook, Says His Lawyer. *The Irish Times.*

Preston, J. (2006, Oct. 17). Lawyer, Facing 30 years, Gets 28 Months, to Dismay of U.S. *New York Times.*

Ramzey, A. (2017, Sept. 22). Kim Jong-Un Called Trump a "Dotard." What Does That Even Mean? *New York Times.*

Reid, T. 1764/1869. *An Inquiry into the Human Mind on the Principles of Common Sense.* Calcutta: Thanker, Spink.

Reiss, D. M. 2017. Cognitive Impairment, Dementia, and POTUS. In *The Dangerous Case of Donald Trump: 27 Psychiatrists and Mental Health Experts Assess a President,* edited by B. X. Lee, 126–35. New York: Thomas Dunne/St. Martin's Press.

Reiss, S. 2000. *Who am I? The 16 Basic Desires That Motivate Our Behavior and Define Our Personality.* New York: Berkley Books.

———. 2008a. Does Eliot Spitzer have a normal personality? A New Way of Thinking about the Spitzer Scandal. Posted March 12, 2008. *Fifteen Eightyfour: Academic Perspectives from Cambridge University Press* (blog). http://www.cambridgeblog.org/2008/03/does-eliot-spitzer-have-a-normal-personality/.

———. 2008b. *The Normal Personality: A New Way of Thinking About People.* New York and Cambridge: Cambridge University Press.

Res, B. A. 2018. *All Alone on the 68th Floor: How One Woman Changed the Face of Construction.* 2nd ed. North Charleston, SC: Create Space Independent Publishing.

Rhodes, R. 2015. *Why They Kill: The Discoveries of a Maverick Criminologist.* New York: Vintage.

Richtel, M. 2011. As Doctors Use More Devices, Potential for Distraction Grows. *New York Times,* December 14, 2011. https://www.nytimes.com/2011/12/15/health/as-doctors-use-more-devices-potential-for-distraction-grows.html.

Ronell, A. 2002. *Stupidity.* Urbana: University of Illinois Press.

Rosenfeld, S. 2011. *Common Sense: A Political History.* Cambridge, MA: Harvard University Press.

———. 2017. The Only Thing More Dangerous than Trump's Appeal to Common Sense Is His Dismissal of It. *Nation,* March 1, 2017.

Rothe, J. P. 2008. *Driven to Kill: Vehicles as Weapons.* Edmonton: University of Alberta Press.

Rotter, J. B. 1980. Interpersonal Trust, Trustworthiness, and Gullibility. *American Psychologist* 35.1: 1–7.

Roush, W. 2006. Marvin Minsky on Common Sense and Computers That Emote. *MIT Technology Review,* July 13, 2006.

Rubin, J. 2017. Russia's Mark: A Dangerous Fool for a President. *Washington Post,* November 12, 2017.

Rushe, D. 2012. Allen Stanford Sentenced to 110 Years in Jail for $7bn Investment Fraud. *Guardian.* June 14, 2012.

Sapolsky, R. M. 2017. *Behave: The Biology of Humans at Our Best and Worst.* New York: Penguin Press.

Sarno, D., P. Hong, and L. Beale. 2009. Wells Fargo Vows 'Decisive Action' in Alleged Use of Malibu Mansion by an Executive. *Los Angeles Times,* September 12, 2009.

Savransky, R. (2016, March 13). Trump: All I know Is What's on the Internet. *The Hill.*

Schoenmakers, Y. M. M., R. de Vries Robbé, and A. P. van Wijk. 2009. *Mountain of Gold: An Exploratory Research of Nigerian 419-Fraud.* Amsterdam: SWP.

Schneider, M. (2017). The Elementary Education of Donald Trump. *Huffington Post,* May 11.

Schwartz, I. 2018. Trump Knocks Maxine Waters: IQ Somewhere in "mid-60s." *Real Clear Politics,* July 5.

Scott, E. S., and L. Steinberg. 2008. Adolescent Development and the Exploration of Youth Crime. *Future of Children* 18.2: 15-33.

SGI Quarterly. 2005. Three Poisons—The Source of the Problem. *SGI Quarterly,* October 2005. https://www.sgi.org/ru/philosophy/buddhist-concepts/three-poisons-the-source-of-the-problem.html.

Shafer, J. 2015. Why did Brian Williams Lie? *Politico Magazine,* February 5, 2015.

Sherrill, S. (2001, Dec. 9), The Year in Ideas: A to Z; Acquired Situational Narcissism. *New York Times*.

Shapiro, D. 2000. *Dynamics of Character: Self-Regulation in Psychopathology*. New York: Basic Books.

Shilkret, R. 2009. Personal communication, April 12, 2009. South Hadley, MA: Mount Holyoke College.

Shiller, R. J. 2000. *Irrational Exuberance*. Princeton, NJ: Princeton University Press.

Shmoop Editorial Team (2008, Nov. 11). *Decameron Third Day, Tenth Story Summary*. Shmoop University, Inc.

Singer, I. B. 1957. *Gimpel the Fool, and Other Stories*. New York: Farrar, Strauss and Giroux.

Solomon, J. 2012. *DSK: The Scandal That Brought Down Dominique Strauss-Kahn*. New York: Macmillan.

Sophocles (441 BCE/ 1986). *The Three Theban Plays: Antigone, Oedipus the King, Oedipus at Colonus*. Translated by Robert Fagles. New York: Penguin.

Stableford, D. (2016). Conspiracy Theorist Alex Jones Says Donald Trump Called to Thank Him. *Yahoo News*, November 14.

Stanghellini, G. 2000. At Issue: Vulnerability to Schizophrenia and Lack of Common Sense. *Schizophrenia Bulletin* 26, part 4: 775–87.

Stanovich, K. E. 1994. Reconceptualizing Intelligence: Dysrationalia as an Intuition Pump. *Educational Researcher* 23.4: 11–21.

———. 1999. *Who Is Rational? Studies of Individual Differences in Reasoning*. Mahwah, NJ: Erlbaum.

———. 2002. Rationality, Intelligence, and Levels of Analysis in Cognitive Science: Is Dysrationalia Possible? In *Why Smart People Can Be So Stupid*, edited by R. J. Sternberg, 124–58. New Haven, CT: Yale University Press.

Sternberg, R. J., ed. 2002a. *Why Smart People Can Be So Stupid*. New Haven, CT: Yale University Press.

———. 2002b. Smart People Are Not Stupid, But They Sure Can Be Foolish: The Imbalance Theory of Foolishness. In *Why Smart People Can Be So Stupid*, edited by R. J. Sternberg, 232-42. New Haven, CT: Yale University Press.

———. 2004. Why Smart People Can Be So Foolish. *European Psychologist* 9.3: 145-50.

Sternberg, R. J., R. K. Wagner, and L. Okagaki. 1993. Practical Intelligence: The Nature and Role of Tacit Knowledge in Work and at School. In *Mechanisms of Everyday Cognition*, edited by J. M. Puckett and H. W. Reese, 205–27. Hillsdale, NJ: Erlbaum.

Stewart, E. 2018. Starbucks Says Everyone's a Customer after Philadelphia Bias Incident. *Vox*, May 19, 2018.

Stewart, E.-A. 1999. *Jesus the Holy Fool*. Franklin, WI: Sheed & Ward.

Stewart, J. B. 2011. *Tangled Webs: How False Statements are Undermining America: From Martha Stewart to Bernie Madoff*. New York: Penguin Press.

Stone, J.R. (2013). *The Routledge Dictionary of Latin Quotations*. Abingdon, UK: Routledge.

Sundem, G. 2010. *Brain Trust: 93 Top Scientists Reveal Lab-Tested Secrets to Surfing, Dating, Dieting, Gambling, Growing Man-Eating Plants, and More!* New York: Three Rivers Press.

Taback, S. 2005. *Kibitzers and Fools: Tales My Zayda (Grandfather) Told Me*. New York: Viking.

Takakusu, Junjirō. 1901. Tales of the Wise Man and the Fool, in Tibetan and Chinese. *Journal of the Royal Asiatic Society of Great Britain and Ireland*, n.s. 33.3: 447–60.

Tapper, J., and B. Kuhlman. 2006. The Macaca Heard Round the World. *ABC Nightline*, August 17, 2006. https://abcnews.go.com/Nightline/story?id=2322630&page=1.

Terrace, V. (1979). *The Complete Encyclopedia of Television Programs, 1947–1979*. New York: A.S. Barnes.

Tesser, A. 1980. When Individual Dispositions and Social Pressure Conflict: A Catastrophe. *Human Relations* 33.6: 393–407.

Tesser, A., and J. Achee. 1994. Aggression, Love, Conformity, and Other Social Psychological Catastrophes. In *Dynamical Systems in Social Psychology* , edited by R. R. Vallacher and A. Nowak, 95–109. San Diego: Academic Press.

Thorndike, E. L. 1921. Intelligence and Its Measurement: A Symposium. *Journal of Educational Psychology*, 12.3: 123–47.

Toobin, J. 2015. *The Run of His Life: The People v. O. J. Simpson*. New York: Radom House.

Trivers, R. 2011. *The Folly of Fools: The Logic of Deceit and Self-Deception in Human Life*. New York: Basic Books.

Trump, D. J., with T. Schwartz. 1987. *Trump: The Art of the Deal*. New York: Ballantine Books.

Tuchman, B. W. 1984. *The March of Folly: From Troy to Vietnam*. New York: Random House.

Turing, A. M. 1950. Computing Machinery and Intelligence. *Mind* 59.236: 433–60.

Tusser, T. (1580/ 1878). *Five Hundred Pointes of Good Husbandrie*. London: Trubner.

Tutzauer, F. 1984. A Catastrophe Theory Model of Child Abuse. *Journal of Family Issues* 5.3: 321–42.

Tversky, A., and E. Shafir. 1992. The Disjunction Effect in Choice under Uncertainty. *Psychological Science* 3.5: 305–10.

urbandictionary.com. 2018. s.v. "Boo Boo the Fool." https://www.urbandictionary.com/define.php?term=boo+boo+the+fool.

Urbina, I. 2008. A Palm Beach Enclave Stunned by an Inside Job. *New York Times*, December 15, B1, B3. https://www.nytimes.com/2008/12/15/business/15palm.html.

Van Boxsel, J. 2003. *The Encyclopedia of Stupidity*. Translated by A. Pomerans and E. Pomerans. London: Reaktion

Van der Maas, H. L. J., R. Kolstein, and J. van der Pligt. 2003. Sudden Transitions in Attitudes. *Sociological Methods & Research* 32.2: 125–52.

Wachtler, S. 1997. *After the Madness: A Judge's Own Prison Madness*. New York: Open Road Media.

Wason, P. C. (1968). Reasoning About a Rule. *Quarterly Journal of Experimental Psychology*. 20.3: 273–281.

Wagner, R. K. 2002. Smart People Doing Dumb Things: The Case of Managerial Incompetence. In *Why Smart People Can Be So Stupid*, edited by R. J. Sternberg, 42–63. New Haven, CT: Yale University Press.

Ward, V. (2019). *Kushner, Inc.: Greed. Ambition. Corruption. The Extraordinary Story of Jared Kushner and Ivanka Trump*. New York: Macmillan.

Webster, C. D., and M. A. Jackson, eds. 1997. *Impulsivity: Theory, Assessment, and Treatment*. New York: Guilford Press.

The Week Staff. 2018. When will self-driving cars take over? *Week*, November 17, 2018.

Weiner, T. 2015. *One Man Against the World: The Tragedy of Richard Nixon*. New York: Henry Holt.

Weiser, S. (2008, Oct. 5). Repeat After Me: Greed is Not Good. *Los Angeles Times*.

Wen, L., and J. Kosowsky. 2013. *When Doctors Don't Listen: How to Avoid Misdiagnoses and Unnecessary Tests*. New York: Thomas Dunne Books/St. Martin's Press.

Whittlesey, L. H. 1995. *Death in Yellowstone: Accidents and Foolhardiness in the First National Park*. Lanham, MD: Rowman & Littlefield.

wicktionary.com. 2018. s.v. "folly." https://en.wiktionary.org/wiki/folly.

Williams, P. 2013. Bones of Contention: A Florida Man's Curious Trade in Mongolian Dinosaurs. *New Yorker*, January 28, 2013.

Wolfe. T. 1987. *The Bonfire of the Vanities*. New York: Farrar, Straus, Giroux.

Wolfensberger, W. 2003. *Leadership and Change in Human Services: Selected Readings from Wolf Wolfensberger*. London: Psychology Press/Routledge.

Woodward, B. 2018. *Fear: Trump in the White House*. New York: Simon and Schuster.

Yaffe, G. 2004. *Manifest Activity: Thomas Reid's Theory of Action*. Oxford: Clarendon Press/Oxford University Press.

Zimbardo, P., and R. Sword. 2017. Unbridled and Extreme Present Hedonism: How the Leader of the Free World has Proven Time and Again He Is Unfit for Duty. In *The Dangerous Case of Donald Trump: 27 Psychiatrists and Mental Health Experts Assess a President*, edited by B. X. Lee, 25–50. New York: Thomas Dunne/St. Martin's Press.

Zuckoff, M. 2005. *Ponzi's Scheme: The True Story of a Financial Legend* . New York: Random House.

———. 2006. The Perfect Mark: How a Massachusetts Psychotherapist Fell for a Nigerian e-mail Scam. *New Yorker* , May 15, 2006, 6.

Index

About the Author

Stephen Greenspan received a PhD in developmental psychology from the University of Rochester and was a postdoctoral fellow in developmental disabilities at UCLA's Neuropsychiatric Institute. He has held several faculty positions, and retired as professor emeritus of educational psychology at the University of Connecticut. He serves often as an expert forensic witness in criminal and civil cases where cognitive impairment is a mitigating factor. His focus has been on social and personal competence, including such things as social intelligence, adaptive behavior, gullibility, and most recently, foolishness. He now lives in Northern California, after having spent the previous twenty years in the Denver area. He writes a blog for *Psychology Today* on the topic of human incompetence.

Made in the USA
Middletown, DE
04 June 2024